6738347

NOTES

on the

PROPHECY AND
LAMENTATIONS

of

JEREMIAH

"The Weeping Prophet"

by

H. A. IRONSIDE

LOIZEAUX BROTHERS
Neptune, New Jersey

FIRST EDITION, OCTOBER 1906
TENTH PRINTING, SEPTEMBER 1973

PUBLISHED BY LOIZEAUX BROTHERS, Inc.
*A Nonprofit Organization, devoted to the Lord's Work
and to the Spread of His Truth*

PRINTED IN THE UNITED STATES OF AMERICA

CONTENTS.

LAMENTATIONS.

Preface to New Edition

After the lapse of some twenty-two years this book is to be reissued, and my publishers have asked me to go over it carefully and make any corrections desired, ere plating it. This I have done. Slight changes have been made here and there, not more than a dozen in all, and a few sentences added for greater clearness. It is a matter of surprise on my part and of real gratitude to God that I see nothing to alter so far as the teaching is concerned. The principles of interpretation I accepted years ago seem clearer to me now than ever. The great outlines of the teaching of the book have only become confirmed in my mind with the passing of the years. I hold, through grace, to-day, what I held when I began these "Notes" nearly thirty years ago. I am more than ever persuaded of their dispensational correctness, and I send the book forth again, in full confidence that it sets forth the truth of God.

—H. A. IRONSIDE.

September, 1928.

PREFACE

The book now before the reader consists not so much of a commentary upon the books of Jeremiah and Lamentations, as of a series of meditative studies, which have been jotted down at intervals in a busy life during a period of nearly five years. This accounts in great measure for the fragmentary character of much that is here presented.

It is hoped, however, that, unfinished as the book may appear from either an expository or a literary standpoint, it may be found helpful in exercising the consciences of the Lord's people and in quickening their spiritual affections, as well as in opening up a portion of Scripture which to many is almost like an unexplored region.

Students generally find difficulty in a careful survey of these books because of the arrangement of the chapters, so utterly regardless of chronological order. To help such, an attempt has been made to present the different prophecies and historical incidents in their true relationship, at the end of the book. It is impossible to speak authoritatively concerning every particular portion, and the thoughtful reader may even be able to improve upon the order there given.

The great prophetic chapters (30, 31, 50, and 51) have been treated more fully than others because of the many existing misconceptions as to God's past, present and future dealings with Israel and Judah (to which the first two chapters designated relate), and, to our mind, the baseless speculations in regard to the rebuilding of literal Babylon, which are, we believe, fully met in the latter two chapters.

The book is not written for the critical scholar, but it is put forth in the hope that it may be suited ministry for the sheep and lambs of the flock of Christ.

The author desires to acknowledge help received from Mr. J. N. Darby's outlines of Jeremiah and Lamentations in his excellent "Synopsis of the Books of the Bible;" as also from the brief paper on Jeremiah by Mr. J. B. Stoney in his "Discipline in the School of God."

May the Master of Assemblies be pleased to make these pages a help to open up a part of His unerring Word for genuine profit to numbers of His people.

—H. A. IRONSIDE.

[1906]

INTRODUCTORY

In taking up the study of the writings of Jeremiah it is not purposed to attempt a full exposition of the books of this the tenderest of all the prophets. My only thought is to jot down notes of what has been particularly impressed on my own heart in going over them, in the hope that others, especially young Christians, may, like myself, find benefit.

The prophecy with its poetical appendix forms a portion of Scripture abounding in soulful, stirring appeals. If we think of prophecy merely as foretelling the future (and especially unfolding the glories of Messiah's kingdom), we shall not find it nearly so full as either Isaiah, Ezekiel, or Daniel, with which it is commonly classed as being one of the major prophets. It has not the majesty of the first, the extended vision of the last, nor the wondrous imagery of the other; but none of these characteristics would be expected in a series of messages chiefly intended for the conscience. If, however, we think of prophecy in its New Testament sense, as that which brings the soul into the presence of God, we realize at once how fully this is the case here. The same is true in great measure of Ezekiel, but it would seem that there the people are practically given up from the start, their defection is so complete; part of them already having been carried into captivity, as in the case of the prophet himself (Ezek. 1 : 1) : but in Jeremiah, in the first half of the book at least, we have evidently ministry with a view to recalling wandering hearts to the One they had forsaken. It is their restoration to God as a means of deferring the already announced judgment (2 Kings 22 : 12-20) that is now before us. This stamps the book as a whole, and gives character to it. What in Ezekiel is expressed in picture—the slow and reluctant leaving of the Shekinah (chap. 10 : 4, 18, 19)—is, in the earlier book, brought before us in the earnest pleadings and conscience-rousing entreaties of the Spirit in the tender-hearted Seer, sorrowing so deeply over the fallen condition of his people.

I have often been struck by what seemed to be a characteristic likeness in Jeremiah and Nehemiah. Both were actuated by the same fervent love for the people and city of God. Both were men of broken and contrite spirits, who trembled at the word of the Lord. Both were very easily moved men, tears being frequently common to them. In the earlier servant, however, there is perhaps more exaltedness of character, more self-forgetfulness, than in the later one. For instance, Nehemiah says: "Remember me, O God, concerning this, and wipe not oɪt my good deeds that I

have done" (chap. 13: 14) ; a sentiment frequently repeated. Jeremiah never spoke like this.
Once only he cries, when he sees his message is
rejected, and hope of the repentance of Judah
is gone, and they are devising evil devices against
him: "Remember that I stood before Thee to
speak good for them, and to turn away Thy wrath
from them" (chap. 18: 20). He was a less in-
trepid man naturally, however, than the other,
the weakness of his heart being again and again
manifested, though this only gives better opportunity (as in the case of Gideon and Ezra) for
God to display His power. "When I am weak,
then am I strong," is the "irresistible might of
weakness," which relies upon "One who is
mighty."

Nehemiah, too, seems to be more of what people call a patriot than the man who advised submission to the Babylonian yoke; but in this it is
clear that each had the mind of God for the time
in which he lived. One stood at the ending of a
path of declension and backsliding; the other, at
the beginning of a new era of temporary restoration and blessing. Men of God both were. May
we emulate what His grace wrought in each.

Coming, then, to the book of Jeremiah itself,
we notice that it divides naturally into two main
parts, with an appendix added by a later hand,
though of course equally inspired by the Holy

Ghost. In chapters 1—24 we hear the gracious
pleadings of Jehovah with His erring and rebellious people. This portion is moral rather than
devoted to foretelling events. Chapters 25—51
give in more detail the judgments of God, by
means of Nebuchadnezzar, resultant upon the rejection of the previous messages; with, however,
promises of future blessing and restoration at the
expiration of seventy years' captivity. The whole
present interval of scattering, since the cutting
off of Messiah, is passed over in silence. "Thus
far the words of Jeremiah." Chapter 52 is the
historical account of the carrying out of the predicted but long-delayed judgment: compare it
with 2 Kings 24: 18-20; 25: 1-17. The closing
verses intimate that as the prophecies of vengeance were thus fulfilled, so shall those be that
told of restoration, for Jehoiachin is not allowed
to die in prison, but is taken into favor by the
king of Babylon—earnest of what is yet to come.

In the Lamentations we are permitted to hear
the outpourings of the heart of the grief-stricken
prophet bewailing the accomplishment of that
which he himself had predicted. How gladly
would this dear servant of God have had all his
prophecies prove false and himself be put to
shame, had the people but been spared! In this
he is blessedly unlike Jonah, who was angry when
grace was shown to the repentant Ninevites, at

the possible expense of his prophetic reputation, or of his probable desire that Nineveh, from whom Israel had suffered, might not go unpunished. What makes Jeremiah's sorrow the more bitter is that it has all been deserved by a rebellious and stiff-necked people; but he still turns to Jehovah for succor and renewal. "Turn Thou us unto Thee, O Lord, and we shall be turned; renew our days as of old."

Oh that those who seek to care for the sheep and lambs of the flock to-day were more characterized by the love and self-abnegation that marked this dear servant of God, whose spirit was not soured by rejection as ours often is, but whose love was only the deeper as the objects of it heaped upon him insult and ignominy. In this, how like the true Man of Sorrows! In fact, so marked is this, that the rabbis have sought to find in Jeremiah the patient Sufferer of Isa. 53. To only One, as we know, can such words really apply; but it speaks volumes for Jeremiah's loving endurance in his deep, deep grief, that *he* should be the "other man" (Acts 8: 34) whom Christ-rejecting doctors put in the very place of the Holy Sufferer of Calvary. May *we* be more and more conformed to His blessed ways down here, who "has left us an example that we should follow His steps."

Notes on the

PROPHECY AND LAMENTATIONS
of
JEREMIAH

————

CHAPTER I

A VESSEL CHOSEN AND FITTED

(Chapter 1.)

The account of Jeremiah's call to the prophetic
office is very instructive and deeply interesting.
The thoughtful reader feels at once how intensely
human was the man, how condescendingly gracious the Lord. On the part of the servant there is
naught but backwardness and trembling when
commissioned to be the bearer of Jehovah's message to His backslidden people. It would be at
best but a thankless task; for people away from
God, yet proudly ignorant of their condition, do
not, as a rule, show much gratitude to the man
who seeks to turn the light on and manifest things
as they really are. It is, generally speaking, a far
more pleasant and agreeable task to preach the
gospel to poor lost sinners than to minister to
the needs of wayward saints. None but a man

who is himself very low before God can accomplish it successfully. If I would wash my brother's feet, I must stoop to do it.

But in this, as in all true service, one's reliance must be upon God, who never sends a messenger without putting in his mouth the word he is to speak; and never bids one undertake a service for which He does not qualify the servant. So with Jeremiah. His confidence is to be in the God of resurrection, who had before made a dry stick to bud, and blossom, and bring forth almonds, and who delights to take up the foolish, the weak, the base, and the despised things, and use them to confound the wise, the mighty, and the noble, "that no flesh should glory in His presence" (1 Cor. 1: 26-29). This is the secret of His so acting. Worship in His presence all can, and should, who have been brought to Himself through sovereign grace; praise and adore Him they freely may; but glory before Him they shall not. All must own that they are but vessels of mercy, who have nothing which they have not received, and He must ever be the Giver, for "it is more blessed to give than to receive." Impossible that the saved sinner should have the more blessed part.

It is not, therefore, brilliant men whom He depends on, nor men of self-sufficiency and self-confidence, but it is ever His delight to fill the empty vessel and then use it to suit Himself. "We have this treasure in earthen vessels, that the excellency of the power may be of God, and not of us" (2 Cor. 4: 7).

Looking, then, a little carefully into this preliminary chapter, we note that Jeremiah was evi-

dently quite a young man ("a child,"* he says,
ver. 7) when the word of the Lord came to him,
in the days of the godly king Josiah—himself but
a youth, as it was in the thirteenth year of his
reign, and he was but eight years of age when
he succeeded his wicked father Amon as King
of Judah (2 Chron. 34: 1). The prophet's ministry covered a period of over forty years under
the kings; and when royalty had departed from
Judah and her princes, and thousands of her people had gone into captivity, he is still found at
his post standing for God among "the poor of the
flock" left in the land, looking forward to the destruction of the very power to which he had previously urged submission, and which had been
permitted to desolate Jehovah's heritage.

Of his early years, before his divine call to
publicly proclaim the word of the Lord, we have
no authentic record. Scripture is silent regarding him, save for occasional references (2 Chron.
35, 36) to his later ministry, corroborating, if
corroboration were needed, his own account in the
books before us. His father's name, Hilkiah; his
service, that of a priest; his home, Anathoth of
Benjamin—these he tells us in the first verse, but
details there are none. Men may be curious to
know of the training and early life of those afterwards celebrated; but God makes no attempts
merely to satisfy idle curiosity. In divine things
all counts for nothing until the soul really begins
with God. That memorable time in the case of
this young priest (that is, the time when he con-

---

* This is the same word that the angel applies to
Zechariah—"Speak to this *young man*" (Zech. 2:4).

sciously had to do with Him) was evidently about the date above mentioned. Like John the Baptist, he was sanctified even before his birth, and ordained to be a prophet, not merely to fallen Judah, but to the nations. We do not know, however, that he was aware of his exalted mission until this time.

There had already been a measure of revival and blessing in the land; outwardly, at least. Just a year previously, Josiah had commenced to purge Judah and Jerusalem from the remains of the idolatrous worship which Manasseh, though humbled and repentant, had not been able to remove, and which the infamous and unhumbled Amon had but furthered and endorsed. The book of the law had not yet been recovered; nor was it until some seven years later (2 Chron. 34). That precious volume was still hidden (where, doubtless, some faithful one had only too safely stored it, in the dark days preceding) in the still unrepaired house of the Lord. In His own time, He who caused it to be written and who watched over it would see that it was brought forth. Till then, and even in connection with it later, He would speak through a prophet.

And right here it may be well to note Jeremiah's place in connection with the other prophets whose writings we have. It was probably about a century since Isaiah had, if tradition speaks truly, been sawn asunder (see Heb. 11: 37) by the fathers of those who now professed to worship Jehovah at Jerusalem. Hosea, Joel, Amos, Micah, and Nahum, all of them for a time at least contemporary with Isaiah, had long since passed off the scene; leaving the nation apparently as hardened as ever. Zephaniah and Habakkuk were both still living, though we have no mention as to whether it was their privilege to "speak often one to another." Ezekiel and Obadiah were also his contemporaries during his later years—Ezekiel only among the captives in Babylon. Daniel prophesied subsequently in the palace of the conquerors. He, it will be remembered, was a student of the writings of his great predecessor, and from this book learned of the appointed seventy years' duration of the captivity. Jonah had been much earlier than any (2 Kings 14: 25), but we know little of the nature of his ministry beyond his mission to the great Gentile city of Nineveh. The remaining three minor prophets, Haggai, Zechariah, and Malachi, were the bearers of Jehovah's message to the remnant restored to their land. Between Jeremiah and the last a period of about three hundred years is generally assigned.

We turn back now to our chapter. Just how the Lord spoke to Jeremiah we are not informed. Abruptly he is told: "Before I formed thee in the belly I knew thee; and before thou camest out of the womb I sanctified thee, and I ordained thee a prophet unto the nations" (verse 5). It is the divine sovereignty that is at once brought before him. He is given to understand from the first that it is the eternal, omniscient, omnipotent Jehovah with whom he has to do. The natural man may shrink from this, but how the soul of the saint delights to dwell upon it! "Known unto God are all His works from the beginning of the creation." Nothing ever takes Him by surprise.

Consequently, with Him, there can be no after-thought. All was foreseen long, long before its actual occurrence; everything was provided for. Satan, sin, and their attendant evils, have in no wise interfered with His purpose, "who worketh all things according to the counsel of His own will." Where had His grace found manifestation, had not sin been permitted? All the glory of the Cross must have had no place if the serpent's entrance into the garden of delight had been denied. Evil, dreadful as it is, is but the dark background that throws into relief His wondrous purposes of love and grace.

It is well for the soul of the believer to grasp this and rest upon it. However much one's spirit may be chafed and fretted and vexed by abounding iniquity, it is well to remember that there is One who abides in eternal peace—"the peace of God." Not that He is indifferent to the evil; but He sees, as we cannot, how blessedly all shall yet result to the glory of the Son of His love. How different must have been our thoughts of Him had our guilt never given occasion for His emptying Himself of His dignities to become a little lower than the angels for the suffering of death! We should never have known Him as Man had not sin necessitated for us a Mediator. Had He sovereignly chosen to become such, though we needed Him not, we could only call Him Lord and not know Him as Saviour, whose precious blood had redeemed us to God: how little could we then have appreciated Him! It is our deep and bitter need which has revealed to us the heart of

God. Very different must have been Adam's thoughts of Him when forbidden the tree, and when clothed by His own hand in coats of skin.

Nor need any one who has learned God in the person of Christ fear to dwell upon His electing love: it is but the assurance of his eternal safety. Others, who as yet cannot call Him "Father," need not question whether they are shut out from a share in it; for His word to all is, "Whosoever will, let him take the water of life freely." Drink, and you shall know that the draught was prepared for *you*, as though no other needed it.

The Lord's word to Jeremiah brings before the mind a lovely passage in the 139th psalm. Space forbids quoting it in full, but we may cull from it what seem its choicest portions, commending it all to the reader's quiet meditation when time and opportunity afford.

After the acknowledgment of the divine omniscience as to his present condition in vers. 1-5, and the divine omnipresence in vers. 7-12, the heart of the singer is absorbed in the contemplation of the thoughtfulness of the divine foreknowledge: "For Thou hast possessed my reins: Thou hast covered me in my mother's womb. I will praise Thee; for I am fearfully and wonderfully made: marvelous are Thy works; and *that my soul knoweth right well.* My substance was not hid from Thee, when I was made in secret, and curiously wrought in the lowest parts of the earth. Thine eyes did see my substance, yet being unperfect; and in Thy book all my members were written, which in continuance were fashioned, when as yet there was none of them. How precious also are Thy thoughts unto me, O God! how great is the sum of them! If I should count them, they are more in number than the sand: *when I awake, I am still with Thee"* (vers. 13-18).

With confidence may the trusting soul turn to such a God, and pray, "Search me, O God, and know my heart: try me, and know my thoughts: and see if there be any wicked way in me, and lead me in the way everlasting" (vers. 23, 24). Such might well have been the answer of Jeremiah to the word of the Lord assuring him of His interest and care, long, long before he could in any sense respond to it; but instead, he exclaims, "Ah, Lord God, behold, I cannot speak; for I am a child" (ver. 6). But what difference could that make to One who had known him thoroughly even ere He had formed him? He could make no mistake in His choice of a servant. Had not He Himself made man's mouth? And would He now, who had all resources in Himself, cast His ambassador upon his own? Ah, that would be altogether unlike God. Like Moses in Midian, Jeremiah had not yet learned Him aright, nor had he learned himself. The great lesson of no confidence in the flesh and of full confidence in God had to be put before him. The former, one might think he had in measure learned already; but had he truly done so, he would not have been disheartened when he reflected on his inability. It was simply natural backwardness: the flesh itself was not really denied. Otherwise he would neither have been troubled if he lacked ability, nor exalt-

ed if he possessed it. Without it, God was enough.
With it, God must still be all, or it would avail
nothing.

In the answer of Jehovah, it is He who assumes
all responsibility. The servant has but to obey.
He will attend to the question of power; and, as
we say in New Testament language, of "gift."
"Say not, I am a child" (ver. 7). In short, say
nothing about self at all. In spiritual things a
giant has no more place than an infant. What he
was or was not, was of no importance. How well
had the apostle Paul learned this, to say in 1 Cor.
3: 7, "So then neither is he that planteth anything" (and it was *himself* who had done so in
this case), "neither he that watereth, but God that
giveth the increase."

"Thou shalt go to all that I send thee, and whatsoever I command thee, thou shalt speak. Be not
afraid of their faces, for I am with thee to deliver thee, saith the Lord." This settled everything. As of a later prophet, we read, "Then
spake Haggai *the Lord's messenger in the Lord's
message,* unto the people, saying, I am with you,
saith the Lord" (Haggai 1: 13). The remnant
then were in the state Jeremiah was in before,
weak and fearful; but immediately upon the proclamation of such a message, we read of a stirring
of the spirits of the leaders and of all the people.

It has often been noticed, too, that the last that
Mark records of the risen and ascended Lord is
His working with those who went forth preaching; and He it was who confirmed the word with
signs following. Thus, for service, if we enter
into His thoughts, it ceases to be a question of

our weak self or our strong self, and becomes
one of *Himself*. The instrument may be feeble,
but it is upheld and used by an all-powerful Hand.

In Jeremiah's case, He who made man's mouth
put forth His hand and touched the lips of the
fearful servant, thus putting His own words into
the prophet's mouth. This in fact is what con-
stitutes a man a prophet. Isaiah's touch is unlike this, perhaps, in some respects. In his case
he had been learning his vileness and innate depravity. The seraphim flew with a live coal from
off the brazen altar of judgment, where the burnt
offering (the blessed answer to all that man is)
was going up as a sweet savor to God. Wrath
having been borne by Another, it removes sin and
terror from the self-confessed and repentant sinner. *That* touch, to Isaiah, spoke of cleansing.
This, to Jeremiah, tells of power. He who
cleanses also fits for service: this is the double
lesson the two prophets bring before us. Not
that Isaiah was not fitted to serve: he was, as
the subsequent verses show (Isa. 6); but that
is not what is there emphasized.

Jeremiah is then set over the nations and the
kingdoms. He is commissioned "to root out, to
pull down, to destroy, to throw down, to build up,
and to plant" (ver. 10). That is, he must tell of
judgment and desolation, of overturning and destruction; but great and terrible though Jehovah's vengeance must be, it is not judgment without mercy, for of restoration and recovery, of
blessing and renewal, he is also to speak. He that
scattereth Israel will regather it in His own appointed time; heavy though the hand of affliction

must fall upon the nations, yet the time will surely come when "the earth shall be full of the
knowledge of the Lord as the waters cover the
sea" (Isa. 11: 9; Hab. 2: 14).

All this is assured in the vision that follows.
The rod of the almond-tree is a symbol easily
read in connection with Num. 17. It speaks of
God's Christ declared to be the Son of God with
power by resurrection of the dead (Rom. 1: 4).
It is as the God of resurrection, the One who
intervenes when all the power of nature is at an
end, that Jeremiah was to know the Lord. It is
because He is such, that the building and planting is certain, though there be first the breaking
down and uprooting. The almond, the Hebrews
called "the hastening tree," because of its early
budding when the cold of winter had scarcely
passed away. "I will *hasten* My word to perform it" is the divine comment on the vision
(vers. 11, 12).

The word to Habakkuk a few years later
(though, as previously noted, he was contemporary with Jeremiah) is, "Though it tarry, wait
for it; because it will surely come, it will not
tarry" (Hab. 2: 3). This, the writer of the
epistle to the Hebrews quotes, but changes the
pronoun, and by the Spirit's direction a Person is
brought before us, and it reads: "Yet a little
while, and He that shall come will come, and will
not tarry" (Heb. 10: 37). It is the Lord Jesus
Himself who will bring in the blessing, predicted
by the prophets, for Israel and the earth. It is
that same blessed Person for whom we now wait
for our full blessing in heaven.

The Rod of the hastening-tree, when He came in grace, was to Israel but as a dry stick, and worthless. Hidden away from the eyes of men, He has "budded and brought forth buds, and bloomed blossoms, and yielded almonds." He has been laid up in the sanctuary above. The rod in the ark tells of the resurrected Man on the throne. (See Num. 17, throughout.)

By and by (how soon none can tell) the once despised Jesus will appear in glory, and all nations will delight in His shadow and find strength in His fruit, while the eye will be gladdened with the beauty of His blossoms; "for how great is His goodness, and how great is His beauty!" (Zech. 9: 17).

Till then, alas, there is the "seething-pot" (ver. 13), into which "His own," who "received Him not," have been cast. This is, doubtless, akin to the smoking furnace of Egypt (Gen. 15). Of old, Pharaoh had been their oppressor. Nebuchadnezzar was now to be their captor (vers. 14-16), though the full scope of the vision goes on evidently to the gathering of all the nations against Jerusalem. The seething pot* is pictured in all its horror in the last chapter of Zechariah. "Behold, the day of the Lord cometh, and thy spoil shall be divided in the midst of thee. For I will gather all nations against Jerusalem to battle; and the city shall be taken, and the houses rifled, and the women ravished; and half of the city shall go forth into captivity, and the residue of the people shall not be cut off from the city." But

---

* Note also Ezek. 24: 2-14 in this connection.

when the flames are fiercest, and the people seem about to be utterly consumed, the Almond-tree will stand again where He stood ere He was laid up in the sanctuary—upon the Mount of Olives. "The Lord my God shall come, and all the saints with Thee" (ver. 5).

Having beheld the visions of the Rod and the seething pot—simple, yet how expressive!—Jeremiah is further encouraged and warned. He is to gird his loins as for arduous service. Standing before the Lord, he is to "speak unto them all that I command thee" (ver. 17). He had but One to please, and he is not to be dismayed at the faces of the opposers: lowering they may be, but he is made as a defenced city, an iron pillar and a brazen wall against kings, princes, priests and people, as he stands in the strength of the Lord. If afraid, it will be evidence that he has not yet done with flesh and blood, and he will be confounded before them. If undismayed, they may fight against him, but prevail they cannot, for "I am with thee, saith the Lord, to deliver thee." This was to be his strength. On it he could rely. The promise is twice repeated, for God designs to give him full witness—he need have no fear (vers. 18, 19).

In the next chapter we find him in his public ministry. He has had to do with God in secret. He is now ready to face the people openly.

CHAPTER II

ENTREATY AND WARNING

(Chap. 2:1—3:5.)

Jeremiah's first expostulation with his people —at least, the first recorded—is certainly a most remarkable address for one who said, "I cannot speak, I am but a child." It would be difficult to find any portion of Scripture that would surpass it in genuine pathos and tenderness, not to speak of eloquence. The earnest pleading of the insulted and forgotten Lord, His grace and compassion towards the guilty nation, blended with solemn warnings of dreadful days to come if the heart is not turned back to Him—all together make up a discourse that might have moved the very stones; but alas, we read of no response on the part of hardened, wilful Judah.

The opening words are remarkably beautiful. "I remember thee, the kindness of thy youth, the love of thine espousals, when thou wentest after Me in the wilderness, in a land that was not sown. Israel was holiness unto the Lord, and the first-fruits of His increase. All that devour him shall offend: evil shall come upon them, saith the Lord" (vers. 1-3). How He delights to recall the first love of His people, when their hearts beat true to Himself and joy welled up in their souls at the thought of His dwelling among them (Ex. 16) !

Do we not well remember that it was so with

us when first we knew Him to be really our Saviour-God and ourselves to be His forever, when the confidence of our hearts was established in His grace? How much He was to us then! What a poor thing this world seemed, with all its glittering baubles! How gladly we turned from everything we had once delighted in to go out after Himself revealed in Jesus! He was outside this scene, the rejected One; we, too, then, must be separated from it. That which had before been as the well-watered plains of Egypt to us now became as a desert, parched and dry, in which was nothing for our hearts. With deepest joy we exclaimed, "All my springs are in Thee," and sang exultingly of the "treasure found in His love," which had indeed "made us pilgrims below."

Those were truly bright and happy days when first Christ dwelt in our hearts by faith: days when He joyed in us and we in Him. But, may we not ask ourselves, is it so now? Must He look back and say, "I remember," or does He find us still occupied with Himself, still gladly and cheerfully counting all below as dross and dung for Him, still exclaiming, "One thing I do"? Alas, that it should be ever otherwise! But the first complaint He had to make against the newly-founded Church, when all else was going on well and orderly, was this: "Thou hast left thy first love" (Rev. 2).

"Go forth, O ye daughters of Zion, and behold king Solomon with the crown wherewith his mother crowned him in the day of his espousals, and in the day of the gladness of his heart"

(Cant. 3:11). If our joy was great, how deep was *His* when first our hearts were won for Himself! Beloved, do we give Him joy now as to our practical ways, and our heart's affections from which our ways spring? Or is His Spirit grieved on account of our cold-hearted indifference—our heartlessness? for is it not worse than coldness? Let us turn, then, to His further gracious words in the portion before us.

"What iniquity have your fathers found in Me, that they are gone far from Me, and have walked after vanity, and are become vain?" (ver. 5.) Just think that *He* should ask that question—He to whom they owed everything! He had delivered them from bondage and brought them safely through a desert land, to their inheritance in the land of blessedness. He had planted them in a beautiful country to eat the fruit thereof and the goodness thereof! Alas, they had *defiled* the land. They had turned His grace into lasciviousness; they had made His heritage an abomination. They walked after things that could not profit (vers. 4-8). Terrible indictment! Base ingratitude! But oh, beloved, let us ask ourselves, Are we any less guilty than they? Nay, have we not known a far greater deliverance, a more wonderful preservation, a more costly inheritance; and yet, have not our hearts, too, gone after the vain and unprofitable things of earth? Have we not forgotten that the cedar-wood, the hyssop and scarlet, were cast into the burning of the heifer (Num. 19)—that, for faith, all the glory of this world came to an end on the cross? That tree on which He hung, that testified to His entire rejection by

this world, has it *really* separated us from the
scene where He has been set at nought? Do we
still want favor, power and place where He found
only rejection, a cross, and a tomb? How, then,
is this? What iniquity have our hearts found in
Him that they can thus turn from Him so ruth-
lessly? Ah, charge *Him* with this we cannot.
Let us confess that it is in ourselves alone the
iniquity is found. It is *we* who have changed
our glory for that which doth not profit. Well
may He say: "Be astonished, O ye heavens, at
this, and be horribly afraid, be very desolate,
saith the Lord. For My people have committed
two evils: they have forsaken Me, the fountain
of living waters, and hewed them out cisterns,
broken cisterns, that can hold no water" (vers.
12, 13).

But has He changed towards those who have so
changed towards Him? Far be the thought:
though He loves His own too much to permit
them to prosper in the paths of disobedience. He
chastened Israel with scourge after scourge, but
His heart of love remained unchangeably the
same. They might blame Him for what He could
so easily have prevented, as we are in danger of
doing; but He can say, "Hast thou not procured
this unto thyself, in that thou hast forsaken the
Lord thy God, when He led thee by the way"
(ver. 17)? He must make the backslidden in
heart eat of the fruit of his own devices (Prov.
14: 14) in order to turn the heart back from
its devices to Himself, the source of all blessing.

It is in vain to turn to Egypt, or Assyria—
each speaking of different aspects of the world;

for how can one who has known Him ever find refreshment and rest anywhere else? The waters of Sihor (supposed to be the mystic Nile, coming from no one knew where) could no longer satisfy those who once rejoiced in rain direct from heaven. Egypt is the world as we knew it when we groaned beneath the sense of its cruel bondage: Assyria is rather the world as the open enemy of the people of God. How can His own look for comfort in either of these? Yet how true it is that the heart when turned from Himself soon sinks back to the dead level of the things from which it was once delivered, and sometimes also is found ranged against the very truths it once enjoyed! In such a condition, when other remedies have failed, it is not seldom that the principle enunciated in ver. 19 has to be used to bring the wandering one to his senses. "Thine own wickedness shall correct thee, and thy backslidings shall reprove thee: know therefore and see that it is an evil thing and bitter, that thou hast forsaken the Lord thy God, and that My fear is not in thee, saith the Lord God of hosts." This is, one might say, His *last resource* (if souls are not otherwise brought back to Himself) to "deliver unto Satan for the destruction of the flesh, that the spirit may be saved in the day of the Lord Jesus" (1 Cor. 5). It has often been said that a child of God out of communion with the Father will stoop to evil reprobated even by the world—and this is doubtless true—until the very depths of the depravity is used of God to correct and reprove. So it was in the case of David, who, confessing his sin, acknowledged that

he had been left to fall so low "that Thou might-
est be justified when Thou speakest, and be clear
when Thou judgest" (Psa. 51). So, too, with
Peter. Self-confidence had characterized him for
some time, and his self-confidence at last corrected him; his dreadful backsliding reproved him.
And thus it was with the wretched man of 1 Cor.
5. He must be left to himself—given over to
Satan till, as a result, his brokenness and penitence can be pressed, in 2 Cor. 2, as a reason for
his being again received into the fellowship of
the assembly. Blessed it is to know, as already
intimated in the preceding chapter, in the wisdom of God, that sin must serve. The waters below, though they speak of sinful self-will, shall
yet be made to bring forth abundantly to the
glory of God, as in the fifth day's work in Gen. 1.
This is not, in any sense, to excuse sin, but the
contrary. Its very hideousness is used of God to
humble and bring very low the soul that has wandered from Him.

As we continue to look at the passage before
us, it is well to remember that while the nation,
as such, was in covenant-relationship with Jehovah, it was not yet the New Covenant, but that
entered into at Sinai. It still looked for something in man, who had said when his bonds were
broken and he was delivered from the yoke, "I
will not transgress" (ver. 20). But, far from
continuing in that covenant, they had sinned and
broken it from its very ratification. He had
planted them a noble vine. They had by their
ways become a degenerate plant of a strange vine
unto Him (ver. 21). Nor was their resource in

themselves: "For though thou wash thee with nitre, and take thee much soap, yet thine iniquity is marked before Me, saith the Lord" (ver. 22). The covenant under which they had placed themselves had only manifested their guilt and helplessness. God alone would be their resource: and we know He was yet to send a Saviour whose precious blood does for every believing sinner what no "soap and nitre" (no human effort) ever could do—cleanse from every sin. But this it is not yet the province of Jeremiah to make known. His present object is to impress upon them their condition, their utter hopelessness, unless they return to the Lord; so he next likens them to the untameable wild ass of the desert, refusing all correction. Exhorted to submission, they reply, "There is no hope: no; for I have loved strangers, and after them will I go" (vers. 24, 25).

Still they were not entirely without a measure of shame and apparent penitence, for even at this time revival had begun among them; but, with the mass at least, there was no real conscience-work. "*As* the thief is ashamed when he is found, *so* is the house of Israel ashamed" (ver. 26). They were ashamed to have the light turned on their idolatry, but not ashamed of the sin itself. Not that they had utterly given up all faith in Jehovah. Idols might do when things went well outwardly. In their trouble they turned to God. How much do we know of this to-day!

But if they seek not His face in times of quietness, He will not be found of them in the day of their sorrow, unless it is with true self-judgment and confession of their sin (vers. 27, 30).

How sad the reproach of vers. 31, 32—"O generation, see ye the word of the Lord. Have I
been a wilderness unto Israel? a land of darkness? Wherefore say My people, We are lords; we
will come no more unto Thee? Can a maid forget
her ornaments, or a bride her attire? yet My people have forgotten Me days without number."
This opened the way for all else: it was quite unnecessary to dig deep (as the word "secret
search" is said to mean, ver. 34) to find the evidence of the sin they refused to acknowledge. Ah,
let God but be forgotten, let the soul be estranged
from His presence, and most godless practices are
indulged in unblushingly, and with a degree of
self-confidence and effrontery that is amazing!
But His word to such is, "The Lord hath rejected
thy confidences, and thou shalt not prosper in
them" (ver. 37). This did not mean, however,
that He had done with them. Far from it. He
might chastise and punish them, but He loved
them still, and assures them of it; for although
to a wife put away, who had become another
man's, her first husband would not return, despite the lewdness of Judah, He cries after her,
"Yet return again to Me!" (chap. 3:1). What
patient, matchless grace is this! Have we, too,
wandered from Him? Have we forgotten the
word that says, "Ye adulterers and adulteresses,
know ye not that the friendship of the world is
enmity with God" (James 4: 4)? Oh, then, in
contrition of heart and self-judgment, may we
turn again to Himself, confessing the evil of our
unhallowed love for that which is so opposed to
His holiness, and prove the sweetness of His re-

storing mercy. Our God has withholden the rain
(ver. 3) that we might prove the barrenness of
a life out of communion with Himself; but He
longs for the moment when, realizing the depth
of our backsliding, the heart turns back to Himself with this cry: "My Father, Thou art the
guide of my youth!" (ver. 4).

Observe here, that though He would have Israel
cry "My Father," this is far different from crying "Abba, Father" by the Spirit of adoption,
which we have, but they had not. Nationally
Israel was God's son (Hos. 11:1; Ex. 4:22, 23).
It is only since the Cross that believers know Him
in the individual relationship of Father—not
merely national adoption—and, having life from
Him, as the One revealed by the Son in resurrection as "My Father and your Father." Our privileges are far greater than theirs. How much
holier should be our lives!

CHAPTER III

(Chaps. 3:6—6:30.)

The next prophecy is a more extensive one, going on to the end of the sixth chapter, and was uttered during the reign of the pious king Josiah (3: 6) ; but at what particular time we are not told. The details of the departure from God of both the northern and southern kingdoms (the former one already in captivity) are here more fully gone into; but there are interspersed precious promises of restoration and blessing upon their repentance which the goodness of God will yet lead them to, though it be through deepest tribulation.

"Backsliding Israel" had openly revolted from Jehovah from the day that Jeroboam's golden calves were set up. God's centre was disowned and His Word (see especially Deut. 12) despised. It is an oft-noted fact that of only one of their kings do we find it said that he sought the Lord, and then only when pressed by the Syrian invasion (2 Kings 13: 4, 5) ; on which occasion, as in the period of the Judges (to which they had practically returned, for "every man did that which was right in his own eyes"), "The Lord gave Israel a saviour, so that they went out from under the hand of the Syrians; and the children of Israel dwelt in their tents as beforetime." But though God was gracious, responding to the fee-

blest evidence of felt need, the people were unchanged: "They departed not from the sins of the
house of Jeroboam . . . and there remained the
grove also in Samaria." This was but one instance of the many in which He said, "Turn thou
unto Me," but she returned not. Finally, as an
adulterous wife, she was put away when the ten
tribes were carried to Assyria (vers. 6, 7).

"Her treacherous sister Judah's" case, however, was quite different. She had, as a rule, professed obedience to the Lord. At least open idolatry had not always characterized her. Backsliding was not so much her continual sin as treachery. A strict attention to the outward ordinances
of the temple worship, but the heart going after
the filthiness of the nations, was generally her
course; as it had been even in the days of Solomon—who built the house of Jehovah, and erected
altars to the gods of his heathen wives!

This is what markedly characterizes much of
what is called Christendom to-day. There is talk
of devotedness to the Lord, a prating of loyalty to
Christ; but alas, alas, how little is known of separation from that which dishonors Him! In fact,
the position of Jeremiah in this book must be very
much that of the man to-day who would stand for
Christ and walk in the truth. Judah had, after
all, but copied Israel, though not always so openly.
"Yet for all this her treacherous sister Judah
hath not turned unto Me with her whole heart,
but feignedly, saith the Lord" (ver. 10). The
king, and many more associated with him in the
revival that was then beginning, were doubtless
real; but there were not wanting those, as An-

anias and Sapphira in the early days of the
Church, who sought a reputation for piety and
devotedness while never truly separated from the
abounding iniquity. This is a great snare, and
only too common in our own day. It is, in fact,
the very essence of Laodiceanism. Lukewarmness
in divine things is treachery against Christ. Better to be cold than this. So he says here, "The
backsliding Israel hath justified herself more than
treacherous Judah" (ver. 11). She made no attempt to conceal her condition, at any rate. He
gives her a gracious invitation to return (even
though He had given her a bill of divorce), coupled with an assurance that He was married to
her still! (vers. 12-14). Precious it is to know
that her sons will, in the "age to come," ask the
way to Zion and return to Himself. But one
thing His holiness demands: "Only acknowledge
thine iniquity" (ver. 13). His mercy longed to
go forth; His anger was already well-nigh over-
past; but confession there must be. She must
sit in judgment on her ways, and repent of her
backslidings. The confession must be clear, and
the evils specified. No mere general acknowledgment of failure will suffice: (1) "Thou hast
transgressed against Me, (2) and hast scattered
thy ways to strangers; (3) ye have not obeyed
My voice."

Nor can it be merely a national repentance.
Nations, as such, do not repent. It must be individual work; so He says, "Turn, backsliding
children" (or sons), though the figure of a wife
is still maintained; but the nation will be saved
in the remnant. "I will take you one of a city

and two of a family and will bring you to Zion; and I will give you pastors according to My heart, which shall feed you with knowledge and understanding" (vers. 14, 15).

Jeroboam, with many successors to follow his steps, had been an evil shepherd, had led them in false ways hitherto, the fruit of which they were now eating; but He had for them shepherds who would delight to direct their feet to green pastures where the soul would find nourishment in the things of God.

It may be well to state here that it is of a literal return of the scattered Israelites, to a literal Zion in the land from whence they were carried, that the prophet speaks throughout, as we shall see more particularly when we look at chapters 30 and 31. The words are too plain and explicit to require spiritualizing, as has falsely been done.

In the 16th verse we have the last mention of the ark of the covenant; as in 2 Chron. 35:3 we have its last historical notice. There was no ark in the second temple. There will be none in that depicted by Ezekiel for the Millennium. A mere legend, for we cannot count it as anything more, tells us that at the destruction of the city and temple Jeremiah hid the ark in a cave, as also the altar of incense. This story is recorded in 2 Macc. 2: 48, an apocryphal record of very dubious authority. However that may be, we are assured that "in those days" (the days of the coming kingdom), "saith the Lord, they shall say no more , The ark of the covenant of the Lord: neither shall it come to mind; neither shall they remember it; neither shall they visit it; neither

shall that be done any more;" or, according to
R. V. margin, "neither shall they miss it, neither
shall it be made any more." Of old, under the
first covenant, it was the throne of the Lord in
the midst of Israel: but *Jerusalem* shall be called
"the throne of the Lord; and all the nations shall
be gathered unto it, to the name of the Lord, to
Jerusalem: neither shall they walk any more
after the imagination of their evil heart" (ver.
17). In that day the Lord Jesus, whom it typified,—the One in whom the wood and gold, hu-
manity and divinity, are found in one Person,—
will Himself be in their midst; the ark, that but
feebly foreshadowed Him, will no longer be
needed.

In the end of the chapter, from ver. 19 to the
close, we have the repentance of the people already made good by faith. It is a prophecy of
what will yet be when they will realize that it
is vain to hope for salvation from any but Jehovah, so long neglected. This will take place after
the Lord has saved the tents of Judah first (Zech.
12).

The first two verses of chapter 4 give us His
response to their cry of anguish, and the promised blessing when in reality they return to God.

From this point the message is to Judah, and is
a call for more than mere surface work, such as
was then going on. No real fruit for God could
be expected where they were sowing on unbroken
and thorn-choked ground (ver. 3). The plowshare
of conviction must overturn the hardened soil of
the heart. Not the natural flesh alone, but the
heart must be circumcised (ver. 4). "For he is

not a Jew which is one outwardly; ... but he is
a Jew which is one inwardly; and circumcision is
that of the heart, in the spirit, and not in the
letter" (Rom. 2:28, 29). And the same apostle
declares the true circumcision is to have "no confidence in the flesh" (Phil. 3:3). If the message
,was unheeded, then judgment must take its
course; and already the Gentile destroyer was on
his way. Vers. 5 to 13 furnish us a vivid picture
of the coming fall of Jerusalem by the hand of
Nebuchadnezzar. So astounding is this announcement that the prophet is himself astonished (ver.
10), and can scarcely credit that the Lord will
so deal with His people.

There is but one door of escape, which he points
out in ver. 14—"Wash thy heart." This can only
be by reception of the Word, and allowing it to
work in the conscience. He immediately goes on
to enlarge on the surely coming overthrow of the
city, in most awe-inspiring language (vers. 15-
21). But the people of Judah were the very
opposite to what the apostle desired for the Roman saints (Rom. 16:19)—they were "wise to do
evil, but to do good they had no knowledge" (ver.
22).

The coming desolation of the land is graphically depicted in ver. 23 to the end. It is not the
earth, but the land of Palestine, that is before
him, as the companion scripture, Isa. 24, clearly
shows. The language is doubtless highly poetical,
yet fully to be relied on,—perhaps one should say
rather *figurative,* than poetical, as the latter expression has been much abused of late.

The subject is continued in the fifth chapter,

only with more perspicuity. Individuals are more brought before us. How fallen must have been their state when the prophet had to say, "Run ye to and fro through the streets of Jerusalem, and see now, and know, and seek in the broad places thereof, *if ye can find a man*, if there be any that executeth judgment, that seeketh the truth; and I will pardon it" (ver. 1). Does not this tell us what might have been had Abraham but had faith to plead further for Sodom? He stopped at *ten* (Gen. 18). Ten could not be found. Here, judgment could be averted for *one*. Alas, they had all alike despised the chastening of the Lord (ver. 3), and turned from the truth. This amazed Jeremiah the prophet. He could scarcely credit the utterly apostate condition of his nation. There must surely be righteous ones somewhere. He would seek them out. "Therefore I said, Surely these are poor; they are foolish: for they know not the way of the Lord, nor the judgment of their God. I will get me unto the great men, and will speak unto them; for they have known the way of the Lord, and the judgment of their God: but these have altogether broken the yoke and burst the bands" (vers. 4, 5). His visit to the great we have not here (we may get many such later), but only proving that ignoble and noble are all one in the rejection of the word of God. So judgment must eventually have its way, though some years elapsed ere its fulfilment. Of this he continues to speak in vers. 6-19.

How terrible the indictment of ver. 7!—"When I had fed them to the full, they then committed adultery, and assembled themselves by troops in the harlots' houses." What a word for the people of God to-day! How awful to contemplate the yet patent fact that those who profess to be part of that Church, blessed with all spiritual blessings in Christ, should ever turn wantonly to the world and its follies, as Judah had done before—though they were on a much lower plane, their blessings being earthly and temporal. "Shall I not visit for these things? saith the Lord: and shall not My soul be avenged on such a nation as this?" (ver. 9). To Christendom He says, "I will spue thee out of My mouth!" (Rev. 3:16). "And it shall come to pass, when ye shall say, Wherefore doeth the Lord our God all these things unto us? then shalt thou answer them, Like as ye have forsaken Me, and served strange gods in your land, so shall ye serve strangers in a land that is not yours" (ver. 19). Sowing is followed by reaping: dreadful was the reaping of Israel; more dreadful will be the reaping of apostate Christendom—"Babylon the Great" (Rev. 17, 18).

Their moral condition is further exposed in words too plain to need comment (vers. 20-29), and all summarized in the last verse. "A wonderful and horrible thing is committed in the land; the prophets prophesy falsely, and the priests bear rule by their means; and My people love to have it so: and what will ye do in the end thereof?" (ver. 30). Solemn words! Ponder them carefully, my reader, and see if they be too severe to describe the great world-church of to-day.

Jerusalem's evil condition fully manifested, the sixth chapter opens with a call to the children of Benjamin to flee from her midst. Only thus could they escape being partakers of her sins. They remained and fell with her. To those entangled with religious corruption in our day the word is, "Let every one that nameth the name of the Lord depart from iniquity" (2 Tim. 2). "Come out from among them, and be ye separate . . . touch not the unclean thing" (2 Cor. 6). Later, to dwellers in the spiritual Babylon, the cry will go forth, "Come out of her, My people, that ye be not partakers of her sins, and that ye receive not of her plagues" (Rev. 18).

The present is no time for temporizing. He who has saved us, and is Lord of all, looks for clear-cut separation from all spiritual or ecclesiastical as well as carnal or fleshly evil, in sanctification to Himself. To Christendom as a whole, as to Judah then, there is little use to make appeals, nor does the Lord do it. "Their ear is uncircumcised, and they cannot hearken: behold, the word of the Lord is unto them a reproach; they have no delight in it" (ver. 10). So it has often been noted that after the days of Pergamos, in Rev. 2 and 3, the call is alone to the overcomer —not to the mass.

What made things all the more dreadful in Jeremiah's time was the mockery of the false prophets, who stilled the fears of the guilty people and prophesied smooth things, thus turning aside the keen edge of the truth. Love of reward was at the bottom of their course. Can any be so charged to-day? "From the least of them even unto the greatest of them every one is given to covetousness; and from the prophet even unto

the priest every one dealeth falsely. They have
healed also the hurt of the daughter of My people slightly, saying, Peace, peace; when there is
no peace" (vers. 13, 14). So also in Ezekiel's day
(chap. 13:10-12), which was nearly contempora-
neous with this.

But the truth rejected did not alter its character. They would have to learn by judgment
what they had no ears for by the word of the
prophet. Meantime the call to any individual
having a heart for God goes out; but there is no
response. "Stand ye in the ways, and see, and
ask for the old paths, where is the good way, and
walk therein, and ye shall find rest for your souls.
But they said, We will not walk therein. Also I
set watchmen over you, saying, Hearken to the
sound of the trumpet. But they said, We will
not hearken" (vers. 16, 17).

It is to "that which was from the beginning"
God ever directs His people in times of failure.
Man is continually running after something new,
and thus away from God, for He is of old, from
everlasting. Evolution there is none in the truth
for the dispensation. It is always evil to turn
from it. There is no restoration apart from turning back to it. There is no room for develop-
ment outside the Book.

The message rejected, the nations are called on
to acknowledge the justness of Jehovah's dealings
with so rebellious a people (vers. 18-21), and the
chapter closes with the judgment reaffirmed:
"Reprobate silver shall men call them, because
the Lord hath rejected them."

CHAPTER IV

"WHAT AGREEMENT HATH THE TEMPLE OF GOD WITH IDOLS?"

(Chaps. 7-10.)

In this section it is more the temple that is before us, and the incongruity of professing great reverence for it while idolatrous practices and their accompanying evils are not only tolerated but diligently persisted in. The prophet had been addressing the people rather as a civil community before. Now he sees them in connection with the newly-cleansed house of Jehovah. His message is addressed to those "that enter in at these gates to worship the Lord" (ver. 2). This is shown to be all a mere pretence, for while they talked loudly of the temple—made it their rallying-cry, so to speak—their ways were anything but in accordance with the holiness that became God's house. "Trust ye not in lying words, saying, The temple of the Lord, the temple of the Lord, the temple of the Lord, are these. For if ye thoroughly amend your ways and your doings; if ye thoroughly execute judgment between a man and his neighbor; if ye oppress not the stranger, the fatherless, and the widow, and shed not innocent blood in this place, neither walk after other gods to your hurt; then will I cause you to dwell in this place, in the land that I gave to your fathers forever and ever" (vers. 4-7).

Nothing can be more obnoxious to God than to have His name vauntingly connected with unrighteousness. How terrible to hear some now-adays prate of "the authority of the Lord in His assembly," and talk of "divine ground," while deliberately refusing to execute judgment between a man and his neighbor, disclaiming all such responsibility! Nay, even worse, seek to foist it upon the Righteous One who dwells in the midst of His people! Strange that the important word, "Follow *righteousness*, faith, charity, peace, with them that call on the Lord out of a pure heart" (2 Tim. 2:22), should be so overlooked! Such is Rome's principle: sad it is, and solemn, to see those who should know better, following, in this at least, in her wake. We can rest assured no amount of professed regard for the assembly of God will atone for the neglect of righteousness. "The righteous Lord loveth righteousness." It is with Him who is "the holy and the true" with whom we have to do—He in whom there is "no darkness at all."

Nothing can be more abhorrent to Him than the dreadful state described in vers. 8-10. It is the divorce of position from condition—the making much of ecclesiastical place, while the walk is utterly at variance with the truth connected with it. Position is important. Nothing, in fact, is more so; but let us be careful to maintain the corresponding practice. Those who, through grace, have been gathered out of unscriptural systems to the precious name of the Lord Jesus Christ alone, should see to it that their walk is consistent with their privileged place.

The next verse, it will be noted, is referred to by our Lord when He made a whip of small cords and drove the money-changers and venders from the courts of the temple (Matt. 21:13). On that occasion He connected two scriptures together. The first was from Isa. 56:7—"My house shall be called a house of prayer for all people." This shall yet be true when Christ's kingdom is set up in power; but when the King appeared in lowliness, His judgment was, "Ye have made it a den of thieves," as Jeremiah had said before: "Is this house, which is called by My name, become a den of robbers in your eyes? Behold I, even I, have seen it, saith the Lord."

As a result, like Shiloh, it was to be left desolate, and the false worshipers were to be cast out from their land; nor would prayer avail for them now. Judgment must have its way (vers. 12-16).

"The queen of heaven" was an object of worship then as with Rome now; for it is well known that Mariolatry was but the continuation of the worship of the false goddess here referred to, universally acknowledged under various names. "The children gather wood, and the fathers kindle the fire, and the women knead their dough, to make cakes to the queen of heaven, and to pour out drink offerings unto other gods, that they may provoke Me to anger" (ver. 18). Terrible it is to see the evils of that dark day actually followed by a fast apostatizing Christendom at the present time! "Do they provoke Me to anger? saith the Lord: do they not provoke themselves to the confusion of their own faces?" (ver. 19). Fury and wrath unquenchable must they reap who have so grievously departed from the true God (ver. 20).

Though the ritual service of the temple, had been re-established, through king Josiah, yet, among the mass, the question of obedience had been entirely forgotten: "They hearkened not, nor inclined their ear, but walked in the counsels and in the imagination of their evil heart, and went backward, and not forward." And this had characterized them from the day He had brought them out of Egypt, though He had sent prophets to them again and again, "daily rising up early and sending them: yet they hearkened not unto Me, nor inclined their ear, but hardened their neck: they did worse than their fathers" (vers. 21-26). The prophets' ministry, it is plain, had become hopeless. The word of God was still to be proclaimed; nothing was to be kept back, but all hope of national response was at an end. The verdict was already pronounced: "This is a nation that obeyeth not the voice of the Lord their God, nor receiveth correction: truth is perished, and is cut off from their mouth" (ver. 28). The Lord had rejected them; let them mourn and cut off the hair, as a woman put to shame, for they are denominated "the generation of His wrath."

Terrible was to be the desolation resulting upon their casting off. Tophet, the high place of the valley of Hinnom, where the children were sacrificed upon the heated brazen arms of Moloch, was to become the valley of slaughter in which they should bury until there was no more place, while fowls and beasts devoured the unburied bodies of the residue. "Then will I cause to cease from the cities of Judah, and from the streets of Jerusalem, the voice of mirth and the voice of gladness, the

voice of the bridegroom, and the voice of the
bride: for the land shall be desolate" (vers. 30-
34). Even the very bones of the kings and princes
of Judah, as well as of the priests, the prophets,
and the inhabitants of Jerusalem, would be
brought from their tombs and strewed before the
heavenly bodies which they had worshiped in
life; while for the residue, death will be preferable to the terrors of that evil day. Doubtless
this all had a fulfilment in the Chaldean conquest
and the later Maccabean times; but as "no prophecy of the Scripture is of any private interpretation," it likewise pictures the direful tribulation yet to come.

It is not because Jehovah delights in judgment
("His strange act") that His people must be so
visited. It was the inevitable result of their own
waywardness. Theirs was a "perpetual backsliding;" and though oft pleaded with, they repented
not, but "every one turned to his course, as the
horse rusheth into battle" (chap. 8: 5, 6). Though
they boasted of their wisdom, they had not the
discernment of the migratory birds. "Yea, the
stork in the heaven knoweth her appointed times;
and the turtle-dove and the crane and the swallow
observe the time of their coming; but My people
know not the judgment of the Lord" (ver. 7).
Of the same character was the Lord's word to the
scribes—"Can ye not discern the signs of the
times?" Yet they said, "We are wise, and the
the law of the Lord is with us;" but the word
of God was practically written in vain for them
—not denied, as it is not always denied to be
His Word to-day, by many who politely bow it

out and profess veneration for it while walking
in disobedience to it. "Peace, peace," such may
say, but true peace there is not. Priest and people alike deal falsely with the Sacred Oracles; as
a result, the time of visitation cannot be long
delayed.

From ver. 14 of chap. 8 to the end of chap 10
we have a most touching lamentation over the
fallen estate of the people who have been "put to
silence" by God; that is, who are so clearly
proven to be guilty before Him that they are
speechless in His presence. Jeremiah enters most
deeply into all their feelings, even wailing with
them, "The harvest is past, the summer is ended,
and we are not saved" (chap. 8: 20). It is a temporal salvation that is referred to, of course. The
day of God's patience with them as a nation is
ended, and all hope is now vain. How striking
is the impassioned cry, "Is there no balm in
Gilead? Is there no physician there? Why then is
not the health of the daughter of My people recovered?" (See also chap. 46: 11). Alas, too
deep is the wound for Gilead's balm to heal!

"Oh that my head were waters, and mine eyes
a fountain of tears, that I might weep day and
night for the slain of the daughter of my people!"
Well has Jeremiah been called the "Weeping
Prophet." His was not the pharisaic spirit that
could build its own reputation for holiness on the
ruined testimony of others. Israel was *his* people. He would not be viewed as other than a part
of the desolate nation—he identifies himself fully
with it. True, he longs to flee from them to a
wayfarer's lodge in the wilderness, as did David

in Ps. 55: 6-8; but he is one with them still,
Their ways grieve him to the soul, as they must
one in fellowship with God about them ; but
for themselves he has tenderest love and compassion. Sad that it should ever be otherwise with
any of God's people now. Yet, alas, a hard, judging spirit often accompanies outward separation
from evil. How easy to forget that we are all
part of a ruined Church, and all share in the responsibility of that ruin. With Jeremiah, we see
that while he is obliged to make known to his people their deep, deep sin and departure from God,
he does so with breaking heart, as one who longs
after them all and is full of heaviness on their
account.

How graphic is the language of ver. 21, descriptive of the decimating plague following the
horrors of war: "Death is come up into our win-
dows, and is entered into our palaces, to cut off
the children from without and the young men
from the streets." In such a world as this, how
strange that a man should glory in the fleeting
things of time and sense! Yet how needful to our
souls ever to keep in mind the verses following:
"Let not the wise man glory in his wisdom,
neither let the mighty man glory in his might; let
not the rich man glory in his riches: but let him
that glorieth glory in this, that he understandeth
and knoweth Me, that I am the Lord which exer-
ciseth loving-kindness, judgment, and righteousness in the earth: for in these things I delight,
saith the Lord" (vers. 23, 24).

In the close of the chapter, Israel uncircumcised
in heart is put on a level with the uncircumcised

nations about them. They must be judged with
the idolatrous nations whose ways they had followed.

Of the 10th chapter I need say little. It is
much like the 44th of Isaiah. It gives us Jehovah's condemnation of idolatry, and contrasts
with the stocks and stones, to which His people
had turned, Him who is "the portion of Jacob,"
"the former of all things," who would fain have
comforted the afflicted nation, but must "sling
out the inhabitants of the land" as from a mighty
catapult, causing them to cry, "Woe is me for
my hurt!"

The 11th verse is in Chaldee, that the heathen
might in their own tongue read the condemnation
of their idolatry.

Solemn are the words with which this portion
is brought to a close: "Lord, I know that the way
of man is not in himself: it is not in man that
walketh to direct his steps. O Lord, correct me,
but with judgment, not in Thine anger, lest Thou
bring me to nothing."

Judgment, unsparing, will fall on the heathen;
chastisement, leading eventually to restoration,
must be meted out to His own.

CHAPTER V

THE BURNED BRANCHES AND THE SWELLING OF JORDAN

(Chaps. 11, 12.)

I have but little to say on these two chapters, solemn and searching as they assuredly are. It is the continued expostulation of Jehovah with the people who were ever upon His heart, however much they had loved to wander.

He goes back to the beginning, the time of their sorrow and slavery when He found them in Egypt and brought them out of the iron furnace. In the joy of deliverance they had sworn obedience to His commandments, but their whole subsequent history had only manifested their faithlessness; in result of which the curse—the only thing the law could give to them or any other—rested upon them (chap. 11:1-8).

Again and again warned and entreated, both Israel and Judah had broken the covenant and joined themselves to idols (vers. 9, 10). Judgment, at last, must fall upon them, and they would cry in vain for deliverance to their self-chosen gods, powerless to save. Altars to their shameful idols were seen everywhere; but no prayer nor cry of need went up to *Him* who alone could deliver: now He declares, "I will not hear them in the time that they cry unto Me for their trouble" (vers. 13, 14). She whom He still called "My beloved" had no longer any place in His house, for on the ground of her responsibility all had been forfeited.

Ver. 16 is doubtless the text of the apostle's dissertation in the 11th of Romans. The branches in the olive tree of blessing,"fair, of goodly fruit," are to be destroyed with the fire of judgment. The apostle indeed tells us what the prophet does not— that wild olive branches were to be grafted in their place; though, if they continue not in God's goodness, they too shall be cut off, and Israel grafted in again; for "God is able."

Jeremiah himself speaks in vers. 18-20, taking, as another has said, "the place of the faithful remnant who have the testimony of God." Persecuted, he appeals to the One on whose errands he ran, and He to whom vengeance belongs assures him of righteous recompense upon "the men of Anathoth;" for it was true of him as of our Lord that a prophet in his own country and city is without honor.

It is quite in keeping with the Old Testament and God's government to find Jeremiah here praying for the destruction of these enemies of the Lord. It is certainly not the grace of the gospel, but according to the righteousness of God's moral government. We see the same thing in the fifth chapter of Revelation, which of itself should show that the souls under the altar are clearly *Jewish* martyrs in the tribulation period, after the present dispensation of grace is closed, and not Christian martyrs, whose prayer would rather be, "Father, forgive them," or, "Lay not this sin to their charge."

In chap. 12 the prophet pleads with God in regard to the vengeance soon to fall. There is something intensely beautiful and touching in the

holy familiarity with which he addresses the High
and Lofty One that inhabiteth Eternity. One is
reminded of Abraham overlooking the cities of
the plains. "Righteous art Thou, O Lord, when
I plead with Thee: yet let me talk with Thee of
Thy judgments: Wherefore doth the way of the
wicked prosper? wherefore are all they happy
that deal very treacherously? . . . Thou art near
in their mouth, and far from their reins."

How gracious of God to be thus "talked with!"
Submissively, Jeremiah pours out his heart; not
in complaint, but as seeking to know the mind of
the Lord, and yet pleading that all may not be
engulfed in the common ruin, but that the wicked
may be separated from the mass, for the slaughter, and thus blessing come upon the mourning
land (vers. 1-5).

In the answer of God, it is made known to him
that the mass are far from His thoughts of
righteousness; and the prophet must have a deepened and more solemnizing sense of their iniquity.
He has been but running with footmen; and as
they have hastened on in sin, he has been grieved
at heart; but, like horses prepared for battle,
like a charge of cavalry, is he to see the abounding evil: how can he contend with such? Thus
far he has been in the land of peace, and hoping
that widespread indignation might not be poured
out; yet he has been wearied by their sin and rebellion. He is to see the judgment of God poured
out in all its fury, as the swelling waters of Jordan in harvest-time (Josh. 3:15), sweeping all before them. In that day, both the righteous and the
wicked will suffer in the desolating woes that are

to be poured upon Judah. How, then, will he do? Even his nearest kinsmen will reject the word he brings, and deal treacherously with him (vers. 5, 6).

It is too late to plead for them. Jehovah has forsaken His house and left His heritage. His "dearly beloved" is to be given into the hand of her enemies. Like a lion roaring in the forest, they have proudly defied Him; now, like a speckled bird persecuted of the birds of the wood, the assembled nations shall devote her to destruction. Their pastors had spoiled them as a ruined vineyard and trodden His portion beneath their feet, and no man laid to heart the desolation ensuing; so from one end of the land to the other the sword of the Lord should devour and no flesh have peace. The awful reaping time had come, the day of the fierce anger of Jehovah (vers. 7-13).

In the last section of the chapter a word is addressed to the surrounding nations. "His evil neighbors" He calls them, thus intimating His concern for Israel still; for they were not only *Israel's* neighbors, but His. Then blessing is foretold both for the chosen people about to be scattered and to any among the nations who turn to their God—which looks on to the Millennium. The nation of Israel shall yet be the centre of God's dealing with the earth, and shall be the means of blessing to the surrounding peoples. "But if they will not obey, I will utterly pluck up and destroy that nation, saith the Lord" (ver. 17).

CHAPTER VI

THE MARRED GIRDLE: "WILT THOU NOT BE MADE CLEAN?"

(Chap. 13.)

"Thus saith the Lord unto me, Go and get thee a linen girdle, and put it upon thy loins, and put it not in water" (ver. 1).

The Lord would now teach by what is evidently a vision, as it is hardly to be supposed that Jeremiah actually carried the girdle all the way to the river Euphrates. On the other hand, if a literal occurrence, it but exemplifies his obedience to the commands of God. The girdle, is the sign of service, as is evident in many scriptures. The Lord Jesus frequently so speaks of it, as in Luke 12: 35, where He bids His servants have "their loins girded about," and in the 37th verse of the same chapter, where He tells of His perpetual service for His redeemed throughout the ages to come. In John 13 we see Him as the girded servant washing His disciples' feet, that they may be cleansed from earthly defilement and thus "have part with Him;" and when He appears in glory to the beloved disciple on the isle of Patmos, He is "girt about the breasts with a golden girdle."

Israel had been Jehovah's girded servant from of old; but, alas, a faithless one, as Christendom has been since. The girdle was the sign of service. Jeremiah gets one, and girds himself therewith. The word of the Lord comes again, telling him: "Take the girdle that thou hast got, which is upon thy loins, and arise, go to Euphrates, and hide it there in the hole of the rock" (vers. 3, 4). So should the faithless nation be carried away to Babylon and be defiled, by the Euphrates. Jeremiah does as he is commanded. "After many days" (indicative of the captivity by the Euphrates where they were about to be carried) he was sent to get it again; but, "behold, the girdle was marred, it was good for nothing" (ver. 7). The application is readily made: captivity would not change the state of the people's heart. Only genuine self-judgment could effect that. Israel had been caused to cleave to the Lord as a girdle to the loins of a man, "that they might be unto Me," He says, "for a people, and for a name, and for a praise, and for a glory: but they would not hear" (ver. 11). Therefore they must as an untrustworthy servant be put away.

By the parable of the bottle their emptiness is set forth (ver. 12). They shall be filled, not with the joy of the Lord, but with the wine of strong delusion, which will make them drunk with self-confidence and lead them to destruction.

The prophet's soul enters fully into this awful word, and he cries as from an anguished heart, "Give glory to the Lord your God before He cause darkness, and before your feet stumble upon the dark mountains, and, while ye look for light, He turn it into the shadow of death, and make it gross darkness. But if ye will not hear it, my soul shall weep in secret places for your pride; and mine eye shall weep sore, and run down with

tears, because the Lord's flock is carried away
captive" (vers. 15-17). He sees his light-reject-
ing people about to be given up to judicial darkness. He would still arouse them to the solemnity
of their condition. If they sleep on and refuse
to hearken, he will weep bitterly as his own predictions come to pass.

There are differences between the darkness of
nature, the darkness of choice, and the darkness
of judgment. In Eph. 4:18 we read of the Gentiles "having the understanding darkened, being
alienated from the life of God through the ignorance that is in them, because of the blindness"
(or hardness) "of their heart." The result of
long years of turning away from God is that men
are born in natural darkness. God has, however,
sent the Light into this scene of gloom; but in
John 3:19, 20 we learn that "this is the condemnation, that light is come into the world, and
men loved darkness rather than light, because
their deeds were evil." This is deliberate, wilful
darkness. In such manner had the men of Judah
and Jerusalem refused to come to the light when
God was speaking to their consciences by His
prophet. The inevitable result must be judicial
darkness. They would be given up to the darkness they had chosen. So will it be, in an even
more dreadful sense, with highly favored Christendom after the Church has been caught away to
be forever with the Lord. "God shall send them
strong delusion, that they should believe the lie
[of the Antichrist]: that they all might be
judged who believed not the truth, but had pleasure in unrighteousness" (2 Thess. 2:11, 12).

By commandment of the Lord, our prophet addresses himself directly to the king and the queen as the responsible leaders—probably Jehoiakim and his consort. He calls upon them to humble themselves and sit down. Their warlike preparations could be of no possible avail. It was *repentance* that was needed, not arms and soldiers. The captivity was decreed. Judah, as Israel before, should be borne away from their land. "Them that come from the north" (ver. 20) refers to the Babylonian army. How touching and yet solemn the question put to the unfaithful king, "Where is the flock that was given thee, thy beautiful flock?" The king had not been to them an example of subjection to God, but rather of defiance to Him. So he is asked, "What wilt thou say when I shall punish thee?" As a travailing woman's pains come suddenly, so should his sorrows take him; as indeed they did very shortly after (ver. 21). And if the question is asked "Wherefore come these things upon me?" the answer is, "For the greatness of thine iniquity are thy skirts discovered, and thy heels made bare" (ver. 22).

Could they then make themselves pure in the sight of God? Far from it. It was just as impossible for them to do good who had been accustomed to do evil, as for the Ethiopian to become white or the leopard to change his spots. How little do the modern apostles of the religion of culture enter into this! As no account of washing can alter the black skin of the negro, so no merely human effort to reform can effect a real change if there be not first a divine work in the soul.

"Altogether unprofitable," they should be scat-

tered as the worthless stubble is carried away by
the wind of the wilderness. This was their due
reward ("the portion of thy measures"), because
they had forgotten the Lord and trusted in false-
hood (vers. 25, 26). Sin had made them as an
utterly reprobate and loathsome adulteress, whose
shame was to be openly manifested. Idolatry
had been their ruin. "Woe unto thee, O Jerusalem!" he cries; but because God is gracious and
long-suffering still, he entreats, "Wilt thou not be
made clean? When shall it once be?" Alas, alas,
they were turning away in their folly from the
only One who could cleanse them, and the black
clouds of doom were fast gathering overhead.

CHAPTER VII

FAMINE—TEMPORAL AND SPIRITUAL

(Chaps. 14, 15.)

Of old, when Jehovah "led Jacob like a flock," and brought the people of His love out of the cruel bondage of Egypt, He set before them blessing and cursing, life and death, good and evil. Earthly prosperity and honor were to accompany fidelity to God. No foe could harm, no drought afflict, no famine or sickness decimate Israel, so long as they were careful to obey the word of the Lord and walk according to His statutes. On the other hand, all these sore trials should certainly follow in the wake of indifference to God and rebellion against His Word.

It is therefore quite in harmony with His ways that we find the people of Judah in great distress for lack of food and water. The real famine was within. The outward misery was but the reflection of the moral state. Deeply touching, and highly poetical too, is the seer's description of the desolation wrought in the land: "Judah mourneth, and the gates thereof languish; they are black unto the ground; and the cry of Jerusalem is gone up. And their nobles have sent their little ones to the waters: they came to the pits, and found no water; they returned with their vessels empty; they were ashamed and confounded, and covered their heads. Because the ground is chapped, for there was no rain in the

earth, the plowmen were ashamed, they covered
their heads.   Yea, the hind also calved in the
field, and forsook it, because there was no grass.
And the wild asses did stand in the high places,
they snuffed up the wind like dragons; their eyes
did fail, because there was no grass" (chap. 14:
2-6).

The language is most pathetic, the condition of
the people heartrending. The children cried, with
parched tongue and fever-cracked lips, for drink;
but there was no water to be had. They went in
vain, at the behest of the hopeless nobles, to the
dry wells. There was no refreshment there. All
farming operations were at a standstill. No rain
meant no crops and no food. The very beasts of
the field shared in the general desolation. The
hind, tenderest of animals, forsook her offspring
"because there was no grass;" the eyes of the
wild asses failed as they looked for a few spears
of herbage.

There was no yearly-overflowing river for
Canaan. "It was a land that drank water of
the rain of heaven;" a land that the Lord watched
over continually. He it was who gave refreshing
showers in abundance, or who withheld according to the state of His people. The river of
Mizraim might flow on unceasingly, and flood its
valley year by year, let the condition of the
Egyptians be as it would, but it was otherwise
in the land of Jehovah. And we may learn from
this to-day. Men of the world are often allowed
to prosper despite utter ungodliness. Alas, they
are lifted up on high to fall more terribly in the
end! On the other hand, the children of God are

under His special care, and "whom the Lord loveth He chasteneth" (or disciplineth) for their eternal good. The sheep of Christ have not wool so thick but that if they wander from the Shepherd's side they feel every cold blast of this world. A Christian out of communion must pass under the rod. To Israel it was said, "You only have I known of all the families of the earth; *therefore* will I punish you for your iniquities." The principle is the same for us now.

In the next three verses Jeremiah again takes the place of the mediator, and tenderly pleads for those who were called by the name of the Lord. He acknowledges their sin as his own. It is *"our* iniquities," *"our* backslidings," and *"we* have sinned." Merit he does not plead; but "for Thy name's sake" is his cry. "O the hope of Israel, the Saviour thereof in time of trouble, why shouldest Thou be as a stranger in the land, and as a wayfaring man that turneth aside to tarry for a night? Why shouldest Thou be as a man astonished, as a mighty man that cannot save? Yet Thou, O Lord, art in the midst of us, and we are called by Thy name; leave us not" (vers. 8, 9). The grief of the prophet, and yet his implicit faith in Jehovah, alike stir the soul. He who would have delighted to show mercy to His people had become as a visiting stranger, so far as their realization of His presence was concerned. In the rejected One, however, is the only "hope of Israel." He had not actually withdrawn Himself. The Shekinah was still in the temple. He abode "in the midst" of them though unrecognized and unsought by the mass.

His answer is, "They have loved to wander, they have not refrained their feet, therefore the Lord doth not accept them; He will now remember their iniquity, and visit their sins" (ver. 10). It was impossible that the Holy One could go on with iniquity. Judgment must begin at the house of God. He loved them too much to let them take their own way with impunity. So He says, "Pray not for this people for their good."

In the New Testament we read, "There is a sin unto death: I do not say that he shall pray for it" (1 John 5: 16). If chastisement is despised, and the Spirit of grace insulted, there comes a time when it is too late for supplication or entreaty. As a last act of God's holy government, the erring one is cut off, and the case left for the Judgment Seat of Christ. We have examples of this in Ananias and Sapphira, both of them cut off in their transgression. So with some in the Corinthian assembly that dishonored the Lord at His table in the memorial Supper. The Holy Spirit says, "For this cause many are weak and sickly among you, and many sleep." And so it was with Israel in the case before us. It was too late for grace alone to be exercised. They must know to the full the government of God. Neither fasting nor offerings would be of any avail to turn aside the sword, the famine, and the pestilence (ver. 12).

Jeremiah, however, continues to plead; and now on the ground that the people had been misled by false prophets, who had spoken smooth things, and thus led their hearers to suppose that sin was a light thing. For answer, the Lord tells him these evil teachers shall bear their judgment, and be consumed with the rest; but this cannot free their followers, who delighted in them because of their own wicked desires. "If the blind lead the blind, *both* shall fall into the ditch!"

In these verses what a solemn picture we have of Christendom as we know it! Satan's ministers turning their hearers away from the truth unto fables! Wolves in sheeps' clothing posing as servants of Christ, yet shaking the confidence of the simple in the truth and authority of the Scriptures, ridiculing and assailing the great and holy truths of the atonement and the eternal judgment awaiting those who trample under foot the blood of Christ! But alas, the listeners will fall in the doom of the preachers! Wanting smooth things, they refuse the truth when presented to them, and cling to deceivers from sheer love of sin. Together they shall "perish in the gainsaying of Core" (Jude 11).

The pathos of the balance of the chapter is beyond description. The prophet, broken-hearted, is inconsolable. He forms one of a trio, with Moses and Paul, who could all alike be cut off themselves if their people might but be saved.

The famine and the sword were doing their deadly work in city and field, and there was no healing. So stirred is his soul that he cannot but continue his agonized intercession: "Do not abhor us, for Thy name's sake; do not disgrace the throne of Thy glory; remember, break not Thy covenant with us" (ver. 21). It is like Joshua's cry of old, "The Egyptians will hear of it." But when the people of God dishonor Him by their lives, He will not spare needed discipline, even though the uncircumcised glory over Him. Better that "the cause of Christ" be disgraced before the world than that His people be permitted to go on in sin. God will vindicate His name in His own way and time.

The solemn answer of Jehovah in the first nine verses of chap. 15 gives no hope of deliverance. Even though Moses and Samuel stood to entreat for them, they would not be heard. The people must "go forth;" and if they despairingly ask, "Where?" the awful answer is, "Such as are for death, to death; and such as are for the sword, to the sword; and such as are for the famine, to the famine; and such as are for the captivity, to the captivity" (ver. 2). The sword, the dogs, the fowls, and the beasts of the earth, are alike appointed to carry out the work of destruction: and any escaping these would be carried into all the kingdoms of the earth; and this because their share in the sin of Manasseh had never been repented of. None should pity nor care; for having forsaken the Lord, He would stretch out His hand against them. Young and old must be destroyed. "It is a fearful thing to fall into the hands of the living God;" for "our God is a consuming fire."

As the full extent of God's sentence bursts upon his soul, Jeremiah is overcome by a sense of almost unutterable desolation. How deeply he feels his helplessness and loneliness, as one man endeavoring to stand for God and seeking the good of those who hate and despise Him! His prayers seem to be unavailing. God apparently refuses to hearken to his voice. The people, on their part, turn a deaf ear to his messages. He cries out in anguish, "Woe is me, my mother, that thou hast borne me a man of strife and a man of contention to the whole earth! I have neither lent on usury, nor have men lent to me on usury; yet every one of them doth curse me" (ver. 10).

The Lord at once replies in tenderest compassion and assures him that with himself and any who really seek His face, "it shall be well in the time of evil and in the time of affliction," but due punishment must be meted out to the workers of iniquity.

Encouraged by this evidence that his cry has not really been unheard and unheeded, he can now pray with fuller assurance; for Jehovah knows and will remember and visit at the appointed time. "For Thy sake," he cries, "I have suffered rebuke:" then he tells of what had been his solace in times of indifference and rejection—the word of God (vers. 15, 16). "Thy words were found, and I did eat them; and Thy Word was unto me the joy and rejoicing of my heart: for I am called by Thy name, O Lord God of hosts." Here we have two things intimately connected elsewhere in Scripture—the *Word* and the *Name*. "Thou . . . hast kept My Word, and hast not denied My Name" (Rev. 3: 8). See, also, Rev. 2: 13—"My Name" and "My faith"—that which is declared by the Word.

Jeremiah, the separatist (2 Cor. 6: 14-18; Isa. 52: 11) of his day, who, much as he loved the people of the Lord, yet had to turn sorrowfully from fellowship with them in their evil course,

had to learn—as all others must who, in a day of
declension, seek to walk in holy separation unto
God—that "he that departeth from evil maketh
himself a prey" (Isa. 59:15). He was a man,
as we have seen, characterized by much tenderness of heart, and certainly by intense affection
for the heritage of Jehovah (chap. 9:1-3); yet
faithfulness demanded that he walk apart from
them, testifying against their ways; and as a result he had to say, "Every one of them doth hate
me." So also Paul could ask the Galatians, "Am
I therefore become your enemy because I tell
you the truth?" (Gal. 4:16), when witnessing
against their departure from the faith once delivered to the saints: and to the Corinthians he
says, "I will gladly spend and be spent for you;
though the more abundantly I love you, the less
I be loved" (2 Cor. 12:15). These dear men of
God are seen pursuing their well-nigh solitary
way at times, finding their refreshment and
strength in the Word and the Name, though denied much as to godly fellowship with others.

In ver. 17 Jeremiah says, "I sat not in the assembly of the mockers, nor rejoiced; I sat *alone*
because of Thy hand." It was in this very period
of loneliness for the Name's sake, when he could
say, "For Thy sake I have suffered reproach,"
that the Word of God was more to him than ever
before. The Lord's people gave him only grief,
but His Word filled him with joy. His heart
might almost break as he contemplated their
apostate condition. It was made to rejoice when
he turned to the sure Word of God.

Job and David in their times could speak in

similar terms. The former is heard crying out, "I have esteemed the words of His mouth more than my necessary food" (Job 23:12), and this at a time when the ways of God with His dear servant seemed quite inexplicable, and he floundered in the vain effort to find Him out. Still "the words of His mouth" he loved to dwell upon, and, relying on them, dared to say, "When He hath tried me, I shall come forth as gold" (ver. 19).

The exalted shepherd, in the "Psalm of the Laver" (119), sweetly celebrates the preciousness and cleansing efficacy of the Word, and in verse 3 joins with "the weeping prophet" in declaring, "Thy testimonies have I taken as an heritage forever; for they are the rejoicing of my heart." And again, he says, "I esteem all Thy precepts concerning all things to be right; and I hate every false way" (ver. 128). See also vers. 97, 113, 119, 163.

Thus we have patriarch, ruler, and prophet, alike testifying to the fulness and richness of the testimonies of the Lord. And that Word—fuller and richer now because of added treasures, making known the hitherto secret things—shall *Christians* now treat it with indifference? *Many*, it is to be feared, find little to interest them in its sacred pages. And the reason is not far to seek—there is so little practical separation from evil, and so little cleaving to the Lord with purpose of heart. Of one thing we can rest assured. Those who really enter into what is involved in being gathered in truth to the Name of the Rejected One, will invariably find His Word an un-

failing source of delight. Heart-identification
with Christ results in heart-appreciation of His
Word. The great *desideratum* is to go on quietly
and humbly with the Lord Jesus Christ, and to
walk apart from the abounding iniquity (both in
its gross and its pleasing forms) of these last
days. Then let the Word of God be the man of
your counsel. Make it your daily companion.
Search its precious pages prayerfully and per-
severingly. Soon you will learn to feast upon it
with ever-increasing delight.

An aged Christian once said, "When first converted, I commenced reading the Bible. I read it
for ten years, and I thought it a very nice book.
I enjoyed it greatly. I read it for ten years more,
and I thought it a wonderful book—it thrilled my
soul. I read it for ten years more, and I thought
it the most surpassingly precious book in the
world. It was as food and drink to me. Now I
have been reading it for forty years, and I am
filled with delight and amazement at its beauties
and depth every time I open it." May the reader
and the writer know more of this increasing love
for its "sure testimonies." Thus we shall find our
delight in walking with Him, even though, as in
Enoch's day, all the world should take another
course.

That separation from evil is the mind of God
for His servants is brought out clearly in the few
remaining verses of this portion. "Therefore thus
saith the Lord, If thou return, then will I bring
thee again, and thou shalt stand before Me: and
if thou take forth the precious from the vile,
thou shalt be as My mouth: let them return unto

thee; but return not thou unto them" (ver. 19).
Whatever others might think, say, or do, Jeremiah is to walk apart; alone, if need be, from all
the abounding evil; not to be amalgamated with
it, or with those in it, in the vain hope of doing
them good. If others took the same position as
he, well and good; he would have their fellowship in his path of separation: but the word is
plain, "Return not thou unto them."

In 2 Tim. 2 the same principle is enforced for
the guidance of the man of God in the declension
and ruin of the Church. He is to "purge himself" from all that is contrary to the word of
God, and from those who tolerate and condone the
ecclesiastical lawlessness of the day. So shall he
"be a vessel unto honor, sanctified and meet for
the Master's use." This is not, of course, to say
that a mere Pharisaic separation from saints
who do not see eye to eye as to details of doctrine or practice is enjoined by Him who would
have His people endeavor "to keep the unity of
the Spirit in the bond of peace." Unity is not
necessarily uniformity. But the call is to separation from what is unholy and offensive to God.
Unspiritual Christians, as well as worldlings, will
doubtless misunderstand and abuse the one who
acts upon this "saying of God," but He will see
to the consequences if we but yield implicit obedience to His revealed will. He promised to make
Jeremiah as a wall of brass, and assured him
that though "they shall fight against thee, they
'shall not prevail against thee: for I am with thee
to save thee and to deliver thee, saith the Lord.
And I will deliver thee out of the hand of the

wicked, and I will redeem thee out of the hand of the terrible" (vers. 20, 21).

God was for him, who could be against him? His faith in this would be severely tested as the darkness deepened and the thunders of judgment roared more loudly. But "I am with thee" is sufficient for every trial. Devils may rage, men may gnash their teeth in malicious hatred, Providence itself may seem to oppose; but the man who can rest in faith upon the promises of the Eternal shall never be put to shame.

CHAPTER VIII

SIN WHERE THE BLOOD SHOULD BE!

(Chaps. 16, 17.)

In the portion of the "Word of the Lord" which now claims our attention, we no longer hear the tender supplication of the seer on behalf of Judah. He pleaded unweariedly while there seemed to be hope of averting the threatened disaster. But there was no repentance on the part of the people, and the holiness of God's character demanded that sin, in those so closely linked with His Name, be not passed over lightly. The present section is a solemn indictment on His part showing why His hand must be against them, however much His heart may still be for them.

The prophet is bidden to refrain from marriage, for connubial bliss was not to be thought of under the present sad conditions. Children born in such circumstances were only being introduced into a scene of sorrow and grief, with the prospect of an unlamented death before them (vers. 1-4). Parents and offspring alike would be involved in the general ruin.

He is neither to go to the house of mourning nor to the house of feasting. In neither are God's judgments owned, nor His Word bowed to. Why should he go to join the general lamentation when the mind of the Lord had been clearly revealed? "For I have taken away My peace from this people, saith the Lord, even loving-kindness and mercies" (ver. 5). To seek to comfort them in their hardness of heart would be but to turn aside the keenness of the chastisement. He must leave them severely alone. They were in the hand of God.

The same thing comes out in the New Testament in connection with discipline in the assembly. Wicked persons are to be withdrawn from and put away from the company of the saints. The moment there is brokenness of spirit manifested, the compassions of those who are spiritually minded will at once flow forth; but in any way to condone or encourage persons persisting in ungodliness, and under the Lord's discipline, is only to hinder restoration and blessing.

It is evident from verse 6 that many heathen customs were being regularly practised by the people of Judah. The announcement that none should "cut themselves, nor make themselves bald" for the dead, would not have been made had it not been practised; that was a plain defiance of Deut. 14: 1, 2: "Ye are children of the Lord your God: ye shall not cut yourselves, nor make any baldness between your eyes for the dead. For thou art a holy people unto the Lord thy God, and the Lord hath chosen thee to be a peculiar people unto Himself, above all the nations that are upon the earth." Alas, that Jehovah's "peculiar people" should have so far corrupted themselves as to have fallen into the most degrading practices of the pagan nations about them! So true is it that "evil communications corrupt good manners." The cutting themselves and making baldness were in honor of heathen deities, notably Baal, the sun-god, who was worshiped under various names.

The Revised Version probably gives the more
exact rendering of the next verse (7) : "Neither
shall men break bread for them in mourning, to
comfort them for the dead; neither shall men
give them the cup of consolation to drink for their
father or their mother." This is the first mention in sacred Scripture of breaking bread and
drinking a cup of consolation in remembrance of
the departed. The Lord Jesus instituted such a
feast on that "same night in which He was be-
trayed." He gave new significance to the breaking of bread by declaring that it set forth the
bruising of His precious body for our sin upon
the cross of shame; while the cup became to us
"the cup of blessing," even "the communion of
the blood of Christ," "shed for many for the re-
mission of sins."

It is clear that to have had no one break bread
nor drink the cup of consolation in memory of
one who had died would have betokened utter forgetfulness. So our Lord has said, "This do, for
the keeping of Me in mind" (literal rendering).
Well may our hearts respond—

> "With joy and sorrow mingling,
> We will remember Thee."

Jeremiah is to join in no memorial feasts, nor
yet in seasons of mirth. In the grief and the joy
of the people he can have no part. He is forbidden to go into "the house of feasting, to sit
with them to eat and to drink. For thus saith
the Lord of hosts, the God of Israel: Behold, I
will cause to cease out of this place in your eyes,
and in your days, the voice of mirth, and the voice

of gladness, the voice of the bridegroom, and the voice of the bride" (vers. 8, 9). So stupefied and insensate had they become that, like their children in the days of Messiah, though mourned unto, they lamented not; though piped unto, they danced not. Neither their joy nor their sorrow led to a recognition of the One who was dealing with them in these various ways; hence their grief should only become deeper, and their laughter be turned into anguish of heart.

It was quite to be expected that, when "all these words" were proclaimed, so seared would be their consciences, that they would ask, "Wherefore hath the Lord pronounced all this great evil against us? or what is our iniquity? or what is our sin that we have committed against the Lord our God?" (ver. 10.) The hardening effect of sin is one of its appalling results. Even "when the Son of Man shall come in His glory," and "shall sit upon the throne of His glory," and all nations be gathered before Him, there will be those who, with amazing effrontery, shall ask, "When saw we Thee ahungered, or athirst, or a stranger, or naked, or sick, or in prison, and did not minister unto Thee?" while conscious of the fact that they had neglected His servants and His Word all their days.

Jeremiah's reply to the gainsayers is that their fathers had ever been characterized by disobedience to God, and they had outdone them by far; therefore they were to be cast out of their land. They had walked after other gods in Canaan: now they should be carried away to the countries where these false deities were especially recognized, and there they should "serve other gods day and night" (vers. 11-13).

Their casting off, however, shall not be forever. "He that scattered Israel shall gather him." Just as He of old brought them up from the land of Egypt, so shall it be said in the near future, "The Lord liveth, that brought up the children of Israel from the land of the north, and from all the lands whither He had driven them:" and He adds, "I will bring them again into their land that I gave unto their fathers" (vers. 14, 15). For centuries "the tribe of the wandering foot" have proved the truth of His Word in regard to their dispersion; and the prophecies relating to their return and restoration shall be as literally carried out. The going up from Babylon, in the days of Ezra and Nehemiah, in no complete sense fulfilled this promise. A few thousand, a mere handful, were brought back at that time, only to be scattered again with their rejection of Christ. When the "times of restitution of all things, spoken of by the prophets," shall have come, Israel shall then be saved; as it is written, "There shall come out of Sion the Deliverer, and shall turn away ungodliness from Jacob: for this is My covenant unto them, when I shall take away their sins" (Rom. 11:26, 27). Meantime it is the "times of the Gentiles;" the "holy city" is trodden by the Gentiles; blindness is fallen upon Israel "until the fulness of the Gentiles be come in." This is the universal testimony of the prophets, strangely overlooked by multitudes who, it is to be feared, read their Bibles to find confirmation for theories of their own, in place of reading in the fear of God, to get His mind.

It is interesting to notice how complete the in-gathering is to be in the latter day—yet only after the people have passed through the last and great tribulation by which the godly and faithful ones are manifested, and the unrepentant apostate part of the nation cut off. Vers. 16-18 tell of this: "Behold, I will send for many fishers, saith the Lord, and they shall fish them; and after I will send for many hunters, and they shall hunt them from every mountain, and from every hill, and out of the holes of the rocks. For *Mine eyes are upon all their ways*: they are not hid from My face, neither is their iniquity hid from Mine eyes. And first I will recompense their iniquity and their sin double; because they have defiled My land, they have filled Mine inheritance with the carcases of their detestable and abominable things." From every corner of the earth God will seek out His "lost sheep of the house of Israel" and bring them back to their land. Many return in unbelief, and judgment will be visited accordingly; but the result will be the reestablishment of the repentant remnant in the home of their fathers, and the rebuilding of the tabernacle of David. During all their wanderings His "eyes are upon all their ways." This is most strikingly brought out in the little book of Esther, where He is found watching over and caring for them even though unrecognized and unsought.*

---

* For an exposition of this interesting and instructive portion of Scripture the reader is referred to "Notes on the Book of Esther," by the same writer.

Do these lines meet the eye of a tried and distressed saint who has been tempted by Satan to believe that God has forgotten and cares not for him? Surely the words are as true of every Christian as of every Israelite, "Mine eyes are upon all their ways." Oh, look up, dear doubting one, and faint not beneath the chastening of the Lord! for His eyes never lose sight of you for one moment, and His heart is ever concerned about you. He is taking careful note of all your circumstances, and "He hath said, I will never leave thee nor forsake thee." Sweet it is to trust where all is dark, and to sing with childlike faith, "My times are in Thy hand!"

Israel's enlargement shall result in blessing for the nations too: "For if the fall of them be the riches of the world, and the diminishing of them the riches of the Gentiles; how much more their fulness?" And "if the casting away of them be the reconciling of the world, what shall the receiving of them be but life from the dead?" (Rom. 11: 12, 15.) So we are told in verses 19 to 21 that the Gentiles shall come to restored Israel and to Israel's God saying, "Surely our fathers have inherited lies, vanity, and things wherein is no profit." Turning to the only true God in confession and repentance, He will make them to know Himself.

The prophet gets but a glimpse of that day of glory, as if the Lord would cheer the weak heart of His servant by rolling back the dark clouds for a moment and giving him a sight of Messiah's reign when He shall, as the Sun of Righteousness, arise with healing in His wings. Jere-

miah must now return to the sterner business of
showing the people their iniquity.

"The sin of Judah," they are told, "is written
with a pen of iron, and with the point of a
diamond: it is graven upon the table of their
heart *and upon the horns of your altars*" (chap.
17:1). This tells the awful tale in a very pronounced way. *Their sin was written down where
the blood of atonement should have been.* This
was why there must be unsparing judgment. God
had ordained that for the sin of a priest, or of
the whole congregation, the sacrificial blood
should be put upon the horns of the golden altar,
the altar of sweet incense, to make atonement for
it, that their fellowship with Himself might be
maintained. (See Lev. 4:7, 18.) If a ruler, or
one of the common people, sinned, the blood was
to be put upon the horns of the brazen altar, the
altar of burnt offering, that all might know the
sin had not caused the Lord to give up the sinner, but to provide a righteous ground to forgive him. (See Lev. 4:25, 30.) Alas! in the
times of Jeremiah, while the offerings of Jehovah were neglected, the offerings of the false gods
of the nations were smoking under almost every
green tree. Therefore His holy eye sees—not the
blood that was ordained to speak of the sacrifice
of His beloved Son, but sees the sin of guilty
Israel graven upon their hearts and upon the
horns of their altars! Therefore Jehovah's
"Mountain in the field"—Jerusalem—where He
had set His Name, the place where His honor
dwelt, should be given, with all its treasures, for
a spoil and a prey to their enemies, while their

high places should be given up to sin in all their borders (ver. 3).

It was not that He delighted in judgment, but that they had themselves given up all title to their inheritance. By turning aside from the commandments of the Lord and ignoring the appointed offerings and the sprinkling of blood, they had forfeited all claim to their land. They must be carried away to a country wherein they should be strangers; for He could say, "Ye have kindled a fire in Mine anger which shall burn forever" (ver. 4).

Such is ever man's history when placed in a position of responsibility. From Adam in Eden, to a world blessed under Messiah in the Millennium, one word gives his story — failure. He cannot be depended upon. "Cursed is the man that trusteth in man, and maketh flesh his arm, and whose heart departeth from the Lord. For he shall be like the heath in the desert, and shall not see when good cometh; but shall inhabit the parched places in the wilderness, in a salt land and not inhabited" (vers. 5, 6). Israel's history, as well as that of all the race, should surely teach one the important lesson of "no confidence in the flesh." But alas with most, *one* at least is considered trustworthy, even one's self.

"Blessed is the man that trusteth in the Lord, and whose hope the Lord is. For he shall be as a tree planted by the waters, and that spreadeth out her roots by the river, and shall not see when heat cometh, but her leaf shall be green; and shall not be careful in the year of drought, neither shall cease from yielding fruit" (vers. 7, 8).

This is the blessed man of the first psalm — the man whose food is the word of God, whose confidence is in the Lord alone—the perfect example of which is our Lord Himself. How little do we, who know Him as our Saviour, practically follow Him in this! When all goes well it is easy to deceive ourselves and think that we are trusting in the Lord, when in reality we are resting on an arm of flesh. The time of trial proves where our confidence really is. "If thou faint in the day of adversity, thy strength is small."

But "the heart is deceitful above all things, and desperately wicked;" and God Himself asks, "Who can know it?" He answers it by saying, "I the Lord search the heart and try the reins" (vers. 9, 10). "The deceitful heart" is what all men have by nature—the depravity resultant upon the fall. In Isa. 44: 20 we read that "a deceived heart hath turned him aside;" and in Deut. 11: 16 Moses warns against the heart being deceived. In these passages, however, it is not the condition of man by nature, but the result rather of listening to the suggestions of the devil —the arch-deceiver. All have a *deceitful* heart: those only have *deceived* hearts who are not subject to the Word of God. He who tries the reins and searches the heart is going to give to every man according to the fruit of his doings. "Whatsoever a man soweth, that shall he also reap." It is vain to fight against the government of God, for "as the partridge sitteth on eggs and hatcheth them not, so he that getteth riches, and not by right, shall leave them in the midst of his days, and at his end shall be a fool" (ver. 11).

Jehovah's throne is high and glorious; yea, He is the high and lofty One that inhabiteth eternity. All men are but as the small dust of the balance before Him. "They that depart from Me," He says, "shall be written in the earth" (ver. 13). What a vivid light this casts upon the striking scene in the eighth of John! There, when the scribes and Pharisees brought to Jesus the poor woman taken in adultery, He stooped down and *wrote upon the ground.* In their lofty pride they pressed Him for judgment. He, looking into man's heart, bade the one without sin among them cast the first stone, and once more stooped down to write them in the earth—the sentence of death is upon them all! Feeling the exposure of His Word, they went forth from the convicting light of His presence one by one, leaving the sinner alone with the Saviour.

In psalm 22 the Lord says, "Thou hast brought Me into the dust of death." "Death," says the apostle, "passed upon all men because all have sinned" (Rom. 5). The Lord in grace stooped to the dust of death to save all who turn to God in repentance. Those who refuse His grace must be "written in the earth;" that is, they are appointed to death from which they might have been saved had they but accepted the Lord Jesus as their Deliverer from the wrath to come. He is "the fountain of living waters," where all who will may drink and have life forevermore.

The 14th verse is the prophet's cry, voicing their need of God's salvation—"Heal me, O Lord, and I shall be healed; save me, and I shall be saved: for Thou art My praise."

Alas, they only scoff and cry, "Where is the word of the Lord? let it come now" (ver. 15). It is the taunt of skepticism. As for Jeremiah, he has no unholy anxiety to see his prophecies of doom fulfilled. He had not desired the woeful day. His own inclinations had not led him to assume the role of a prophet, but God was witness that what he had given utterance to had been in sincerity as it was revealed to him. Jehovah was his hope in the day of evil, when his adversaries would be confounded and dismayed.

It may seem, at first sight, like a break in the chain of thought as we pass from what has just been claiming our attention to the paragraph relative to the Sabbath with which this portion of the prophecy is concluded. It should be remembered, however, that the Sabbath was the weekly memorial of Israel's covenant relation with Jehovah. It was to be kept sacred as a perpetual reminder of their deliverance from Egyptian bondage (Deut. 5 : 15) ; and it pointed forward to the final rest, when, all man's labor ended, the redeemed should enter into the undisturbed bliss of the new creation (Lev. 23 : 3). Therefore the state of the people was ever manifested by the estimation in which they held Jehovah's holy day. If they "called the Sabbath a delight," and rejoiced in its privileges, there was good evidence that their hearts were true to Himself. If on that day they did their own pleasure and neglected the ordinances of the law relative thereto, no further proof need be sought as to their wretched state.

In order to bring this out beyond controversy,

Jeremiah is bidden to go and stand in the gate (the place of judgment) and cry in the hearing of the king and all the inhabitants of Jerusalem, as they passed in or out of the city, "Hear ye the Word of the Lord. . . . Take heed to yourselves, and bear no burden on the Sabbath day, nor bring it in by the gates of Jerusalem; neither carry forth a burden out of your houses on the Sabbath day, neither do ye any work, but hallow ye the Sabbath day, as I commanded your fathers" (vers. 19-22). This summons as to the Sabbath would be a reminder of God's past deliverance and future promise. But man prefers his useless labor. "They obeyed not, neither inclined their ear," but deliberately turned away from hearing the message and refused the instruction.

Even at this late day they were promised a continuance of the divine favor if they thus returned to God, and manifested their subjection to Him by hallowing the seventh day. From all the cities of Judah and Benjamin the people should throng to Jerusalem as in the days of old, and once more sacrifices and offerings should be accepted by the Lord at their hands. But if they persisted in their refusal to hearken unto Him, then the city, with all its palaces, should be utterly consumed. Surely never were a people more tenderly entreated or more faithfully warned; but the "evil heart of unbelief in departing from the living God," was in them. Entreaties and commands alike had but fallen on ears wilfully closed—bent, as it were, on their own destruction!

It is easy enough to censure them; but oh,

reader, let us examine our own ways, and ask ourselves whether *we* too may not be refusing Him who now speaks to us both by their example and by His Word. Departure from God and coldness of heart are the order of the day. The last great apostasy is fast hastening on. The Scriptures of truth are being readily surrendered at the behests of a host of veneered infidels who, parading as Christian ministers, are decrying every fundamental truth of the Bible.

CHAPTER IX

LESSONS FROM THE POTTER'S HOUSE

(Chaps. 18, 19.)

Many are the Scripture similes taken from the potter's house. The manufacturer of earthenware utensils was a man of no mean repute among the Hebrews, nor yet among the surrounding nations. In 1 Chronicles 4: 22, 23, the potters are among those who "dwelt with the king for his work." They were under the royal patronage and the royal eye. They speak of that communion with the Lord which is an absolute essential if there be work in accordance with His mind. The laborer must dwell *with* Him if he would be "well-pleasing to Him."

In Ps. 2: 9 and Rev. 2: 27 Messiah takes the part of the offended potter, dashing in pieces the unworthy vessel. Isaiah in chapters 29: 16 and 64: 8 of his magnificent prophecy, and Paul in Rom. 9: 20, 23, use the same figure as this chapter in Jeremiah brings before us. God is the Potter, we are but the clay in His hands. (See also Isa. 30: 14.)

The feet of the great image of Gentile power and dominion in Dan. 2: 41 are part of iron and part of potter's clay; the iron speaking of strong authority, the pottery of the unstable masses; all alike to be smitten by the Stone that shall soon fall from heaven at the second appearing of earth's rightful King.

It is noticeable, too, that with the money paid for the betrayal of the Lord Jesus, the "potter's field" was purchased to be a place to bury strangers in. This earth is but the Potter's field. It was ever His own: but in a most solemn sense it was purchased by the suffering of the Son of God; and what a vast burial-place it is! He, the heavenly stranger, was buried in it Himself; but He rose in triumph, and is alive forevermore. Soon, from earth and sea, He shall call into life the dust of all His saints to share His excellent glory; and, later, awake the unrepentant by the summons to judgment!

Solemn and needful lessons are to be learned in the house of the potter—lessons for puny man's pride and self-sufficiency. And the Lord said to Jeremiah, "Arise, and go down to the potter's house, and *there* I will cause thee to hear My words" (chap. 18:2). In unquestioning obedience he goes to the appointed place of instruction arriving just in time to find the potter working a vessel on the wheels : marred in his hands, he takes it up anew, and as Jeremiah looked on "he made it again, as it seemed good to the potter to make it" (vers. 3, 4).

At once the word of Jehovah came to His servant. Taking what had just occurred before his eyes, He likened it to the way in which He was about to deal with marred, sin-disfigured Israel; and not with Israel only, but, later, with many nations of the earth. The grand lesson of the divine sovereignty with which he first began his course in the school of God (chap. 1) is now illustrated and amplified for his soul's benefit.

"Then the word of the Lord came to me, saying, O house of Israel, cannot I do with you as this potter? saith the Lord. Behold, as the clay is in the potter's hand, so are ye in My hand, O house of Israel" (vers. 5, 6).

This being an incontestable fact, none could deny His righteousness in sparing a nation, as He spared Nineveh, after sentence of judgment had gone forth—provided the guilty people should turn from their evil way and seek His face. This they all admitted. The other side would be less readily received, but equally true. If He had blessed a nation, and had spoken "concerning a kingdom to build and to plant it," if it turned from the path of obedience to His voice and did evil in His sight, He would repent of the good with which He had said He would benefit them (vers. 7-10). The first proposition was the only ground for hope left to Judah and Israel. The last meant their undoing, for it pictured their case exactly.

Therefore Jeremiah is to go again to the men of Judah and to the inhabitants of Jerusalem with the warning that the Lord had devised evil against them; but he is also to exhort them to return from their iniquitous course, and to make their ways and their doings good (ver. 11). On their part, however, there was no sign of penitence—not to speak of repentance. With that awful boldness that so often characterizes men away from God, they replied, "There is no hope: but we will walk after our own devices, and we will every one do the imagination of his evil heart" (ver. 12). They had committed them-

selves to a course of rebellion and treachery, and
they desired nothing better than their own godless way. Who can tell the depths to which even
one who has known much of divine care and
guidance can sink when once a good conscience
has been put away?

The Lord's patience and grace are markedly
manifested in the following verses, albeit His
long-tarrying judgment must soon be carried out.
Who among the heathen had heard of anything
so horrible as that which the virgin of Israel had
done? Had the snow of Lebanon ceased to supply the cold flowing waters of the springs? (See
R. V., ver. 14.) In other words, had His gracious
provision for their refreshment failed, that they
should have forgotten Him and have burned incense to vanity? They had stumbled in their
ways, from the ancient paths, had walked in by-
paths and in a way not cast up—that is, in a way
that He had not marked out for them. Their
land should be made desolate, so that every
passer-by should be astonished, and they themselves should be scattered as with an east wind
—the wind of adversity. How have the centuries
since testified to the truth of these words!

At the time they were uttered the prophet's
hearers refused to credit them; and playing on
the words of Jehovah, they said, "Come, and let
us devise devices against Jeremiah." They would
make *him* the responsible party, and they sought
to wreak their vengeance on the servant, in place
of bowing to the words of the Master. With vain-
glorious self-confidence, they cried, "The law shall
not perish from the priest, nor counsel from the

wise, nor the word from the prophet!" They referred, of course, to their own false priests, teachers, and prophets, whom God had not sent nor
anointed. "Come, and let us smite him with the
tongue," said they, "and let us not give heed to
any of his words" (ver. 18). In place of con-
tending with them, Jeremiah makes his supplication to the One who had sent him; for "the servant of the Lord must not strive." At the very
moment when they in their bitter hatred and
hostility had "digged a pit" for his soul, he
prays, "Remember that I stood before Thee to
speak good for them, and to turn away Thy wrath
from them" (ver. 20). But because they despised their own mercies, and persisted in their
wilful course, he makes intercession, as Elijah
had done, against them, and calls for the fulfilment of his prophecy (vers. 21, 23).

In the first verse of chap. 19 he is sent to get
a potter's earthen bottle, and is told to take elders
of the people and of the priests with him as witnesses.

Going forth unto the valley of the son of Hinnom, the place where the refuse of the city was
afterwards burned, but which at this time was
still the theater of the performance of the abominable rites of Moloch-worship, he was to proclaim once more to the kings of Judah and the
inhabitants of Jerusalem both the guilt of the
people and the judgment that was about to be
meted out to them (vers. 2-5). The Valley of
Hinnom should soon be known as the Valley of
Slaughter; for as they had slain their sons in
that dreadful Tophet as offerings to Baal and

Moloch, He would cause them to fall there by the sword of their enemies, and would give their unburied carcases to be meat for the fowls of heaven and the beasts of the field (vers. 6-9).

The bottle was then to be broken in the sight of the ancients, as he proclaimed Jehovah's message: "Even so will I break this people and this city, as one breaketh a potter's vessel, that cannot be made whole again: and they shall bury them in Tophet, till there be no place to bury" (ver. 11). Such should be the end of their rejection of God for the idols of the heathen.

Returning from Tophet, or the valley of Hinnom, "he stood in the court of the Lord's house, and said to all the people, Thus saith the Lord of hosts, the God of Israel: Behold, I will bring upon this city and upon all her towns all the evil that I have pronounced against it, because they have hardened their necks, that they might not hear My words" (vers. 14, 15). He had warned, pleaded, and entreated, but their hearts had not relented. They must know the bitterness of the cup of His wrath.

CHAPTER X

PASHUR'S NEW NAME AND THE PROPHET'S COMPLAINT.

(Chap. 20.)

With callous indifference, not so much actual persecution, our prophet thus far has had to cope. He is now to experience physical suffering at the hands of one from whom, above many others, better things might have been expected. Pashur, a priest and chief governor in the house of Jehovah, resents the faithful preaching of Jeremiah, and seeks to put a stop to it by forcible means. Scripture is silent elsewhere as to this man, although several other persons by the same name are mentioned in this book. Here we are only told that he was the son of Immer; that is, he belonged to the sixteenth course of the priesthood (1 Chron. 24: 14). He heard that "Jeremiah prophesied these things," and he resolved to make a public example of him. We are told that he smote the prophet, "and put him in the stocks that were in the high gate of Benjamin, which was by the house of the Lord" (vers. 1, 2). He was thus ignominiously exposed to the taunts of the vulgar multitude. For a part of a day and a night he seems to have been left in this position; then, on the morrow, his persecutor "brought him forth out of the stocks."

The degradation and suffering had in nowise daunted the man of God. Naturally, as we have

seen, a timid, backward man, he is now bold as
a lion, in accordance with the promise made to
him by the Lord when he began his ministry.
The man who has so often wept over the stony-
hearted men of Judah and Jerusalem has now no
fears for himself, nor yet any soft words for the
renegade priest. Abruptly he declares, "The Lord
hath not called thy name Pashur, but Magor-
missabib" (ver. 3). Pashur is commonly said to
mean "prosperity." He should never prosper
more, for he had lifted up his hand against the
Lord's anointed and rejected His Word. Magor-
missabib means "terror" (or fear) "on every
side." Such should be his future condition. A
terror to himself and to all his friends, living
in abject fear for his own life from day to day,
this should be his reward till carried away in
captivity to Babylon; and there he must die and
be buried in the land of the uncircumcised.

We read not of any reply on the part of the
false priest. The power of Jeremiah's words
must have struck deep, however much he hated
him; so he seems to have dismissed him from
his presence.

And now we find the man who could be so
bold before the despiser of the word of Jehovah,
in brokenness and even fear before the Lord. He
was no stoic. He felt most keenly the reproach
of his position. From verse 7 to the end of the
chapter we have a kind of soliloquy. He pours
out first his complaints, then his praises, and
again his remonstrances, into the ears of the
Lord of Hosts. "O Lord, Thou hast persuaded
me, and I was persuaded" (R. V.): Thou art

stronger than I, and hast prevailed: I am in derision daily, every one mocketh me." He did not court persecution and taunts: on the contrary, it stung him to the quick to be thus despised, and to find his messages derided. But Jehovah had persuaded him. He believed; therefore had he spoken.

His preaching from the beginning had been of violence and spoil; hence the word of the Lord was made a reproach unto him, and a derision daily (ver. 8). Had he prophesied smooth things and given utterance to sentiments calculated to soothe the people in their sin, he would have been held in honor and esteem. But this could not be, for he had to proclaim the words given him by the Lord.

So painful was it to his sensitive nature to meet with reproach and rejection everywhere, that he had made up his mind not to prophesy further. "Then I said, I will not make mention of Him, nor speak any more in His name." This, however, was for him an impossibility. "His word," he says, "was in my heart as a burning fire shut up in my bones, and I was weary of forbearing, and I could not stay" (ver. 9). "Woe is me," declared the apostle of the Gentiles, "if I preach not the gospel." Men sent forth by God with a message from Himself are unable to be at rest if that message is unproclaimed. How different this is to the perfunctory service of multitudes of modern clergymen! "A burning fire" must have vent, and if the word of God be thus surging up in one's breast he simply *must* preach. To seek to *imitate* this is but folly. Any spiritual person, and many utterly godless ones, can readily detect the difference between giving forth that which has been implanted in the inmost soul by the Holy Spirit, and the mere vaporings of a wrought-up sermon.

The very "defaming of many on every side" but served to cast Jeremiah the more on God, and nerve him, if we may so speak, in the conflict for the truth he proclaimed. Those who professed friendship for him, his "familiars," watched for his halting, and hoped he might be enticed, that they might be avenged on him. Fear was round about as he had declared to Pashur. But he could say, "The Lord is with me as a mighty terrible one: therefore my persecutors shall stumble, and they shall not prevail: they shall be greatly ashamed; for they shall not prosper" (the reference here is clearly to the name Pashur) : "their everlasting confusion shall never be forgotten" (ver. 11). Therefore to Jehovah of Hosts, the One that tries the righteous and sees the reins and the heart, he commits his cause, and pleads that he may see the divine vengeance upon the enemies of Judah's peace. Strong in faith, he counts the things that are not as though they had already come to pass, and cries in his exaltation of spirit: "Sing unto the Lord, praise ye the Lord: for He hath delivered the soul of the poor from the hand of evil doers" (ver. 13). It is not "He *will* deliver," but faith says, "He *hath* delivered."

Who would suppose that the same man would be in this truly blessed state of soul at one moment, and perhaps immediately afterwards be plunged into the abyss of the few remaining verses? Ah, it is an experience common to most of the children of God. While faith is in exercise, all is bright. When self is looked to, all becomes dark. In the verses we have been considering, the Lord has been before the prophet's soul. In those to follow, it is with himself he is occupied. The result is a sudden depression of his spirit, akin to that of Job when "he opened his mouth and cursed his day" (Job 3:1). In fact, one can scarcely resist the conclusion that Jeremiah was quite conversant with the book that relates the ways of the Lord with the chief of the land of Uz. By comparing the entire third chapter of Job with these five verses, it will be seen how much alike are the complaints of each of these devoted men.

Our prophet curses the day of his birth and the man who bore the news to his father that a man child had been born unto him. He wishes he had been slain from the womb, or that he might never have been born. "Wherefore," he asks in despair, "came I forth out of the womb to see labor and sorrow, that my days should be consumed with shame?" It is the breaking down of a weak and tender heart when the eye has been turned for the time from the God of his salvation. He who knows the deepest feelings of the soul estimated all aright, and in the balances of the sanctuary weighed the grief of His stricken servant.

CHAPTER XI

THE SIEGE AND CAPTIVITY FORETOLD

(Chaps. 21-24.)

The various prophecies of Jeremiah as set before us in this book do not follow any chronological order. The series recorded in chapters 21-24 belong to the last days of Zedekiah, in whose time the final carrying away to Babylon took place. The next series were uttered in the fourth year of Jehoiakim, and the ones following in his first year. Nevertheless there is evidently a divine purpose in thus grouping them, as they follow a definite moral order showing how utterly hopeless was the state of the people. Nebuchadrezzar had already commenced the siege of Jerusalem when this portion opens. The form of his name, it will be noticed, is slightly different to that found in the book of Daniel and elsewhere, even in the latter portion of this same book. The spelling as given here agrees better with the inscriptions of late years unearthed in Babylonia than the other, which was probably a Hebraized form. This mighty potentate had, when still a prince, conquered Palestine and Jerusalem, but had left Jehoiakim, brother of Jehoahaz, upon the throne as a tributary to Babylon. From Palestine Nebuchadrezzar marched into Egypt, having already routed the armies of Pharaoh-Necho. While here, tidings of the death of Nabopolassar, his father, reached him, whereupon he returned at once to Chaldea with his light troops, in order to make sure of his succession to the throne. The balance of his army, convoying a number of captives of royal lineage, followed later by a more circuitous route.

Soon after this, Jehoiakim rebelled against him (as recorded in 2 Kings 24:1), and was punished by being carried captive to Babylon. His son Jehoiachin, or Jeconiah, was placed on the throne; but he too rebelled very soon afterwards. Nebuchadrezzar marched again to Jerusalem, and carried him also captive with about ten thousand of the people. It was at this time that Ezekiel and Mordecai were carried to Babylon.

The victorious Chaldean made Mattaniah, uncle of the deposed monarch, king in his stead, changing his name to Zedekiah. Mattaniah meant "Gift of Jah." Zedekiah means the "Justice of Jah." This Jewish prince was a most ungodly man, though but a youth of one-and-twenty when he ascended the throne, and his reign lasted seven years. Of him it is recorded that "he did that which was evil in the sight of the Lord, according to all that Jehoiakim had done. For through the anger of the Lord it came to pass in Jerusalem and Judah, until He had cast them out from His presence, that Zedekiah rebelled against the king of Babylon" (2 Kings 24:19, 20).

The Chaldean army appeared once more before the devoted city, and a long siege began, which lasted almost an entire year. It was during this time of distress and perplexity that Zedekiah sent Pashur the son of Melchiah, and Zephaniah the son of Maaseiah the priest, to Jeremiah. Of the first of these two messengers we shall hear more when we come to consider the thirty-eighth chapter. Zephaniah we shall also meet with as we pursue our meditations. He is mentioned by name on several occasions, and on none to his credit (Jer. 29:25; 37:3; 2 Kings 25:18).

The very fact of Zedekiah having revolted and broken his pledges to the king of Babylon manifested his unbelieving and unsubject heart. God had sent the conqueror against Judah because of sin. That evil unrepented of, no human prowess could avail to effect deliverance. Yet the Judean monarch had thought to break off the yoke by force of arms. Now, in his helplessness, he sends to Jehovah's prophet, but gives evidence of no sense of wrong-doing; consequently his petition is utterly devoid of any expression that might speak of contrition or repentance. His message is, "Inquire, I pray thee, of the Lord for us; for Nebuchadrezzar king of Babylon maketh war against us; if so be that the Lord will deal with us according to all His wondrous works, that he may go up from us" (ver. 2). It all sounds pious, but he had not framed his ways or his doings to turn unto the Lord. He feels himself to be in a tight and difficult place. He would avail himself of divine power, if possible, while ignoring divine claims upon him. He is neither the first nor the last that has so acted. For him, however, as for any such, there is no answer of peace. Jeremiah bids the messengers return to their master, and say that not only does Jehovah refuse to fight *for* him, but He will fight *against* them, even to turning back the weapons of war in their hands. The city shall be delivered to the Chaldeans, and the bulk of the inhabitants shall die of the sword and a great pestilence. Those that are left, including Zedekiah, shall become the captives of Nebuchadrezzar and be carried away to the imperial city on the Euphrates (vers. 3-7).

Yet a choice was to be given to the people. "The way of life and the way of death" should be set before them. All abiding in the city should die, but any who should go out and fall to the besiegers should live; "his life shall be unto him for a prey." The city itself was to be burned with fire (vers. 8-10). As for the house of Judah's king, there was a special exhortation and a warning. The execution of justice morning by morning (see Ps. 101: 8) was called for, and the deliverance of the spoiled out of the hand of the oppressor; otherwise the fury of the Lord should burn against them like a fire which none could quench. Proudly they had said, in their fancied security, "Who shall come down against us? or who shall enter into our habitations?" The Lord Himself was against them, and would punish according to their corrupt and ungodly ways (vers. 11-14).

The result of this reply to the king's message we are not told. We can but infer that it was entirely disregarded, although Zedekiah evidently feared it was the truth, but did not dare act upon it.

In the beginning of the twenty-second chapter we find the prophet sent by the Lord to the royal palace. He was a pre-Christian John Knox, who,

"strong in the Lord and the power of His might,"
though in himself a frail and trembling man,
could be the reprover of kings as well as pastor
of the poor.

There is no hesitancy or uncertainty about his
utterances. It is "the word of the Lord" he
brings. He speaks as "the oracles of God." His
address is a call to righteousness. If the king
will be the leader in turning to God, as he has
been a leader in rebellion against Him, there shall
still enter in by the gates of the royal house
kings sitting upon the throne of David. Otherwise "this house shall become a desolation." As
Gilead and Lebanon for glory and beauty had
they been before Him: they should become as
the dry and parched wilderness; insomuch that
the nations, in wonderment, should ask as they
passed by, "Wherefore hath the Lord done thus
unto this great city?" and the answer would be,
"Because they have forsaken the covenant of the
Lord their God, and worshipped other gods, and
served them" (22: 1-9).

How abundantly the prophetic burden has been
verified, let the centuries witness! Jerusalem is
to-day the pillar of salt to the nations, crying to
all the kingdoms of the earth, "Remember!" The
dead should, at least, find a grave in the land of
their fathers—soon to be hallowed by Messiah's
feet. For them let none weep. For him that
goeth away let them "weep sore," for "he shall
return no more, nor see his native country" (ver.
10).

Shallum, otherwise called Jehoahaz (see 1
Chron 3: 15; 2 Kings 23: 30, 32), had been car-

ried away to Egypt by Pharaoh-Necho about
eighteen years previously, after an evil and
ignominious reign of but three months. Some
perhaps had hope that he, a son of the godly
king Josiah, might yet return as their deliverer,
but the seer declares that "he shall not return
thither any more: but he shall die in the place
whither they have led him captive, and shall see
this land no more" (vers. 10-12). This sentence
was fulfilled very shortly afterwards.

Ever since Josiah's untimely death on the
plains of Megiddo, his unworthy successors had
been characterized by iniquity. "Woe unto him
that buildeth his house by unrighteousness, and
his chambers by wrong," the reprover of kings
goes on—"that useth his neighbor's service without wages, and giveth him not for his work; that
saith, I will build me a wide house," etc. (vers.
13, 14). Jehovah's heart is ever concerned about
the poor and needy. When Josiah did judgment
and justice, it was well with him. He judged the
cause of the afflicted and poverty-stricken; and
this, the Lord declares, was "to know Him."

This crying sin of Jeremiah's age is being
multiplied a thousandfold in these last days.
Rich men heap up wealth by others' labor, and
tread down the poor. In their pride and hauteur
they build themselves palaces and live as though
God had forgotten their iniquitous means of ac-
quisition of wealth. But He that is higher than
the highest is not an unconcerned spectator. He
has said: "Go to now, ye rich men, weep and
howl for your miseries that shall come upon you.
Your riches are corrupted, and your garments

are moth-eaten. Your gold and silver is cankered;
and *the rust of them shall be a witness against
you*" (hoarded riches, while multitudes are in
distress, witness against their possessors), "and
shall eat your flesh as it were fire. Ye have
heaped together treasure for (or *"in,"* R. V.,)
the last days. Behold, the hire of the laborers
who have reaped down your fields, and is of you
kept back by fraud, crieth: and the cries of them
which have reaped are entered into the ears of
the Lord of Sabaoth" (hosts). "Ye have lived
in pleasure on the earth, and been wanton; ye
have nourished your hearts, as in a day of slaughter. Ye have condemned and killed the just; and
he doth not resist you." The hour of Jehovah's
vengeance is about to strike! Meantime the word
to the poor and lowly who trust in His name is:
"Be patient therefore, brethren, unto the coming
of the Lord: . . . the coming of the Lord draweth
nigh" (James 5: 1-8). He will not look on forever in apparent (*only* apparent) indifference.
There shall yet be a righting of all the wrongs
of the ages. The workers of iniquity shall be
visited with swift retribution, as this city of God
was—delivered to the Gentile oppressor for its
manifold wickedness.

It took more than ordinary boldness to enable
a poor priest to face proud Zedekiah and declare, "Thine eyes and thy heart are not but
for thy covetousness, and for shedding innocent
blood, and for oppression, and for violence" (ver.
17)—a solemn and terrible indictment, to which
the wicked king made no reply. His conscience,
as in Herod's case, was on the accuser's side.

Jehoahaz' doom has been pronounced—to die in Egypt. His successor, Jehoiakim, set up by Pharaoh-nechoh, whose name had been changed from Eliakim (2 Kings 23: 34), should have no better fate: he had been carried to Babylon seven years prior to this time, and for him none should lament, but he was destined to die in captivity and to be "buried with the burial of an ass, drawn and cast forth beyond the gates of Jerusalem" (vers. 18, 19; see also chap. 36: 30). Thus one by one the kings of Judah should be destroyed; for in their prosperity the Lord had spoken; but they had wilfully said, "I will not hear." "This," He declares, "hath been thy manner from thy youth, that thou hast not obeyed My voice." Therefore all the shepherds of the people should go into captivity, that they might be ashamed and confounded for all their wickedness; when their anguish came upon them like the pangs of a travailing woman, then might they become gracious and subject to His will.

There was still another Judean king in captivity. Coniah (called variously Jeconiah, Jehoiachin, Joiakim and Joachim) had, after a brief and inglorious reign of a little over three months, been likewise carried to Babylon. For him, too, there should be no return. He must die in the land of the stranger, as "a vessel wherein is no pleasure" (vers. 24, 28).

Thus one by one the men on whom the people had set their hopes were being taken away in judgment. Would they never learn? "O earth, earth, earth, hear the word of the Lord. Thus saith the Lord, Write ye this man childless, a man that shall not prosper in his days: for no man of his seed shall prosper, sitting upon the throne of David, and ruling any more in Judah" (vers. 29, 30). In him the line of Solomonic succession ends. Royalty passes over to the line of David's son Nathan. This explains why we have the two genealogies of our Lord in the New Testament. Matthew gives Joseph's line through this very Coniah. But if Christ came through him, He would not be able to sit upon the throne. In Luke we evidently have the line of Mary the daughter of Heli, Joseph's father-in-law, through Nathan, thus preserving the blood-line of David while avoiding the curse of Coniah.

"Write ye this man childless" is a solemn word for a Christian, if we may venture to spiritualize it. Every one saved by the blood of Christ should covet to be a winner of souls. "He that withholdeth corn, the people shall curse him" (Prov. 11: 26). If my reader has been born again, he is now in possession of a treasure for lack of which needy men and women on every hand are perishing— dying in their sins and going down to a Christless eternity. Oh, see to it that you share with them the great and precious things confided to you. Strive to be one whom God can use in leading others to Himself. "He that is wise winneth souls" (Prov. 11: 30, R. V.). Thus you shall have the joy of beholding your children in the faith who shall be your crown of rejoicing in that day (1 Thess. 2: 19,20). Who can conceive the loss if one must then be written "childless!"

Israel's pastors—that is, their kings—had to a great degree failed to use their exalted office for

the blessing of the sheep confided to their care.
The last four, especially, who reigned in Jerusalem were recreant shepherds, intent only upon en-
riching themselves, and caring nought for the
flock. In the opening verses of the 23d chapter
a "woe" is pronounced upon them for destroying
and scattering the sheep of Jehovah's pasture.
"Ye have scattered My flock, and driven them
away, and have not visited them; behold, I will
visit upon you the evil of your doings, saith the
Lord" (vers. 1, 2). It is a pitiable thing when
the leaders of the people of God cause the simple
to err; when those who are set to guide and protect the flock lead them into by-paths and ex-
pose them to danger. Solemn will be the account-
ing when the Lord shall visit for these things.
By referring to the 34th chapter of Ezekiel the
reader will get a fuller description of the course
of these evil shepherds. See especially vers. 1
to 6. Both there and here there are sweet assurances that, human pastors having so wretchedly
failed, the Lord Himself will gather the remnant
of His flock from all countries whither He has
driven them, and will bring them again to their
folds, where they shall be fruitful and increase
(ver. 3). This has no reference to a conversion
of Jews to Christianity. There is no fold now;
but "one flock and one Shepherd" (John 10: 1⁵,
R. V.). But this promise speaks of a still future
and literal return of the Jews to their land after
the present dispensation has closed, and the
Church is removed to heaven. When thus restored to the home of their fathers, and to their
King (whom they once rejected, saying, "We have

no king but Cæsar"), He shall then "set up shepherds over them which shall feed them: and they shall fear no more, nor be dismayed, neither shall they be lacking, saith the Lord" (ver. 5).

Twelve of these shepherds we know, for our Lord said to the apostles: "Verily I say unto you, That ye which have followed Me, in the regeneration when the Son of Man shall sit in the throne of His glory, ye also shall sit upon twelve thrones, judging the twelve tribes of Israel" (Matt. 19:28). Judas, by transgression, forfeited his place, but Matthias was given the bishopric thus made vacant. Through the promised Messiah are these covenanted mercies of David to be fulfilled. "Behold, the days come, saith the Lord, that I will raise unto David a righteous Branch, and a King shall reign and prosper, and execute justice in the earth" (ver. 5).

This Branch of the Lord's planting is frequently referred to in the prophets. Isaiah tells of His beauty and glory when "the fruit of the earth shall be excellent and comely for them that are escaped of Israel, . . . and the Lord shall have washed away the filth of the daughters of Zion" (Isa. 4:2-4). The entire passage is depicting a Millennial scene. In Zech. 3:8 the Lord says, "Behold, I will bring forth My servant the BRANCH," and He will then "remove the iniquity of that land in one day." Also in chapter 6:12, 13 of the same book, we read: "Thus speaketh the Lord of hosts, saying, Behold the Man whose name is The BRANCH; and He shall grow up out of His place, and He shall build the temple of the Lord; even He shall build the temple of the Lord; and He shall bear the glory, and shall sit and rule upon His throne; and He shall be a priest upon His throne: and the counsel of peace shall be between them both." When vacillating Pilate set Jesus before the multitude, and, unconsciously uttering the words of the prophet, cried, "Behold the Man!" he was directing the gaze of Israel to the Branch of the Lord in whom, though they knew it not, all their hopes were centered.

"In His days . . . Israel shall dwell safely; and this is His name whereby He shall be called, JEHOVAH TSIDKENU—*The Lord our Righteousness*" (ver. 6). Having no title to blessing in themselves, they shall find it all in their once rejected Messiah. Like that great pattern Jew, Saul of Tarsus (1 Tim. 1: 16), they will "be found in Him, not having their own righteousness, which is of the law, but that which is through the faith of Christ, the righteousness which is of God by faith" (Phil. 3: 9). Unto them, as unto us now, He shall be made their wisdom: even righteousness, sanctification, and redemption (1 Cor. 1: 30).

"Therefore, behold, the days come, saith the Lord, that they shall no more say, The Lord liveth, which brought up the children of Israel out of the land of Egypt; but, The Lord liveth, which brought up and which led the seed of the house of Israel out of the north country, and from all countries whither I had driven them; and they shall dwell in their own land" (ver. 8). Some would seek to make the partial return in the days of Cyrus to be the fulfilment of this promise. It is manifestly an erroneous interpretation. In the first place, there was no such universal restoration then, as this verse warrants us to expect; and in the second, Israel did not *dwell* in the land, but were soon scattered again, and are to-day dispersed among all nations. Isaiah plainly tells us that "it shall come to pass in that day, that the Lord shall set His hand again *the second time* to recover the remnant of His people, . . . and assemble the outcasts of Israel, and gather together the dispersed of Judah from the four corners of the earth" (Isa. 11: 11, 12). It is to this second and final deliverance that Jeremiah refers.

We are next introduced to another of the contrasts so frequent in this book. After having, for a brief moment, dwelt upon the glories of Messiah's reign, he gives utterance to his lamentation over the state of his people; so different from what it shall be in that day of Millennial blessing. "My heart within me is broken," he says, "because of the prophets; all my bones shake: I am like a drunken man, and like a man whom wine hath overcome, because of the Lord and because of the words of His holiness" (ver. 9). No unworthy jealousy of others in the prophetic office affected him thus, but his soul was deeply moved as the lying seers were but leading their disciples farther from God, causing them to be at peace in their wretched condition. The whole land mourned by reason of the adulteries and profaneness of the nation, and both prophet and priest were the leaders in the iniquities so commonly practised. Therefore "their

way shall be unto them as slippery ways in the
darkness," and perish at the visitation of the
Lord (vers. 10-12).

Not only in Judah was this the state of things,
but in Samaria, from whence the ten tribes of the
northern kingdom had been carried into Assyria
long before: prophets had arisen who "prophesied
in Baal," and caused the remnant that were left
in the land to err (ver. 13). But it was in Jerusalem that the evil was most manifest. There the
prophets themselves, licentious and untruthful,
strengthened the hands of the evil doers, keeping
them back from repentance, until the city had become as Sodom and Gomorrah for vileness. For
this they (the prophets) should be fed with the
wormwood of His wrath and be made to drink
the water of gall of His judgment (vers. 14, 15).

The people are pleaded with not to hearken
unto them; they were but made vain through
their false prophets, speaking a vision of their
own heart, having received nothing from the
Lord. To those despising Him, they declared,
"The Lord hath said, Ye shall have peace;" and
they assured every one walking after the imagination of his own heart that no evil should
come upon him (vers. 16, 17). As a result, a
whirlwind of the Lord had gone forth in fury,
for He would execute the thoughts of His heart
against prophet and people alike; and *His* counsel and word should stand. In the latter days
they should consider it, and understand that they
were being so dealt with in chastisement for their
departure from Himself (vers. 18-20). These
self-appointed prophets, unsent by God and with

no word from Him, could not cause the people to turn from their evil ways; they but encouraged them in their sin. Alas! that they have had many successors, both in Judaism and in Christendom, must be patent to every thoughtful person. Do not such teachers and preachers abound? And the blind multitude, "having itching ears, depart from the truth" to follow after their self-chosen deceivers. But the eye of the Lord, who is "not a God afar off," is over all, and none can "hide in secret places from Him who fills heaven and earth" (vers. 23, 24).

He heard the lies of the prophets, who spoke out of the deceit of their own hearts, in the dark days we have been considering; and He is taking note of all the empty vaporings of to-day. Instead of His sure and faithful Word, mere idle dreams were being given out as the word of God. "The prophet that hath a dream, let him tell a dream; and he that hath My Word, let him speak My Word faithfully. What is the chaff to the wheat? saith the Lord" (vers. 25-28). All men's brightest thoughts and loftiest imaginings are but as worthless chaff compared with the pure, unadulterated word of God. We "have renounced the hidden things of dishonesty, not walking in craftiness, nor handling the word of God deceitfully; but, by manifestation of the truth, commending ourselves to every man's conscience in the sight of God" (2 Cor. 4: 2), is the utterance of the true minister. How different to Satan's wretched counterfeit!

"Is not My Word like as a fire? saith the Lord; and like a hammer that breaketh the rock in

pieces?" There is a power in the simple truth
of God such as no merely human fancies or phi-
losophies can ever have. It alone can break the
heart of stone. But these prophets, giving out
their dreams and speculations for the people's
acceptance, were actually stealing Jehovah's
words from them. He was therefore against
them; and they would be of no profit to the people (vers. 29-32).

On the other hand, when either priest, prophet,
or any of the people, should come to Jeremiah in
perplexity and fear, asking, "What is the burden
of the Lord?" he is to answer, according to their
folly, "What burden? I will even forsake you,
saith the Lord;" while all who shall profess to
have another "burden" shall be punished, and
"the burden of the Lord" shall be mentioned no
more, "for every man's word shall be his burden"—that is, they shall have no word from God,
but shall be given up to their own thoughts, because they had perverted the words of the living
God. They must therefore bear their judgment,
and know the truth of that which had been
penned by Solomon, "Where there is no vision,
the people perish" (Prov. 29:18). They shall be
"in everlasting reproach and a perpetual shame,
which shall never be forgotten" (vers. 33-40).

The twenty-fourth chapter is added here as an
appendix, because it relates a vision given after
the carrying away of Jeconiah, therefore during
the early part of Zedekiah's reign. Jeremiah was
shown by the Lord, in vision, two baskets of figs
set before the temple of the Lord (ver. 1). The
fig tree is the well-known symbol of Judah na-

tionally; as the vine is of Israel as a whole.
Judah was likened by the Lord Jesus to a "fig
tree planted *in* a vineyard."

In the vision following, (chap. 24 :1-6) one
basket contained good fruit; the other bad figs,
so bad that they could not be eaten. They set
forth the two classes into which Jehovah had divided the people. Those carried away captive by
the Chaldeans had been sent away "for their
good." He would watch over them in grace, and
eventually restore them (the remnant) to their
land, to be once more planted, never to be plucked
up again. This last phrase negatives effectually
the unworthy theory that would consider the
promise fulfilled in the days of Ezra and Nehemiah. Have they not been "plucked up again?"
Surely. But when Jehovah's set time has come,
they shall be established in their land never to
be rooted out of it again. For in that day God
will give them a heart to know Himself: they
shall be His people and He will be their God: for
they shall do what the former remnant never
did—"return unto Him with *their whole heart*"
(ver. 7).

These then are the good figs to be treasured
up by Jehovah. The evil figs, which were utterly
worthless, typified Zedekiah with the residue of
Jerusalem remaining in the land, and those
dwelling in defiance of His Word in the land of
Egypt. They were to be removed into all the
kingdoms of the earth "for their hurt" (as the
others "for their good"), and should be "a reproach and a proverb, a taunt and a curse, in all
places whither" He should drive them: ever pun-

ished by the sword, famine and pestilence until utterly consumed (vers. 8-10). Who but one inspired of God could have so faithfully predicted, long before it came to pass, that which, for over two millenniums, has been a matter of history, familiar to all?

CHAPTER XII

(Chap. 25.)

The "burden" of this chapter antedates that
which we have just been considering by about
seventeen or eighteen years; the date in the first
verse being the fourth year of Jehoiakim and
the first of Nebuchadrezzar. Of the former it is
recorded that "he filled Jerusalem with innocent
blood; which the Lord would not pardon" (2
Kings 24:4). Yet his father was the godly and
devoted king Josiah who had trembled at the
word of the Lord and sought to drive idolatry
from the land. Grace is not inherited. "Ye must
be born again" is of equal force whether applied
to progeny of saint or sinner.

It is to the people of Judah and Jerusalem
that the prophet addresses himself—not to the
rulers as such. For three and twenty years he
had exercised his office among them, declaring
the word of the Lord. Since the thirteenth year
of Josiah, when the reforms were going on, to
the present, when idolatry prevailed everywhere,
he had spoken unto them, "rising early and
speaking," but they would not hearken. Other
servants and prophets had preceded him, but to
them likewise they had turned a deaf ear. The
messages of all had been in a great measure alike.
They said, "Turn ye again now every one from
his evil way, and from the evil of your doings,

and dwell in the land that the Lord hath given unto you and to your fathers for ever and ever: and go not after other gods to serve them, and to worship them, and provoke Me not to anger with the works of your hands; and I will do you no hurt." But there had been no response nor sign of repentance, that He might not be provoked to anger (vers. 2-7).

Because they had thus refused to hearken, the northern army led by Nebuchadrezzar, whom the Lord calls "My servant," should be brought against them and the nations round about them who had seduced them into their idolatrous practices. All joy and gladness, as well as all that told of a people pursuing the ordinary avocations of life, should cease, and the whole land should become a desolation: not forever, however, but "these nations," we read, "shall serve the king of Babylon *seventy years.*"

This period is a most significant one. When Israel were about to enter the land, the Lord told them that every seventh year was to be a sabbath, in which the ground was to lie fallow. The commandment ran, "When ye come into the land which I give you, then shall the land keep a sabbath unto the Lord. Six years thou shalt sow thy field, and six years thou shalt prune thy vineyard, and gather in the fruit thereof; but in the seventh year shall be a sabbath of rest unto the land, a sabbath for the Lord: thou shalt neither sow thy field, nor prune thy vineyard. That which groweth of its own accord of thy harvest thou shalt not reap, neither gather the grapes of thy vine undressed: for it is a year of rest unto the land. And the sabbath of the land shall be meat for you; for thee, and for thy servant, and for thy maid, and for thy hired servant, and for thy stranger that sojourneth with thee; and for thy cattle, and for the beast that are in thy land, shall all the increase thereof be meat" (Lev. 25: 2-7). A promise of assured prosperity, if observed, was also given; for we read, "And if ye shall say, What shall we eat the seventh year? behold, we shall not sow, nor gather in our increase: then will I command My blessing upon you in the sixth year, and it shall bring forth fruit for three years. And ye shall sow the eighth year, and eat yet of old fruit until the ninth year; until her fruits come in ye shall eat of the old store" (Lev. 25: 20-22). There would thus be no lack, but an abundant supply, if they kept the year of rest and gave the land its sabbath; in this way acknowledging the divine ownership, and themselves Jehovah's servants. In Ex. 23: 10, 11 we have the command to observe the sabbatic year more briefly given: but one clause is added, which shows the Lord's grace to the lowly—"That the poor of thy people may eat." He would keep open house, as it were, and the poverty-stricken should avail themselves of His bounty, resting and eating in this year of cessation from the ordinary duties of husbandry.

Not only did He promise blessing if His Word was obeyed; but, through Moses, He solemnly warned them of judgment if they failed to give ear to His commandments. If they walked contrary to Him, He would walk contrary to them; and He declared, "I will scatter you among the heathen, and will draw out a sword after you: and your land shall be desolate, and your cities waste. *Then shall the land enjoy her sabbaths,* as long as it lieth desolate, and ye be in your enemies' land; even then shall the land rest, and enjoy her sabbaths. As long as it lieth desolate it shall rest; *because it did not rest* in your sabbaths, when ye dwelt upon it" (Lev. 26:34, 35). And in verse 43, of the same chapter, He says: "The land also shall be left of them, and shall enjoy her sabbaths, while she lieth desolate without them: and they shall accept the punishment of their iniquity; because, even because they despised My judgments, and because their soul abhorred My statutes."

This word, then, it was that the Lord was about to fulfil. The people were to be transported to Babylon for seventy years.

In the present unsatisfactory state of chronology, one would not build too much on numbers; but it would seem that for the entire period from the dedication of the temple till the destruction of it, the sabbatic year had been unobserved. This was approximately 490 years. Seventy Sabbaths had been neglected. For seventy years they should dwell in the stranger's country while the land kept sabbath.

In 2 Chron. 36:21, when the threatened captivity had actually taken place, it is stated that it was "to fulfil the word of the Lord by the mouth of Jeremiah, until the land had enjoyed her sabbaths: for as long as she lay desolate she kept sabbath to *fulfil threescore years and ten.*" It is impossible to overreach God. Selfish Judah, doubtless, reasoned that time would be gained and wealth more rapidly accumulated if the year of rest were allowed to pass unobserved. They had to learn the truth of the words, "Them that honor Me I will honor, and they that despise Me shall be lightly esteemed." So with many a self-seeking child of God since. Time spent in waiting upon Him has been esteemed as time lost. Many are too busy to give Him His portion. Business, pleasure, everything that begins and ends with self, in short, must come first; leaving little or no time for Him. But He invariably balances things at last. Many a saint has spent long, weary months and years on a bed of languishing, for the simple reason that the things of God were crowded out and neglected in days of health and vigor. Yet, blessed be His name, as in the case of His earthly people, the days of captivity have been made to become days of great fruitfulness. It was in their subjection to the Babylonian yoke that Judah learned to abhor idols. Never has the nation offended on that ground since. The seasons of the Lord's chastening are not lost time. Afterward they yield the peaceable fruit of righteousness to those exercised thereby.

The discipline over, and the lost sabbatic years made up, they were to be permitted to return to their land. "It shall come to pass, when seventy years are accomplished, that I will punish the king of Babylon, and that nation, saith the Lord, for their iniquity, and the land of the Chaldeans, and will make it perpetual desolations. And I will bring upon that land all my words which I have pronounced against it, even all that is written in this book, which Jeremiah hath prophesied against all the nations. For many nations and great kings shall serve themselves of them also: and I will recompense them according to their deeds, and according to the works of their own hands" (vers. 12-14). The overthrow of Babylon would be the signal that Israel's redemption had drawn nigh. Daniel, it will be remembered, was a student of the writings of the former prophets, and it is recorded that he "understood by books the number of the years, whereof the word of the Lord came to Jeremiah the prophet, that He would accomplish seventy years in the desolations of Jerusalem" (Dan. 9:2). He had God's sure word, and he knew that he could rely on it. Jeremiah but spoke the words which, by the inspiration of the Almighty, had been given him.

It is noticeable that Babylon, having been permitted to destroy Jerusalem, and having been the instrument of Jehovah's discipline, should in her turn be utterly destroyed for her manifold abominations.

"Judgment must begin at the house of God." The nations, however, should not escape. Verses 15 to 26 give a list in detail of the various peoples to whose lips the wine-cup of Jehovah's fury must be pressed. To each one Jeremiah is to hand it in turn, to "cause all the nations . . . to drink it." Drinking, they would fall and rise no more (ver. 27).

"And it shall be, if they refuse to take the cup at thine hand to drink, then shalt thou say unto them, Thus saith the Lord of hosts: Ye shall certainly drink. For, lo, I begin to bring evil on the city which is called by My name, and should *ye* be utterly unpunished?" (vers. 28, 29). Nay, it could not be; for, "if the righteous scarcely be saved, where shall the ungodly and the sinner appear?" (1 Peter 4: 18). How the nations were made to drink and to fall before the might of Jehovah has been for long ages a matter of ̄uthentic history.

In martial metre, and with graphic delineation, the day of the Lord's controversy with the nations and their shepherds, or kings, is set forth in the closing verses (30-38). Comment is unnecessary. The simplicity and grandeur of the description need no interpreter.

CHAPTER XIII

DANGER AND DELIVERANCE

(Chap. 26.)

Some time before making the proclamation in the name of Jehovah which we have just been considering, Jeremiah's life had been placed in jeopardy for his faithfulness in showing the people their sins and setting before them the sure judgment about to fall. No exact date is given beyond the statement that it was "in the beginning of the reign of Jehoiakim" (ver. 1).

He had been commanded by the Lord to stand in the temple courts, evidently on the occasion of some one of the yearly feasts; for he was to "speak unto all the cities of Judah which come to worship in the Lord's house." He had no choice as to the matter of the discourse, for he was told to speak "all the *words*" (not merely the thoughts or ideas clothed in language of his own choosing, as the opponents of verbal inspiration would fain have us believe) that the Lord commanded him— diminishing nothing (ver. 2). See 1 Cor. 2:13. Notice that the very words spoken by the apostle were, as in Jeremiah's case, those which the Holy Ghost taught.

If the people of the cities of Judah would hearken, and turn from their evil way, the Lord might repent Him of the evil which He purposed to do unto them because of their iniquities. If they refused to heed the message, and persisted

in their wilful course, He would make His house
desolate like Shiloh, where He had dwelt of old,
and Jerusalem should become "a curse to all the
nations of the earth" (vers. 3-6).

Obedient to "the heavenly vision," the prophet
did as he had been commissioned to do, and all
the people heard his words.

He had barely finished his address when the
priests and the false prophets who were serving
in the courts of the Lord's house, joining with
the rabble, placed him under arrest as a disturber
of the peace of the holy place, and a traitor to
his king and country. The scene must have been
a remarkable one. In large measure he was privileged to be a partaker of the sufferings and reproach of Christ, as yet unrevealed. "Despised
and rejected of men," he heard the multitude
clamoring for his blood. They cried, "Thou shalt
surely die. Why hast thou prophesied in the
name of the Lord, saying, This house shall be
like Shiloh, and this city shall be desolate without an inhabitant?" The pessimist from Anathoth was weakening the hands of the warriors
and disheartening the people. They would put
him out of the way, and thus silence his "tongue
of fire." In all that crowd he was left without
so much as one human friend. A true earlier-day
Antipas, he stood "against all." For we are told
that "*all* the people were gathered against Jeremiah in the house of the Lord" (vers. 7-9).

It is on such an occasion that one would naturally have expected so weak and fearful a man
to be overwhelmed with gloom and even terror.
On the contrary, he is neither crushed nor

affrighted. Bold in his confidence in the word of Jehovah which he had proclaimed, he confronts the raging populace undismayed.

The princes of Judah, learning of the disturbance, came up at once from the palace to the new gate of the temple, where inquiry is immediately instituted. The priests and the false prophets vehemently accuse Jeremiah, saying, "This man is worthy to die; for he hath prophesied against this city, as ye have heard with your ears" (vers. 10, 11).

Jeremiah is permitted to speak for himself. Without the slightest hesitation, and with no apparent concern for the outcome as to himself, he boldly declares, "The Lord sent me to prophesy against this house and against this city all the words that ye have heard." The message was not of the servant, but of the Lord, and the case is one of Judah *versus* Jehovah, whom they hypocritically professed to serve. If they disliked to hear threatenings of judgment and desolation there was a sure way to avoid their fulfilment. "Therefore now amend your ways and your doings, and obey the voice of the Lord your God; and the Lord will repent Him of the evil that He hath pronounced against you" (vers. 12, 13). Not by murdering the messenger, but by heeding the proclamation, could the wrath of Jehovah be turned aside.

"As for me, behold, I am in your hand: do with me as seemeth good and meet unto you." Without a quaver in his voice or a sign of pallor on his cheek, he gives himself up to die if they are determined upon it. Nevertheless he warns them of the result. "But know ye for certain, that if ye put me to death, ye shall surely bring innocent blood upon yourselves, and upon this city, and upon the inhabitants thereof: for of a truth the Lord hath sent me unto you to speak all these words in your ears" (vers. 14, 15). It is the courage of one conscious of his own integrity, relying upon the justice of the Holy One. In a similar spirit did Robert Moffatt of Kuruman bare his breast for the savages' spears, and in like manner Paton of the New Hebrides fearlessly faced the enraged men of Tanna. So have thousands of devoted saints jeoparded their lives for the truth's sake, concerned far more for the ungrateful people to whom they ministered than for their own safety.

The effect of Jeremiah's words is most marked. The princes, and the fickle populace, who a few moments before clamored for his execution, now give their verdict in his favor. "This man," they say, "is not worthy to die: for he hath spoken unto us in the name of the Lord our God" (ver. 16). Alas, that acknowledging this they did not give heed to the exhortation! Then certain elders, Nicodemuses in their time, rose up to speak in his behalf. The case of Micah the Morasthite is first cited: how in the days of Hezekiah he had prophesied, saying, "Thus saith the Lord of hosts: Zion shall be plowed like a field, and Jerusalem shall become heaps, and the mountain of the house as the high places of a forest" (vers. 17, 18; see also Micah 3: 12). Did Hezekiah put him to death for this solemn announcement? On the contrary, had it not been the means of leading him the more to fear the Lord, with the happy result that "the Lord repented Him of the evil which He had pronounced against them?" If they acted contrary to this precedent, might they not procure great evil against their souls? (ver. 19.)

Urijah, another man of God, is next adduced. In his case the king had acted in the contrary manner. Whether evil would result remained to be seen; for it was in the reign of this same Jehoiakim who was now on the throne that Urijah had prophesied in the name of the Lord against the city and the land in terms similar to those employed by Jeremiah. The prophet, filled with fear, had fled to Egypt. Yet king Jehoiakim, bent on his destruction, had brought him out of the land of his refuge and "slain him with the sword, and cast his dead body into the graves of the common people" (vers. 20-23). Thus far the Lord indeed had not avenged this ignominious treatment of His servant; but it might be yet too early to judge of the consequences, and it is left without further comment.

Another man now rises, Ahikam the son of Shaphan, in behalf of Jeremiah, preventing his being given into the hand of the people to be put to death (ver. 24). Thus, once more God vindicated and protected His servant. Had Urijah been a man of similar faith and trust in God, who can say that he too might not have been safeguarded? "The name of the Lord is a strong tower: the righteous runneth into it, and is safe" (Prov. 18:10).

CHAPTER XIV

BONDS AND YOKES

(Chaps. 27, 28.)

Chapters twenty-seven and twenty-eight are intimately connected. Both alike treat of the general subject of passive submission to the Babylonian yoke. Strange as it may seem to those not conversant with the ways of God with man on earth as outlined in the Scriptures, it was He Himself who had raised up Nebuchadrezzar and had given His people and the Gentile nations into his hand. This, and the failure on man's part (especially that of the "head of gold," as the Chaldean monarch was declared to be), will all be found fully detailed in the book of Daniel. It was for Israel and Judah to own God's righteousness in thus causing the dominion to pass from David's house, because of their sin, and to be given to the stranger. This, Zedekiah, as we have seen, did not do; and from the present position it would appear that he and the kings of the surrounding nations, Edom, Moab, Ammon, etc., had attempted an organized coalition against the king of Babylon. Jeremiah is therefore commissioned to warn Zedekiah and his allies of the futility of any such attempt.

The first verse presents a difficulty as it stands in the Authorized Version. It gives the date of the prophecy as being the same as that in the previous chapter, viz., "the beginning of the reign of Jehoiakim the son of Josiah," etc. The Revisers have added a marginal note to the effect that it should properly read, "Zedekiah, king of Judah," as is evident from the 3d, 12th and 20th verses, and the first verse of the next chapter. It is probably a copyist's error: some ancient authorities read as just noted, though the Received Text has Jehoiakim. The Scriptures of the Old and New Testaments are the inspired Word of God, free from all error, as originally written. But this in no sense involves the reception of blunders easily made by translators and copyists. To expunge such minor errors, the patient labors bestowed in the careful comparison of all the manuscripts on hand are of importance and profit; for man has failed in everything to which he set his hand: even while duplicating copies of the sacred oracles.

It was in the early part of the reign of Zedekiah then, Judah's last king, that Jeremiah was bidden to make bonds and yokes and put them first upon his own neck, then send them for a testimony to the kings of Edom, Moab, Ammon, Tyrus, and Zidon, by the hand of their own ambassadors, who had come to Jerusalem to confer with the Hebrew ruler (vers. 2, 3).

Not only was he to give to each the symbolic bonds and yokes, but he was to give them the explanation likewise: "And command them to say unto their masters, Thus saith the Lord of hosts, the God of Israel: Thus shall ye say unto your masters: I have made the earth, the man and the beast that are upon the ground, by My great power and by My outstretched arm, and have given it unto whom it seemed meet unto Me. And now have I given all these lands into the

hand of Nebuchadnezzar the king of Babylon,
My servant; and the beasts of the field have I
given him also to serve him. And all nations
shall serve him, and his son, and his son's son,
until the very time of his land come: and then
many nations and great kings shall serve themselves of him" (vers. 4-7). Resistance for the
present is but folly, and worse than useless. The
king of Babylon was the servant of Jehovah,
though he wist it not. He could but act by divine permission, and it was the will of God to
use him as the scourge to punish the people with
whom He had a controversy. That purpose
achieved, his power should be broken; but till
then no might could stand against his victorious
armies.

The nation refusing to put the neck under his
yoke would incur greater punishment, in the way
of the sword, the famine, and the pestilence, until
they should be utterly consumed (ver. 8).

They were warned against giving heed to
charlatans parading as prophets and diviners, as
also dreamers, enchanters, and sorcerers, who
abounded among the heathen. Such, as a rule,
give the message which they know is most likely
to be received with favor; but when they spoke,
saying, "Ye shall not serve the king of Babylon," they were prophesying a lie, and only the
more drawing down the vengeance of God upon
those believing and acting upon their prognostica-
tions. If the nations would submit to the yoke,
they should be permitted to remain in their own
lands as tributaries to Nebuchadnezzar (vers.
9-11).

To Zedekiah also a personal warning and entreaty was given. He was urged not to rise in rebellion, but to bend his neck to the yoke, thus saving himself and the people. In his court also were false prophets, who predicted the success of his effort to throw off subjection to Babylon, but the Lord had not sent them. They were prophesying lies in His name (vers. 12-15).

To the priests and the people a similar address is directed. The pseudo-prophets had declared, "Behold, the vessels of the Lord's house shall now shortly be brought again from Babylon." This was utterly false; and he pleads with the people not to be deceived. "If," he says, "they be prophets, and if the Word of the Lord be with them, let them now make intercession to the Lord of hosts, that *the vessels which are left* in the house of the Lord, and in the house of the king of Judah, and at Jerusalem, go not to Babylon" (vers. 16-18). For Jehovah had made known to him that not only should there be no present recovery of the sacred utensils now in Babylon, but the brazen pillars and the sea, with all the vessels hitherto allowed to remain in Jerusalem, "which Nebuchadnezzar king of Babylon took not, when he carried away captive Jeconiah the son of Jehoiakim king of Judah from Jerusalem to Babylon, and all the nobles of Judah and Jerusalem," should soon be carried away also and kept in the city of their captivity until the day appointed for His visitation, when He would bring them up and restore them to the holy city (vers. 19-22).

The record of their restoration is given in Ezra

1: 7-11. In His own time the word of the Lord was literally fulfilled, while the testimony of the false prophets was proven to be a lie, as the next incident shows.

"And it came to pass the same year, in the beginning of the reign of Zedekiah king of Judah, in the fourth year, and in the fifth month, that Hananiah the son of Azur the prophet, which was at Gibeon, spake unto me in the house of the Lord, in the presence of the priests and of all the people, saying, Thus speaketh the Lord of hosts, the God of Israel, saying, I have broken the yoke of the king of Babylon" (chap. 28: 1, 2). Hananiah reiterated the statement that the vessels of the Lord's house were soon to be returned from Babylon, even setting a definite time limit —"within two full years." He also predicted the return of Jeconiah, with all the captives of Judah, declaring that the Lord was about to break the yoke of the king of Babylon (vers. 3, 4). Had it indeed been true, Jeremiah would have heartily rejoiced in it; though his own utterances would have entirely failed. Having the secret of the Lord, however, he knew it should be quite the contrary. In reply to Hananiah, he said before all the priests and the people that were assembled in the house of the Lord, "Amen: the Lord do so: the Lord perform thy words which thou hast prophesied, to bring again the vessels of the Lord's house, and all that is carried away captive, from Babylon into this place" (vers. 5, 6).

The meek and faithful Jeremiah—how gladly would he, true lover of Judah as he was, have welcomed such an end to the miseries of his peo-

ple! But he knew it was not to be. "Nevertheless," he continues, "hear thou now this word
that I speak in thine ears, and in the ears of all
the people: The prophets that have been before
me and before thee of old prophesied both against
many countries, and against great kingdoms, of
war, and of evil, and of pestilence. The prophet
which prophesieth of peace, when the word of
the prophet shall come to pass, then shall the
prophet be known, that the Lord hath truly sent
him" (vers. 7-9). He brings no railing accusa-
tion: nor is he drawn into useless argument.
With the earlier prophets, whose writings they
had, his word agreed; while Hananiah's was to
the contrary. If it be fulfilled, then he would
admit that the Lord had sent him. "The servant
of the Lord must not strive."

Hananiah, however, evidently fearing that the
composure of the man of God would have some
weight with his audience, assumes the dramatic;
and taking off the yoke which Jeremiah, in accordance with the Lord's command (chap. 27: 2),
was wearing about his neck, he broke it in pieces,
saying, as he did so, "Thus saith the Lord: Even
so will I break the yoke of Nebuchadnezzar king
of Babylon from the neck of all nations within
the space of two full years" (vers. 10, 11). Error
is generally insistent and dogmatic—the more so,
often, the farther it is removed from the truth.

The servant of Jehovah makes no reply. He
has no reputation to save: he desires not to at-
tach the people to himself by a display of words.
He can afford to wait, for he knows he has the
mind of the Lord, which will be verified in its

ᴏwn time. We simply read, "And the prophet Jeremiah went his way" (ver. 11).

Alone in the presence of God he received a message for the man who had sought to triumph over him and had withstood his words. He was told to go and tell Hananiah that he had but broken yokes of wood: the Lord should make a yoke of iron, and put it upon the neck of all the nations he had before referred to, and the sentence is reaffirmed, that they should serve the king of Babylon (vers. 12-14).

For Hananiah himself a most solemn word was added. He had sinned unto death. In God's holy and righteous government, he must die. "Then said the prophet Jeremiah unto Hananiah the prophet, Hear now, Hananiah: The Lord hath not sent thee; but thou makest this people to trust in a lie. Therefore thus saith the Lord: Behold, I will cast thee from off the face of the earth: this year thou shalt die, because thou hast taught rebellion against the Lord" (vers. 15, 16). Solemn is the responsibility resting upon "vain talkers and deceivers," who, by their "good words and fair speeches," deceive the hearts of the simple. "The Lord will not hold him guiltless that taketh His name in vain." Not alone to profanity does this refer; but to taking upon one the name of the Lord when the life is dishonoring His holiness; or professing to speak in the name of the Lord when one has received no message from Him.

Scarce two months elapsed ere the judgment so solemnly foretold overtook the impostor. "So Hananiah the prophet died the same year, in the seventh month." All God's ways are in righteousness, whether in mercy or in judgment.

CHAPTER XV

THE LETTER TO THE CAPTIVITY

(Chap. 29.)

Not alone to "the poor of the flock," and the haughty rulers who remained in the land, was Jeremiah appointed to minister. He had also a service to render to those who had been carried into captivity. It was not his province to go to them in person and minister among them in the land of their bondage. For this service God had raised up Ezekiel, who was of the number of those who had been deported. He prophesied "among the captives by the river of Chebar" (Ezek. 1:1). By means of a letter, the sorrowing son of Hilkiah was to give the Lord's message to his dispersed countrymen. False prophets had arisen among them who were giving them false hopes. Their captivity had not changed their hearts. He must give them a word of rebuke, as also a word of encouragement to those who had faith to receive it.

"Now these are the words of the letter that Jeremiah the prophet sent from Jerusalem unto the residue of the elders which were carried away captives, and to the priests, and to the prophets, and to all the people whom Nebuchadnezzar had carried away captive from Jerusalem to Babylon; (after that Jeconiah" [that is, Jehoiachin] "the

king, and the queen, and the eunuchs, the princes
of Judah and Jerusalem, and the carpenters, and
the smiths, were departed from Jerusalem;) by
the hand of Elasah the son of Shaphan, and
Gemariah the son of Hilkiah (whom Zedekiah
king of Judah sent unto Babylon to Nebuchadnezzar king of Babylon) saying, Thus saith the
Lord of hosts, the God of Israel, unto all that are
carried away captives, whom I have caused to
be carried away from Jerusalem unto Babylon"
(vers. 1-4). The messengers who carried the letter were sent primarily as ambassadors from
Zedekiah's rebellious court to treat with the great
Chaldean ruler. They bore, however, a message
from a far greater king than either of these, even
from Jehovah of hosts. He deigns to communicate in this way with His captive people.

The first thing He brings before them is that
it was no chance misfortune that had happened
unto them. It was *Himself* who had caused them
to be carried away. If they really believed this,
how it would affect all their ways. They would
see that it was in vain to resist His holy discipline; but it would also, surely, be manifest to
them that He was truly concerned about them;
otherwise He might have left them to pursue un-
hinderedly their self-chosen course. Ah, He loved
them too well for that, as He loves "His own
which are in the world" now far too much to
permit them to go on long in a path contrary to
His mind without causing them to feel the rod
of chastening. Blessed it is to remember that
He deals with us not as enemies, but as sons; for
"what son is he whom his father chasteneth not?"

The entire passage in Heb. 12 is a notable one, often overlooked by tried saints, who thus despise or faint beneath the discipline instead of being "exercised thereby."

For the dispersed of Judah, then, the message is that they are to receive as from *His own hand* their affliction; and in place of trying to effect a deliverance before the appointed time, they are bidden to attend with soberness to the duties of life, and to "seek the peace of the city" in which they were captives, and to "pray unto the Lord for it: for in the peace thereof shall ye have peace" (vers. 5-7).

In a similar strain are the sojourners and pilgrims of a later dispensation addressed, both in Peter's first letter (2: 11-17) and in Paul's first epistle to Timothy (2: 1-4). The former of these passages is especially full, and contains teaching often overlooked in our present restless, not to say reckless, age. "Submit yourselves," we are told, "to every ordinance of man for the Lord's sake: whether it be to the king, as supreme; or unto governors, as unto them that are sent by Him for the punishment of evil doers, and for the praise of them that do well. For so is the will of God, that with well-doing ye may put to silence the ignorance of foolish men: as free, and not using your liberty for a cloak of maliciousness, but as the servants of God." In the other portion referred to, the Christian is instructed to make supplication "for all men; for kings, and for all that are in authority." We will never be at home in this world. It is a great pity if we seek to be; but we are here by the will of the

Lord; and He would have us own in a practical way the great truth that "the powers that be are ordained of God." This will not make worldly politicians of us. We need have no more to do with the government ourselves than had the captive children of Judah in the land of Shinar; but we shall really be the salt, preserving the whole social and political system from corruption. It is not ours to "assert ourselves" and "stand for our rights." We side with Him who came into this scene not to get His rights, but His wrongs. Like Him, then, be it ours to render unto Cæsar the things that are Cæsar's, and to God the things which are His.

"For thus saith the Lord of Hosts, the God of Israel: Let not your prophets and your diviners, that be in the midst of you, deceive you; neither hearken to your dreams which ye cause to be dreamed. For they prophesy falsely unto you in My name: I have not sent them, saith the Lord" (vers. 8, 9). In all ages men have abounded who professed to speak in the name of Jehovah. By the Word of God their professions are to be tested, as also by their fruits. It can never be of the Holy One to cause people to resist divine discipline, and to prophesy peace to those away from God. The diviners here referred to were substituting their own idle dreams (in accordance with the desires of their unsubject hearts) for the burden of the Lord.

He had already given His word, and now reiterates it, that "after seventy years be accomplished at Babylon" He would visit them and perform His good word toward them. (See chap.

25: 11-14.) Then He would cause them to return unto Jerusalem, but not before. Until the prophetic hour should strike, all effort to effect their restoration would be in vain.

"For I know the thoughts that I think toward you, saith the Lord, thoughts of peace, and not of evil, to give you an expected end" (ver. 11). That which they desired was also His desire for them. The looked-for end should surely come, but only in His own time. How precious thus to learn of God's intimate concern in the welfare of each saint! His thoughts toward those who are redeemed by the precious blood of the Son of His love are ever thoughts of peace—never of evil. David entered into this when he cried, "How precious also are Thy thoughts unto me, O God! How great is the sum of them! If I should count them, they are more in number than the sand; when I awake, I am still with Thee" (Ps. 139: 17, 18). But we must never forget that He has declared, "My thoughts are not your thoughts, neither are your ways My ways. . . . For as the heavens are higher than the earth, so are My ways higher than your ways, and My thoughts than your thoughts" (Isa. 55: 8, 9). Though He permit sorrow and disaster to beset our footsteps, He will at last guide us into our destined haven where "there remaineth a rest for the people of God."

Israel's God is ours, and His ways with them but typify His ways with us. "There is an *appointed time* for all upon the earth." For them the set time of their temporal deliverance was the expiration of the seventy years. For us,

the morning of our eternal deliverance will be
ushered in by "the coming of our Lord Jesus, and
our gathering together unto HIM."

The object of their discipline was to lead to
a thorough repentance. That accomplished, they
should call upon Him and He would hearken.
His word ran, "Ye shall seek Me, and find Me,
when ye shall search for Me with all your heart"
(vers. 12, 13). Then He would indeed be found
of them, and would turn away their captivity,
and gather them back to their land.

Because of the disobedience of those who
haughtily said, "The Lord hath raised us up
prophets in Babylon," and who failed to bow to
the rod, a greater judgment should yet be sent
upon the land of their patrimony. Like vile figs
(see chap. 24:8), the rest of the people should
be cast out and destroyed; for when He had
called, they had refused to listen. Thus all hope
of present recovery should be destroyed (vers.
15-19).

Two of the false prophets are mentioned by
name—Ahab and Zedekiah. Their utterances are
plainly declared to be lies, and as a sign they
should be delivered into the hand of Nebuchadrezzar and slain before the eyes of their dupes.
Their fate was to be a terrible one—"roasted in
the fire" for their villainy. This form of punishment was evidently a common one with the king
of Babylon, as we gather from Dan. 3. For these
false prophets there should be no deliverer, as
for the three faithful Hebrews who would not
bow to the image set up in the plain of Dura.
Not only had these men spoken falsely, but their

lives were full of iniquity and lechery, as Jehovah knew and was "a witness" (vers. 20-23).

This concludes the letter to the captivity. It provoked an answer from one of the dispersed who was known as Shemaiah the Nehelamite, or "the dreamer"—a false prophet too, as this name seems to imply. He sent letters to the Jews remaining at Jerusalem, and to Zephaniah the son of Maaseiah the priest, with the rest of the sacerdotal company, affirming that "The Lord hath made thee priest in the stead of Jehoiada the priest, that ye should be officers in the house of the Lord, for every man that is mad and maketh himself a prophet, that thou shouldest put him in prison, and in the stocks" (vers. 24-26). He inquired therefore why Zephaniah had not reproved Jeremiah of Anathoth, who, according to him, had "made himself a prophet." Men, unsent themselves by God, are ever ready to charge the true servants of the Lord with being self-appointed men—so deceiving are the ways of Satan. Jeremiah's letter had told the people, "This captivity is long: build ye houses, and dwell in them; and plant gardens, and eat the fruit of them" (vers. 27, 28). This aroused the ire of Shemaiah, as he evidently considered its effect would be to destroy the poeple's hopes and keep them from rising in rebellion, if Zedekiah's revolt seemed to be successful.

Zephaniah the priest read the letter in Jeremiah's hearing. In response, the word of the Lord came again to him, and he wrote a second epistle to "all them of the captivity." He faithfully denounced the dreamer as a prophet whom the Lord had not sent, and who was causing the people to trust in a lie. Because of this, Jehovah would punish both him and his seed. His family should be utterly extirpated. Not a man should be left "to dwell among this people." He should not be permitted to live to see the good that God promised to do for those now oppressed and scattered, because "he hath taught rebellion against the Lord" (vers. 30-32). Thus the three archdeceivers are doomed. Let the people heed the word of the One they had so often grieved!

CHAPTER XVI

(Chaps. 30, 31.)

Nowhere in Scripture, so far as I am aware, have we clearer instruction as to the final, literal restoration of Israel, preceded by the great tribulation, than in the section which now claims our attention. If read in connection with Matt. 24, 25; Rom. 11; and the books of Daniel and Revelation, it will help much to give a clear outline of what God has in store for His earthly people. Because of its supreme importance in this regard, we shall look at it verse by verse, in place of making as hasty a survey as of some previous portions.

"The word that came to Jeremiah from the Lord, saying, Thus speaketh the Lord God of Israel, saying, Write thee all the words that I have spoken unto thee in a book" (vers. 1, 2). It is necessary that we have clearly before our souls the fact that here, as in all Scripture, God Himself is speaking. "The Lord God will do nothing unless He reveal it to His servants the prophets." Having been pleased thus to announce His purposes for Israel, we can be assured that it is for our profit and blessing to seek to become acquainted with what is so manifestly near to His heart.

"For, lo, the days come, saith the Lord, that I will bring again the captivity of My people Israel and Judah,* saith the Lord: and I will cause them to return to the land that I gave to their fathers, and they shall possess it" (ver. 3). Distinctly we are told that both Israel and Judah—not the latter only—are to be returned to their land. Nor does the temporary restoration at the expiration of the seventy years fulfil the terms of this prophecy; for, when brought back to the home of their fathers, they are to "possess it," which was manifestly not the case with those who returned under Zerubbabel, as their descendants were scattered again among the nations, and remain so to this day. At that time also, though a few from the ten tribes went back with the remnant of Judah, there was no regathering of Israel, as such. When Jehovah's set time to remember Zion has come, twelve thousand from each of the twelve tribes will be delivered out of the hand of the Gentiles. (See Rev. 7.) The number may be figurative, we admit, but it at least implies a goodly company out of each tribe.

"And these are the words the Lord spake concerning Israel and concerning Judah" (ver. 4). Here note again how clearly the northern and the southern kingdoms are referred to. Both have been scattered. Both are included in God's counsels of judgment and grace.

"For thus saith the Lord: We have heard a voice of trembling, of fear, and not of peace" (ver. 5). Before there can be the fulfilment of

---

* Having divided into two kingdoms after Solomon, the ten tribes (forming the bulk of the nation) are distinguished as "Israel;" while the tribes of Judah and Benjamin formed the kingdom of "Judah."

the promises of blessing, there must be the tasting to the full of the cup of Jehovah's indignation. The subject therefore to which these words introduce us is that of "the great tribulation." (See Matt. 24: 21 and Rev. 7: 14.) Before the appearing of Israel's once rejected Messiah and the establishment of the kingdom, the favored nation will be exposed as never before to the power of the oppressor and to the malice of Satan. It is their special punishment for having crucified and slain the Anointed of Jehovah.

"Ask ye now, and see whether a man doth travail with child? wherefore do I see every man with his hands on his loins, as a woman in travail, and all faces are turned into paleness?" (ver. 6). So terrible will be that time of trial, but so sure is the joy to follow, that it is likened to the travail-pains that precede the birth of a child. Strong men will be in anguish as of a woman in her pangs.

"Alas! for that day is great, so that none is like it: it is even *the time of Jacob's trouble;* but he shall be saved out of it" (ver. 7). To the Church the promise is: "Because thou hast kept the word of My patience, I also will keep thee *from* the hour of temptation, which shall come upon all the world, to try them that dwell upon the earth" (Rev. 3: 10). The saints of this dispensation shall be kept *from* the hour of travail. Those of the next period will be saved *out of it:* they will pass through it, but find deliverance at last when the Lord returns in glory. This short but dreadful time of sorrow is emphatically the time of *Jacob's* trouble. Necessarily others will be involved in it. All "earth-dwellers," in fact, will have to suffer while it continues; but it is the special season of Israel's sifting, when God will repay them double for all their sins. Scripture gives no hint of the Church passing through this unparalleled tribulation. It is not for the testing of the members of the Body of Christ, but for the chastisement of Israel.

"For it shall come to pass in that day, saith the Lord of hosts, that I will break his yoke from off thy neck, and will burst thy bonds, and strangers shall no more serve themselves of him: but they shall serve the Lord their God, and David their king, whom I will raise up unto them" (vers. 8, 9). The yoke referred to is that of the last great Gentile power, the ten-horned beast of Rev. 13— the Roman empire revived in its last and awful form. The power of the beast will be destroyed by the appearing in flaming fire of the Lord Jesus Christ with all the armies of heaven (Rev. 17); after which Israel, restored to their land, shall enter into rest under Messiah's beneficent rule. "David their king" refers, doubtless, not to the first son of Jesse who wore the royal diadem, but to the fact that the reign of the Lord is the ful- filment of Jehovah's promise to raise up, of David's line, One to rebuild his fallen tabernacle and to sit upon his throne. "The Lord God shall give unto Him the throne of His father David: and He shall reign over the house of Jacob for- ever; and of His kingdom there shall be no end" (Luke 1: 32, 33). This declaration, communi- cated by Gabriel, has never been fulfilled in the present dispensation. Not for one moment has

the Lord Jesus sat upon David's throne. He now
sits upon His Father's throne (Rev. 3:21; Heb.
1:3). At the end of this age He will rise from
that throne, when His enemies are made His footstool (Heb. 1:13; Ps. 110:1). Then He will de-
scend to earth to fulfil the promise spoken of by
Gabriel and all the prophets.

"Therefore fear thou not, O My servant Jacob,
saith the Lord; neither be dismayed, O Israel:
for, lo, I will save thee from afar, and thy seed
from the land of their captivity; and Jacob shall
return, and shall be in rest, and be quiet, and
none shall make him afraid" (ver. 10). Was this
the case when Judah returned by permission of
Cyrus? Were they in rest? Did none make them
afraid? The book of Nehemiah and the apocryphal records of the Maccabees give the answer,
as also the Gospels themselves. From their return to the destruction of Jerusalem under Titus,
we have one long record of unrest and warfare.
To the near future we must look for the carrying
out of this word.

"For I am with thee, saith the Lord, to save
thee: though I make a full end of all the
nations whither I have scattered thee, yet will
I not make a full end of thee; but I will
correct thee in measure, and will not leave
thee altogether unpunished" (ver. 11). Their
long sojourn among the Gentiles is but the fulfilment of this. The legend of the Wandering Jew,
deathless, yet ever moving on, has its foundation
here. Impossible to destroy the people of Jehovah's choice! Empires may rise and fall, nations
may be blotted out as the meteors of the heavens,

but Israel shall abide, and at last will triumph and bear rule over all the earth.

"For thus saith the Lord, Thy bruise is incurable, and thy wound is grievous. There is none to plead thy cause, that thou mayest be bound up: thou hast no healing medicines. All thy lovers have forgotten thee; they seek thee not; for I have wounded thee with the wound of an enemy, with the chastisement of a cruel one, for the multitude of thine iniquity; because thy sins were increased" (vers. 12-14). Prophets and seers had sought in vain to apply the healing word. Disaster and captivity even had not resulted in recovery. That the wound was utterly incurable so far as human power was concerned, the Cross would soon bring out. God in Christ walked among them in lowly grace. They nailed Him to a gibbet. Disowned by Jehovah, for a time, they must be. Antichrist, the false shepherd, shall bear rule over them in the day of their deepest tribulation. Their "lovers"—that is, the idols in which they had trusted—shall avail them naught. They must know to the full that "it is a fearful thing to fall into the hand of the living God."

The Gentile nations, however, who shall be the means of their affliction, shall in their turn know the rod of Jehovah's wrath. "Therefore all they that devour thee shall be devoured; and all thine adversaries, every one of them, shall go into captivity; and they that spoil thee shall be a spoil, and all that prey upon thee will I give for a prey" (ver. 16). All down through the centuries the nations have been made to know the truth of this verse. None have prospered long who oppressed

Israel. Babylon and Assyria exist not; while
Persia and Greece are still preserved. So among
modern nations. There should be no question
that one source, at least, of the strength of
Britain and the United States is found in this,
that they have, as a rule, befriended the Jews.
On the other hand, the history of the powers who
have stretched out their hands against Jehovah's people, records disaster after disaster.
Spain is witness to this; as, markedly, Russia is
also—that great dominion of Gog.

"For I will restore health unto thee, and I will
heal thee of thy wounds, saith the Lord; because
they called thee an Outcast, saying, This is Zion,
whom no man seeketh after" (ver. 17). Through
the wounded One the wounds of Israel shall yet
be healed, when, no longer outcast, they shall be
called "Sought out, A city not forsaken" (Isa.
62: 12).

"Thus saith the Lord: Behold, I will bring again
the captivity of Jacob's tents, and have mercy on
his dwelling-places; and the city shall be builded
upon her own heap, and the palace shall remain
after the manner thereof. And out of them shall
proceed thanksgiving and the voice of them that
make merry; and I will multiply them, and they
shall not be few; I will also glorify them, and
they shall not be small. Their children also shall
be as aforetime, and their congregation shall be
established before Me, and I will punish all that
oppress them" (vers. 18-20). Temporal blessings await repentant Israel as of old, "when there
was no strange god with him." The city, rebuilt
upon the ancient site, shall be filled with joy and

gladness; young and old shall alike be blessed, as Zechariah also prophesies: "There shall yet old men and old women dwell in the streets of Jerusalem, and every man with his staff in his hand for very age. And the streets of the city shall be full of boys and girls playing in the streets thereof" (Zech. 8:4, 5).

No longer oppressed by the haughty stranger, "their nobles shall be of themselves, and their governor shall proceed from the midst of them; and I will cause him to draw near, and he shall approach unto Me: for who is this that engaged his heart to approach unto Me? saith the Lord. And ye shall be My people, and I will be your God" (vers. 21, 22). There seems to be good reason to believe that the "governor" here spoken of is the same as the prince referred to so frequently in the last five chapters of Ezekiel. (See Ezek. 44:3; 45:7; 46:2, etc.). He will, we gather, be a direct lineal descendant of David, and will be the earthly ruler, subject in all things to the glorified Immanuel. In this day of "the restitution of all things spoken of by the prophets," the hearts of the people will have been fully turned to the Lord—that is, the spared remnant, for the apostate part of the nation will be destroyed in the great tribulation which is brought to our notice once more in the closing verses of this chapter.

"Behold, the whirlwind of the Lord goeth forth with fury, a continuing whirlwind: it shall fall with pain upon the head of the wicked. The fierce anger of the Lord shall not return, until He have done it, and until He have performed the intents of His heart: in the latter days ye shall consider it" (vers. 23, 24). The expression "the latter days" is evidently synonymous with "the time of the end" of Dan. 12, when "many shall be purified, and made white, and tried; but the wicked shall do wickedly: and none of the wicked shall understand; but the wise shall understand" (ver. 10). The fury of the Lord will fall with awful power upon the ungodly part of the nation who own Antichrist's impious sway; but those who refuse "the mark of the beast" (Rev. 13), and who honor Jehovah's Word, will then come into blessing.

Chapter 31 continues the general subject, dwelling more particularly upon the deliverance of the righteous remnant, and the establishment of the new covenant with them. "At that time, saith the Lord, will I be the God of all the families of Israel, and they shall be My people" (ver. 1). The Lo-ammi sentence of Hosea 1:9 will be forever repealed, for it is written: "Yet the number of the children of Israel shall be as the sand of the sea, which cannot be measured nor numbered; and it shall come to pass, that in the place where it was said unto them, Ye are not My people, there it shall be said unto them, Ye are the sons of the living God" (Hos. 1:10).

"Thus saith the Lord: The people which were left of the sword found grace in the wilderness; even Israel, when I went to cause him to rest" (ver. 2). The faithful remnant in the latter day are doubtless referred to. By Ezekiel a similar message is given: "I will bring you out from the people, and will gather you out of the countries wherein ye are scattered, with a mighty hand, and with a stretched out arm, and with fury poured out. And I will bring you into the wilderness of the people" (or nations), "and there will I plead with you face to face. Like as I pleaded with your fathers in the wilderness of the land of Egypt, so will I plead with you, saith the Lord God. And I will cause you to pass under the rod, and I will bring you into the bond of the covenant: and I will purge out from among you the rebels, and them that transgress against Me: I will bring them forth out of the country where they sojourn, and they shall not enter into the land of Israel: and ye shall know that I am the Lord" (Ezek. 20: 34-38). In that unparalleled tribulation period, referred to in Matt. 24: 21, the apostates of Israel will be destroyed by the judgment of the Lord; after which, those who have faithfully sought to walk in His ways will be established in the land.

All this, however, is pure grace; for it is His own loving-kindness that shall attract their hearts to Himself. Hence we read: "The Lord hath appeared of old unto me, saying, Yea, I have loved thee with an everlasting love: therefore with loving-kindness have I drawn thee" (ver. 3). It is His eternal love for them, not theirs for Him, that insures their final blessing. So with us: "Herein is love, not that we loved God, but that He loved us, and sent His Son to be the propitiation for our sins" (1 John 4: 10). When in us, as in Israel, there was naught to draw out that love, save, indeed, our deep and bitter need, He set His heart upon us and wooed us for Himself. In this way had He dealt with His earthly people; and having once set His affections upon them, He will never give them up.

"Again I will build thee, and thou shalt be built, O virgin of Israel: thou shalt again be adorned with thy tabrets, and shalt go forth in the dances of them that make merry" (ver. 4). For centuries their harps have been hung upon the willows, for "how can they sing the Lord's song in a strange land?" But soon the scene of the dance and song led by Miriam on the banks of the Red Sea shall be repeated in grander, fuller measure, when all their enemies are overthrown forever. In that day also they "shall yet plant vines upon the mountains of Samaria: the planters shall plant, and shall eat them as common things" (ver. 5).

The temple at Jerusalem will be rebuilt on a scale of magnificence previously unknown, and the tribes shall once more gather there to celebrate the feasts of Jehovah. "For there shall be a day that the watchmen upon the mount Ephraim shall cry, Arise ye, and let us go up to Zion unto the Lord our God. For thus saith the Lord: Sing with gladness for Jacob, and shout among the chief of the nations: publish ye, praise ye, and say, O Lord, save Thy people, the remnant of Israel" (vers. 6, 7). The "time of the singing" (Cant. 2:12) will have truly come, when the Lord shall turn again the captivity of His people.

"Behold, I will bring them from the north country, and gather them from the coasts of the earth, and with them the blind, and the lame, the woman with child and her that travaileth with child together: a great company shall return thither. They shall come with weeping, and with supplications will I lead them: I will cause them to walk by the rivers of waters in a straight way, wherein they shall not stumble: for I am a Father to Israel, and Ephraim is My first-born" (vers. 8, 9). God was not revealed as Father in an individual sense in the Old Testament. To Abraham He was known as the Almighty, or the All-Sufficient; to Moses, as Jehovah; prophetically, as the Most High; to the remnant in the days of Ezra and Nehemiah, as the God of heaven. The Lord Jesus it was who revealed the Father to *us*—"My Father and your Father," He says. This is blessedly individual. Each saint is a child, and can cry by the Spirit, "Abba, Father." Nationally, Israel was His son. As so recognizing them, He is spoken of as Father, but in no nearer sense. "Doubtless thou art our Father," the future remnant are entitled to say, "though Abraham be ignorant of us, and Israel acknowledge us not: Thou, O Lord, art our Father, our Redeemer; Thy name is from everlasting" (Isa. 63:16). In the book we are studying we have already noticed Jehovah's pathetic appeal: "Wilt thou not from this time cry unto Me, my Father, Thou art the guide of my youth?" (chap. 3:4.) As a Father, often grieved but loving still, He will rejoice over them when once more they ask the way to Zion.

"Hear the word of the Lord, O ye nations, and declare it in the isles afar off, and say, He that scattered Israel will gather him, and keep him, as a shepherd doth his flock" (ver. 10). No tem-

porary restoration can be here contemplated; **no**
gathering to allow of scattering again; but they
shall be brought back to be kept by the faithful
"Shepherd of Israel," nevermore to wander from
the fold.

"For the Lord hath redeemed Jacob, and ran-
somed him from the hand of him that was
stronger than he" (ver. 11). He has never given
up His purpose of redemption. As a nation they
were sheltered by blood from judgment and redeemed by power from Pharaoh's thraldom,
when He brought them out of Egypt. He has
contemplated them ever since from that standpoint. His grace cannot admit of failure to bring
them into fulness of blessing at last, however
much their ways may have necessitated chastisement in the interim. When brought safely
through the time of Jacob's trouble, they will sing
the song both of Moses and of the Lamb (Rev.
15). Their final deliverance is intimately connected with their salvation from bondage in the
past.

"Therefore they shall come and sing in the
height of Zion, and shall flow together to the
goodness of the Lord, for wheat, and for wine,
and for oil, and for the young of the flock and
of the herd: and their soul shall be as a watered
garden; and they shall not sorrow any more at
all. Then shall the virgin rejoice in the dance,
both young men and old together: for I will turn
their mourning into joy, and will comfort them,
and make them rejoice from their sorrow. And
I will satiate the soul of the priests with fatness,
and My people shall be satisfied with My goodness,

saith the Lord" (vers. 12-14). It is an utterly false system of exegesis that would spiritualize all this, and then apply it to the Church in this dispensation. The language is plain and simple. It is a millennial picture, descriptive of the joy of Messiah's kingdom when set up in this world.

In verses 15-17 we have the tribulation period once more referred to, with comforting assurances of blessing eventually. We know well that the words of verse 15 are referred by the Holy Ghost to the slaughter of the infants in Bethlehem, under Herod's cruel edict. "A voice was heard in Ramah, lamentation, and bitter weeping; Rachel weeping for her children refused to be comforted for her children, because they were not." (Comp. Matt. 2: 17, 18.) That was a similar case and an apt fulfilment of the passage, but the two following verses make it evident that a second and more complete fulfilment is contemplated; for it is distinctly stated that the children of which Rachel is bereft shall "come again from the land of the enemy," and that they "shall come again to their own border." It is captivity, and not alone slaughter, that is contemplated. This twofold application of prophecy is very common in Scripture, as witness Peter's citation from the prophet Joel on the day of Pentecost (Acts 2). The words will have a fuller performance in the last days in connection with the ushering in of the kingdom.

From verses 18 to 21 the repentance of the ten tribes (often referred to under the name Ephraim, as the two tribes are included in the term Judah) is vividly depicted. "I have surely heard Ephraim bemoaning himself thus: Thou hast chastised me, and I was chastised, as a bullock unaccustomed to the yoke: turn Thou me, and I shall be turned; for Thou art the Lord my God" (ver. 18). Hosea had declared that "Israel slideth back as a backsliding heifer" (Hos. 4: 16). This is here taken up as their own confession, but they turn to the One so long refused and sinned against. In true self-judgment Ephraim is heard to exclaim, "Surely after that I was turned, I repented; and after that I was instructed, I smote upon my thigh: I was ashamed, yea, even confounded, because I did bear the reproach of my youth" (ver. 19). It is the acknowledgment of the Lord's grace in bringing them back. Smiting on the thigh is, I judge, an expression symbolizing the entering once more into covenant. This breathing after Himself is at once responded to by Jehovah, who exclaims: "Is Ephraim My dear son? is he a pleasant child? for since I spake against him, I do earnestly remember him still: therefore My bowels are troubled for him; I will surely have mercy upon him, saith the Lord" (ver. 20). Hence the call to take the highway leading back from the lands of the nations to their ancestral home in Palestine. "Set thee up waymarks, make thee high heaps: set thy heart toward the highway, even the way which thou wentest: turn again, O virgin of Israel, turn again to these thy cities" (ver. 21). How boundless the grace that owns as a virgin the people that had been so horribly polluted!

"How long wilt thou go about, O thou backsliding daughter? for the Lord hath created a new thing in the earth, A woman shall compass a man" (ver. 22). The so-called "Fathers" were wont to apply this verse to the incarnation. The woman, with them, was the Virgin Mary: the man, her Holy Son. This, however, seems to be quite unwarranted and dubiously fanciful as an interpretation. Is it not more likely that the woman referred to is the virgin of Israel of the preceding passage? In that case the man would possibly be the symbol of power in the hands of the Gentile. (See Nebuchadnezzar's dream in Dan. 2.) Israel, weak as a woman, shall compass, or overcome, the power of the nations. This would harmonize with the context. The verse is confessedly difficult and the meaning obscure.

"Thus saith the Lord of hosts, the God of Israel: As yet they shall use this speech in the land of Judah and in the cities thereof, when I shall bring again their captivity; The Lord bless thee, O habitation of justice, and mountain of holiness. And there shall dwell in Judah itself, and in all the cities thereof together, husbandmen, and they that go forth with flocks. For I have satiated the weary soul, and have replenished every sorrowful soul" (vers. 23-25). When could Jerusalem have been referred to as the "habitation of justice and the mountain of holiness" in the five centuries following the return by permission of Cyrus? Beyond all contradiction these are promises yet to be made good. They refer to Judah, not the Church; therefore the Jews must be brought back to their land and established there in the fear of Jehovah if this word is to be carried out. "The Scripture cannot be broken."

Our prophet has been like a man in slumber while this vision of future glory and rest was unfolded to him. He is now aroused and his heart filled with a sweet, trusting peace as he enters into the purpose of God for his people. "Upon this I awaked, and beheld; and my sleep was sweet unto me" (ver. 26).

The few verses following recall at once the parable of the sour grapes uttered by Ezekiel at about the same time. "Behold, the days come, saith the Lord, that I will sow the house of Israel and the house of Judah with the seed of man, and with the seed of beast. . . . And I will watch over them, to build, and to plant, saith the Lord. In those days they shall say no more, The fathers have eaten a sour grape, and the children's teeth are set on edge. But every one shall die for his own iniquity: every man that eateth the sour grape, *his* teeth shall be set on edge" (vers. 27-30). In Ezek. 18 we find that this proverb had become a common one on the lips of the people of Judah. Blind to their own sins, they attributed their misfortunes to the Lord's anger because of the evil doings of their fathers. This was far from being the case, as both Ezekiel and Jeremiah testify. Their *own* sins had drawn down condign judgment. *They* had eaten the sour grapes, therefore were their teeth set on edge. "The soul that *sinneth*, it shall die." This they will be brought to confess in the time of their greatest sorrow; and as a result, we find Jehovah sowing them once more in their land; building and planting, whereas before He had been obliged to pluck up and afflict.

Following on this, the new covenant will be made with them. It is important to note that while the *blessings* of the new covenant are ours, yet it is never said to be made with the Church. In the epistle to the Hebrews, as in the passage before us, it is distinctly stated that it is to be made with "the house of Israel and the house of Judah" (Heb. 8:8-13). The Mediator of that covenant is the Lord Jesus Christ. The blood of the new covenant is that which He shed for our sins. Therefore believers now rejoice in the distinctive blessings it insures; but it is with the earthly, not with the heavenly, people that the covenant itself is to be made. "Behold, the days come, saith the Lord, that I will make a new covenant with the house of Israel, and with the house of Judah: not according to the covenant that I made with their fathers, in the day that I took them by the hand to bring them out of the land of Egypt; which My covenant they brake, although I was a husband unto them, saith the Lord" (vers. 31, 32). It were folly to speak of a *new* covenant with the Church, when no former covenant had been made with us. In the case of Israel and Judah it is different. They entered into the covenant of works at Sinai. That covenant had two parties to it. If they did their part, God would fulfil His. Alas, on that ground they forfeited everything before ever the tables of the covenant were brought down from the mount! Legal righteousness they had none.

In the new covenant God alone is the respon-sible One; hence they are placed in the position of recipients. It is pure grace. As we, also, are saved on this ground, it is clear that the same principle is operative in both cases; but the new covenant, as such, has its place in connection with them alone. We get the terms of it in the next two verses:

"But this shall be the covenant that I will make with the house of Israel: After those days, saith the Lord, I will put My law in their in-ward parts, and write it in their hearts; and will be their God, and they shall be My people. And they shall teach no more every man his neighbor, and every man his brother, saying, Know the Lord: for they shall all know Me, from the least of them unto the greatest of them, saith the Lord: for I will forgive their iniquity, and I will re-member their sin no more" (vers. 33, 34). There is no possibility of failure here, because all the pledges are on God's side. This covenant, there-fore, once made, shall never be abrogated. It is "an everlasting covenant, ordered in all things and sure." Israel and Judah, one nation in the land—purged, repentant and forgiven—shall never more forfeit Jehovah's favor. Forever they shall be debtors to His grace.

"Thus saith the Lord, which giveth the sun for a light by day, and the ordinances of the moon and of the stars for a light by night, which di-videth the sea when the waves thereof roar; The Lord of hosts is His Name: If those ordinances depart from before Me, saith the Lord, then the seed of Israel also shall cease from being a nation before Me forever. Thus saith the Lord: If heaven above can be measured, and the foundations of the earth searched out beneath, I will also cast off all the seed of Israel for all that they have done, saith the Lord" (vers. 35-37). The vastness of the heavens above and the earth beneath set forth this immeasurable mercy to Israel. In the face of this passage, what possible ground is there left for those to stand upon who teach the ultimate rejection of the once-favored nation?

Mark: it is not here a promise to bring Israel into blessing through the Church, and by incorporation into it. It is their national existence that is pledged, and their blessing as Israelites—not as Christians. They must be restored to their land, recognized once more as a nation, and brought into complete subjection to Jehovah, owning their once rejected Messiah as King and Saviour, or the prophecies of this chapter fall to the ground. All here is intensely literal. Nothing could be more so than the remaining verses, which need no comment. "Behold, the days come, saith the Lord, that the city shall be built to the Lord from the tower of Hananeel unto the gate of the corner. And the measuring line shall yet go forth over against it upon the hill Gareb, and shall compass about to Goath. And the whole valley of the dead bodies, and of the ashes, and all the fields unto the brook of Kidron, unto the corner of the horse gate toward the east, shall be holy unto the Lord; *it shall not be plucked up, nor thrown down any more forever*" (vers. 38-40). To no period of the past can these words apply. In our Lord's time the filthy stench of the valley of Hinnom still polluted the atmosphere. It was in no sense holy unto Jehovah. To the future alone can we look for a fulfilment that shall accord with, and transcend, the promise. "The zeal of the Lord of hosts will perform this."

CHAPTER XVII

All the fervid appeals of the prophet had been apparently wasted on Zedekiah. His heart was bent on departure from God. For over nine years, however, we hear of no positive act of persecution on his part. It is rather the other way. The records indicate that he stood in awe of the solemn and terrible denouncer of his iniquitous ways. His conscience would be, like Herod's, on the accuser's side. In this tenth year of his reign he was in great straits, owing to the fact that the army of the king of Babylon had invested Jerusalem. In his distress he turned not to Jehovah, but brazenly steeled his heart against His words. Jeremiah, particularly, was as a thorn in his side. He determined to silence him. Accordingly he commanded his apprehension, and the prophet was soon placed under arrest and shut up in the court of the prison, which adjoined the royal palace. The ostensible reason given was that by his words he weakened the hands of the people of Jerusalem by declaring that the defence would be in vain; the Lord having assured him that the city was to fall into the hands of the besiegers.

Of Zedekiah, too, he had prophesied only evil. *He* should not escape, but be certainly delivered into the power of Nebuchadrezzar and led to Babylon as a captive (vers. 1-5). All this was

a most unwelcome message for the self-willed
king. Having no thought to humble himself, he
concluded to silence the seer rather than bow to
his message. It has been the common resource
of men in all ages, who being set upon their own
ways are angered when coming judgment is proclaimed.

In the prison Jeremiah is instructed by the
Lord to make what to many would have seemed
a most unwise investment. His cousin Hanameel,
the son of his uncle Shallum, had a field in
Anathoth, which he, doubtless pressed by the
troubles of the times, was desirous of realizing
some money upon. A purchaser would be hard
to find, but he is instructed to go direct to the
very man who had prophesied the captivity of the
people, to whom he offers to sell it, as the "right
of redemption" was Jeremiah's; that is, according to the law he was the *Goel,* or kinsman-
redeemer. By his purchasing the field, it would
not pass from the house of his fathers.

Hanameel accordingly went to the court of the
prison, there to find his cousin in durance vile.
The Lord had already apprised Jeremiah of his
purpose. "Buy my field, I pray thee, that is in
Anathoth, which is in the country of Benjamin,"
he said: "for the right of inheritance is thine,
and the redemption is thine; buy it for thyself"
(ver. 8). Assured that it was from the Lord, the
prophet unhesitatingly bought the property in
question, paying for it seventeen shekels of
silver. The deed was accordingly made out trans-
ferring the property to him, properly attested by
witnesses, all in due order as required by the law
and custom of the time.

The title-deeds seem to have been contained in two rolls. One was open and the other sealed. The open one would probably, under ordinary circumstances, be placed on file in the official archives; the sealed one was to be safely stored away until the seventy years' servitude had come to a close, when it would be of value in determining the portion of Jeremiah's heirs. It was delivered to Baruch, of whom we now hear for the first time, but who was evidently the propheth's amanuensis, and a faithful man. He was instructed to "take these evidences, this evidence of the purchase, both which is sealed, and this evidence which is open; and put them in an earthen vessel, that they may continue many days. For thus saith the Lord of hosts, the God of Israel: Houses and fields and vineyards shall be possessed again in this land" (vers. 9-15). The purchase is thus seen to be a distinct act of faith on Jeremiah's part. God had informed him of the sure return from Babylon of the remnant of the people, upon the expiration of the seventy years. He implicitly believed that word, and therefore bought what seemed to be a piece of ground now worthless, in the possession of which neither he nor his heirs could enter. At the appointed time the sealed title-deeds would put the rightful owner into possession of the field. No thoughtful Bible student can fail to see in this striking incident the key to the understanding of the vision of the seven-sealed book in the Revelation. The latter is unquestionably the title-deed to this world. It remains sealed till the rightful Heir steps forth to claim it. He,

the worthy One, has first to purge His heritage
by judgment, before entering into possession of
it.   The opening of the seals is the declaration
that He is about to enter into His vested rights.

Returning to our chapter, we have, from the
16th verse to the 25th, Jeremiah's prayer upon
the signing of the deeds, followed (from verse
26 to the end) with Jehovah's reiteration of the
promise that the land shall yet be inhabited by
Israel and fields again bought therein.

In his prayer the prophet acknowledges the
power, as also the loving-kindness, of the Lord,
and owns the righteousness of His judgment upon
His people because of their sins. "Ah, Lord
God!" he prays, "behold, Thou hast made the
heaven and the earth by Thy great power and
stretched out arm, and *there is nothing too hard
for Thee*" (ver. 17). This is the ground of his confidence. He reposes upon the word of the Omnipotent God. "Thou showest loving-kindness unto
thousands, and recompensest the iniquity of the
fathers into the bosom of their children after
them: the Great, the Mighty God, the Lord of
hosts, is His name, great in counsel and mighty in
work: for Thine eyes are open upon all the ways
of the sons of men, to give every one according to
his ways, and according to the fruit of his doings"
(vers. 18, 19).   He is owned as the Moral Governor of the universe, who deals with all according to their works.   Nothing is too small for His
notice, or too great for His capacity.   "All things
are naked and open before the eyes of Him with
whom we have to do."   His eyes run to and fro
throughout the whole earth to render to all men

according to the fruit of their doings. He shows Himself strong in behalf of those who seek to honor Him; while, to such as lightly esteem Him, He appears as an enemy. Not that He ever is such—"His mercy endureth forever"—but from the wicked He hides His face.

Jeremiah goes back to the nation's beginning in Egypt, owning the grace that dealt with them in giving deliverance from the cruel oppressor and in bringing them into the land of promise. All He had undertaken had been abundantly fulfilled, but they obeyed Him not; therefore "all this evil" had come upon them (vers. 20-23). Now the Chaldeans surrounded the beloved city, while famine and pestilence raged within. "What Thou hast spoken is come to pass; and, behold, Thou seest it" (ver. 24). Yet the Lord had said, "Buy the field for money, and take witnesses;" even though the city was given into the hand of the Chaldeans (ver. 25). Here he breaks off abruptly, and at once Jehovah answers him by delineating more fully the sin of Israel and Judah, but in assuring him also of the everlasting nature of His covenant with them.

He declares, in verse 27, that He is the God of all flesh, and asks, "Is there anything too hard for Me?"—taking up the expression Jeremiah had used in the beginning of his prayer. Precious it is to have to do with One to whom nothing is impossible. What comfort for His imprisoned servant to know that it was the Almighty upon whom he leaned!

Into the hand of the Chaldeans the city shall surely be given, He goes on to say; and Nebu-

chadrezzar shall take it, destroying the houses
and roofs where incense was offered to Baal, and
drink offerings were poured out unto other gods.
From their youth the course of Israel and Judah
had been only evil. Jerusalem had been to Him
"as a provocation" of His anger "from the day
they built it unto this day;" therefore it should
be razed to the ground (vers. 28-31).

Kings, princes, priests, prophets, and the com-
monalty of Judah and Jerusalem, had all been of
one heart to do evil in His sight. They had
turned their backs upon Him; and though He
gave them instructors who would fain have recovered them to Himself, they had refused to heed
their messages. Even in His own house they had
set up their abominable idols, thus defiling its
sacred precincts, while unmentionable idolatrous
practices (of which He could say, "which I commanded them not, neither came it into My mind")
had they perpetrated (vers. 32-36).

Therefore there was no remedy; He would
give them up until His chastisement had yielded "the peaceable fruit of righteousness." In
that day He will "give them one heart, and one
way, that they may fear [Him] forever, for the
good of them, and of their children after them"
(vers. 37-39). When, in true repentance, they
turned back to Himself, He would "make an everlasting covenant with them," and never more
turn away from them, but would put His fear in
their hearts, that they should not depart from
Him (ver. 40). With His "whole heart and soul"
He will rejoice over them to do them good. How
touchingly human the language used! (ver. 41.)

All the evil prophesied had been and should be fulfilled to the letter. In like manner will He literally carry out all His promises for good. No word of His can by any means fail of accomplishment. Israel restored and the land once more inhabited in peace and safety, "men shall buy fields for money, and subscribe evidences, and seal them, and take witnesses in the land of Benjamin, and in the places about Jerusalem, and in the cities of Judah, and in the cities of the mountains, and in the cities of the valley, and in the cities of the south" (vers. 42-44).

The thirty-third chapter consists of two distinct prophecies, but we group them with the preceding because all alike were given during the time that Jeremiah was shut up in the court of the prison. His body might be in confinement, but none could hinder the communication of divine messages to the soul of the man of God.

The first section includes verses 1 to 18. Like the foregoing, it concerns the restoration to the land, but in no sense limiting it to the return at the expiration of the seventy years in Babylon. "Great and mighty things" God is about to show to His servant. He who, for their sins, has permitted the overthrow of Jerusalem, having hidden His face from it, will assuredly bring it health and cure, revealing unto them "the abundance of peace and truth." He will cause the captivity of both Israel and Judah to return, and give them to know His pardoning grace, cleansing them from all their transgressions (vers. 1-8).

Jerusalem is destined yet to become a "name of joy, a praise, and an honor before all the nations of the earth," for the fame of His loving-kindness towards it shall go out into all the world. In place of the desolation which it must for a time know, its streets shall once more be filled with a joyous, God-fearing multitude who shall chant the praise of their covenant-keeping God (vers. 9-11).

In the country round about shepherds shall once more pasture their flocks with none to make them afraid, when the cities shall be rebuilt and the waste places inhabited, in the day that the Lord will perform all His promises of blessing (vers. 12-14).

At that time the veil that for centuries has covered their hearts will be removed; the lowly Nazarene, once rejected as an impostor, will reappear in glory, to be accepted of all the people as the Anointed of Jehovah. "In those days, and at that time, will I cause the Branch of Righteousness to grow up unto David; and He shall execute judgment and righteousness in the land. In those days shall Judah be saved, and Jerusalem shall dwell safely: and this is the name wherewith she shall be called, *Jehovah Tsidkenu*" ("the Lord our Righteousness," vers. 15, 16). We have already noticed that in chap. 22: 6 it is He who is called by this significant name. Here it is applied to her—that is, to restored Jerusalem. His righteousness shall be put upon her; and clothed in the garments of salvation she shall rejoice beneath Immanuel's sway. The promise made to David shall be fulfilled: he "shall never want a man to sit upon the throne of the house of Israel," and the priesthood likewise shall be established (vers. 17, 18).

The second section is composed of the balance of the chapter—vers. 19 to 26, inclusive. It resembles the affirmation of chap. 31: 35-37, but is even fuller. If the covenant of the day and of the night can be broken, then may His covenant with David be annulled; but as truly as the stars of heaven cannot be numbered, nor the sand of the sea measured, so will He multiply the seed of David and of the Levites that minister unto Him (vers. 19-22).

In their unbelief they had charged Him with violating His pledge and casting off the two families (Israel and Judah) which He had chosen; and the reference in their complaint is probably to the Chaldeans: "They have despised My people, that they should be no more a nation before them" (vers. 23, 24). Their reasoning is utterly at fault. It is *because they are His people* that He "will punish them for their iniquity." Though they pass under the rod, He will not utterly give them up. If His covenant be not with day and night, and if He have not appointed the ordinances of heaven and earth, then He will cast away the seed of Jacob and of David; otherwise He will certainly "cause their captivity to return, and have mercy on them" (vers. 25, 26).

Soon, perhaps in the lifetime of many now upon earth, will He cause these promises to be fulfilled.

CHAPTER XVIII

(Chap. 34.)

The peculiarly vacillating character of Zedekiah and the nobles of Judah is very pronouncedly brought before us in the prophetic message to which our attention is now directed.

The three kings who followed the godly Josiah were apparently all deliberately opposed to Jeremiah, the advocate of submission to Babylon. Their policy was to rely upon Egypt, and by a league with Pharaoh to throw off the Chaldean yoke. Jeremiah, as we have seen, ever counseled the contrary. The king of Babylon had been appointed by God and set over the nations. Egypt was a broken reed. The only safe and right policy was to submit to the authority ordained of Jehovah, and to acknowledge how richly the sins of Israel and Judah had deserved this national degradation.

Zedekiah was set up by Nebuchadrezzar, consequently was not so ardent an advocate of a confederacy with Egypt as his predecessors. In fact, only upon a great triumph of the Egyptian arms did he decide to throw in his lot with that once powerful nation and rebel against his liege lord. He seems to have had sincere respect for Jeremiah, frequently counseling with him; but as he was a man of a double heart and not upright before God, there is a painful lack of obedience to the word of God as thus delivered to him. Finally, when his position became desperate and the city seemed about to fall, he threw the prophet into prison, and refused to hearken to his admonitions. At times, however, conscience seemed to awake, as in the present instance, but, alas, only to be again lulled to sleep. The incident here recorded probably occurred prior to the imprisonment of which the previous section treats. It was an attempt to enforce the law of God, long neglected, upon a vitally important matter, even the recognition of the sabbatic year.

The armies of Nebuchadnezzar (as he is here called), consisting of the Chaldeans and subject legions from "all the kingdoms of the earth of his dominion," were surrounding the devoted city when the prophet was commanded to go and speak to Zedekiah (ver. 1). The message was one of gloom and disaster. The Lord was about to give the city into the hand of the Babylonian spoiler, and the king himself must go into captivity. Nevertheless, as there had been some good things in him—some regard, however slight, for the word of God, some concern for the state of Judah—he was informed that he should not die by the sword, but in peace; and that customary honors upon the decease of princes should be paid to his remains. He would be lamented in a way that had not been done for the former kings (vers. 2-5).

Jeremiah delivered the divine communication as commanded, but we have no word as to the effect upon the unhappy monarch.

The foe had been almost everywhere triumphant; only two of Judah's defenced cities remained unconquered, besides the capital. These were Lachish and Azekah, both west of Jerusalem, and about some fifteen miles apart. These were invested, and all hope of their holding out much longer was vain (vers. 6, 7). It would seem that Zedekiah keenly felt the plight he was in, and in his distress he had made a covenant with all the people to observe the sabbatic year—so far as it affected the relationship of masters and slaves. The portion referring to the land could not be carried out, as all the fields were overrun by the foragers of the Chaldean armies, and the husbandmen carried away or slain.

The law (Ex. 21: 1-6; Deut. 15: 12-18) regulated servitude in Israel by commanding that all male slaves of Hebrew birth, and all maidens not betrothed to the master or his son, should serve at the most but six years, and in the seventh go out free; unless, having been given a wife in bondage, the servant should of his own volition choose to remain with her in his subject condition. Rapacity and covetousness had made this law a dead letter for years. Now, the king and people covenanted to observe it, and to "proclaim liberty unto them; that every man should let his manservant, and every man his maidservant, being a Hebrew or a Hebrewess, go free; that none should serve himself of them, to wit, of a Jew his brother" (vers. 8, 9).

This was fully in accord with the mind of the Lord; and if there had been purpose of heart to continue in it, and genuine repentance because of past sin, it would have been acceptable in His

eyes. But, alas for man's stability when left to
himself! The proclamation was hardly made before it was repealed! Possibly some slight rift in
the dark clouds overshadowing them gave them to
suppose that, after all, the seriousness of their
condition had been exaggerated; consequently
they returned to their old ways, which had never
been truly judged, bringing the servants and the
handmaids once more into subjection (vers. 10,
11).

The Lord, accordingly, once more put a word
in His servant's mouth, and sent him unto the
vacillating and unstable people. He reminded
them of the covenant made with their fathers
when He brought them out of Egypt, and of the
provisions of the year of release, as recorded in
Deut. 15, above referred to. Their action in pro-
claiming liberty He describes as being right in
His sight. In turning from their covenant, and
causing their servants once more to enter into
bondage, they had polluted His name. Now He
would proclaim a liberty against them—even to
the sword, to the pestilence, and to the famine!
(vers. 12-17). It is true of nations as of men
that whatsoever is sown must be reaped. Obedience to the word of God brings blessing. Disobedience is the sure precursor of judgment.
"Righteousness exalteth a nation, but sin is a reproach to any people."

In the most solemn manner had Judah's princes
and people sealed the covenant which their cupid-
ity caused them so readily to violate. They had
"cut the calf in twain and passed between the
parts thereof" (ver. 18). From of old this seems

to have been a customary form for the contracting parties to a solemn covenant. A sacrifice was offered, and the pieces or parts thereof arranged in order on the altar; then the persons pledging themselves passed between the pieces. We see God pledging Himself thus in Abraham's day. The patriarch was instructed to take "a heifer of three years old, and a ram of three years old, and a turtle-dove and a young pigeon" (Gen. 15: 9). All these were typical of the one true sacrifice—the Lord Jesus Christ—each representing Him in some special aspect. The young ox speaks of Him as the patient Servant, providing food for others. The goat is, in Matt. 25, used to picture the sinner, and points, therefore, to Him whom God made sin for us, that we might become the righteousness of God in Him. The ram is the consecration offering, and tells of His submissive obedience unto death. The turtle-dove, as others have suggested, is the bird of love and sorrow; and never was either love or sorrow so great as His. The pigeon, of course, is similar; and both being from the heavens, they pointed to the One who came from heaven to die on earth for our redemption.

Abram, whose name had not yet been changed, took "all these and divided them in the midst, and laid each piece one against another; but the birds divided he not." Each part being placed in order, he kept watch over them, driving away the unclean fowls which gathered to devour them, as the Christian to-day is called to contend earnestly for the great "mystery of piety," suffering no unclean one to rob him of the truth as to "the doctrine of Christ."

Night falling, the watcher wearied, and fell into a deep sleep. A "horror of great darkness fell upon him"—a symbol of the hiding of Jehovah's face, which his seed must in measure experience. It was then that God drew near and reiterated His promise of blessing for the chosen race, but openend up likewise something of their future sorrows, coupled with their final deliverance. Then He confirmed His covenant in a remarkable manner. A smoking furnace was seen, symbol of their affliction in the Egyptian bondage, and, following after it, "a burning lamp, which *passed between the pieces.*" This burning lamp, or, literally, lamp of fire, was the visible manifestation of God's presence. By thus passing between the pieces He pledged Himself, by the Cross of His beloved Son, to fulfil all His covenant. And notice that Abram was not called upon to do likewise. *He* made no pledge. None was asked of him. It was a covenant of pure grace.

In this way, then, the people of Judah had confirmed a covenant in regard to the sabbatic year of release. They had offered to Jehovah a calf, and "passed between the parts thereof." Nothing could have been more solemn. They bound themselves, by the strongest of all vows, to proclaim liberty to every bondman or bondmaid of Hebrew birth. But because there was no true self-judgment, no sincere repentance, they soon fell back to their old ways. As a result, all these unfaithful swearers who "passed between the parts of the calf" should be given up to death; for their so doing was practically a declaration that they would forfeit their lives if they violated their agreement. They should be taken at their word. Jehovah would give them into their enemies' hands; and their dead bodies should have none, like Abram, to drive away the carrion-birds of prey, but they should "be for meat unto the fowls of the heaven, and to the beasts of the earth" (vers. 19, 20). It is a fearful thing to trifle with God. He is a consuming fire. How little even saints realize the solemnity of having to do with Him, the High and Lofty One, who inhabiteth Eternity!

From the last verses (21, 22) we gather that the direct reason for the unfaithful going back of the people had been the withdrawal for a time of the army of the besiegers. They had evidently struck their tents and temporarily left the city to itself. This was taken to mean that the siege was abandoned. Those who before were desperate now became elated and careless. Their complacency was ill-timed. The Lord would command, "and cause them to return to this city, and they shall fight against it, and burn it with fire." The cities of Judah would become a desolation, without an inhabitant.

CHAPTER XIX.

THE HOUSE OF THE RECHABITES

(Chap. 35.)

In striking contrast to the story of vacillation and treachery, recorded in the chapter we have just been considering, is the very instructive incident now brought to our notice.

The prophet is bidden to go to the house of the Rechabites, and, after saluting them, to "bring them into the house of the Lord, into one of the chambers, and give them wine to drink" (vers. 1, 2). This was sometime during the reign of Jehoiakim; therefore a number of years before the broken covenant of the last chapter. There is, however, a beautiful moral order in presenting it in this connection, utterly precluding the impious assumption that the various parts of this book have been thrown together haphazard by some later editor.

These Rechabites were not originally of the stock of Israel. They were Kenites, a tribe, the origin of which is shrouded in mystery. It is commonly supposed that they were Midianites by extraction, as Jethro the father-in-law of Moses belonged to the Kenites (Judges 4:11). Heber the Kenite, with his wife Jael, took the part of Israel in the war with the Canaanites headed by Sisera, who was slain by Jael when he sought refuge in her tent.

In 1 Chron. 2:55 we find the Rechabites numbered with the children of Judah. "These are the Kenites that came of Hemath, the father of the house of Rechab." It is through their valiant representative Jehonadab, the son of Rechab, that they first acquired special prominence. It was he who went out to meet Jehu after he had been anointed king of Israel by the nameless prophet sent by Elisha to Ramoth-Gilead. Having destroyed the vile house of Ahab, and likewise many of the house of Ahaziah king of Judah, Jehu was riding towards Samaria when "he lighted on Jehonadab the son of Rechab coming to meet him: and he saluted him, and said to him, Is thy heart right, as my heart is with thy heart? And Jehonadab answered, It is" (2 Kings 10:15). Dramatically Jehu cried, "If it be, give me thy hand." Upon his doing so, he took him up with him into the chariot, saying, "Come with me, and see my zeal for the Lord." The conclusion is irresistible that Jehu already knew Jehonadab well as a man devoted to the worship of Jehovah, and an abhorrer of idolatry. The piety of his father Rechab is expressed in the name given to his son, the meaning of which is, "Jehovah freely gave." In company with the zealous but cruel king, Jehonadab is found commanding the search to see that no servants of Jehovah were mingled with the worshipers of Baal in the temple of Samaria, prior to their massacre at the order of Jehu. He is not again mentioned until we come down to our present chapter.

In accordance with the word of the Lord, Jeremiah took Jaazaniah, the son of another Jere-

miah, and his brethren, and the whole house of
the Rechabites, and brought them into the chamber of the sons of Hanan, a man of God, in the
temple. Here he set before them pots full of
wine, and said, "Drink ye wine" (vers. 3-5).

Nobly they refused the invitation, giving as a
reason for their conduct the fact that this
very Jehonadab (called here Jonadab the son of
Rechab) had, nearly three hundred years before,
commanded them neither to drink wine, nor to
build houses, nor sow seed, nor plant nor own
vineyards, but to dwell ever in tents, that they
might live many days in the land where they were
strangers. This command they had literally
obeyed from his days until the overrunning of
the country by Nebuchadrezzar. The presence of
his troops had made it impossible for them to
live in their former unguarded manner; so, to
save their lives, they had moved into Jerusalem;
but although thus obliged to dwell in a walled
city, they would not violate the command for-
bidding them to drink of the fruit of the vine
(vers. 6-11). Their reverence for and obedience
to their great ancestor is all the more striking
when the dissolute state of Israel and Judah is
taken into consideration.

They were a living sermon on subjection to
the law, for any who would take cognizance of
them. Hence Jeremiah is bidden to "Go and tell
the men of Judah and the inhabitants of Jerusalem, Will ye not receive instruction to hearken
to My words? saith the Lord" (vers. 12, 13).
Alas, their record had ever been that they only
knew His law in order to break it. From the day

when they made the calf in the wilderness until
the time in which Jeremiah ministered to them,
their history had been one long, shameful account
of disobedience and wilful rejection of His Word.
Long ere this, He, through Isaiah, had cried,
"Hear, O heavens, and give ear, O earth: for the
Lord hath spoken; I have nourished and brought
up children, and they have rebelled against Me.
The ox knoweth his owner, and the ass his master's crib: but Israel doth not know, My people
doth not consider" (Isa. 1: 2, 3). Less respon-
sive than the beasts that perish, they had turned
away their ears from His law, and refused to
walk in the way of His commandments.

Has not this awful indictment a solemn message for Christians? How widespread is the
same wilful spirit even among those who are
"bought with a price," even the precious blood
of Christ! How many of us act as truly *knowing*
our Owner? We are not our own, but His who sold
all that He had to purchase us! What kind of a
bargain has He had? What is our Master's crib
but the holy Word of God, so often neglected and
uncared for in Christian homes! What an abundance of good provender does it contain, and all
for the sheep of Christ! Yet how is it turned
from, while the husks of this world are sought
instead! It is to be feared there is very little
moral difference between the state of Judah in
the days of her downfall and the house of God
to-day. Let us see to it that we learn the lesson
of these faithful Rechabites.

Wine, in Scripture, is the symbol of joy
(Judges 9: 13; Ps. 104: 15). The Nazarite of

old was to refrain from it, for he found not his joy in a ruined creation. The sons of Rechab, as strangers and pilgrims, touch not that which comes from the vine of the earth. They speak, in type, of those who seek a higher, deeper, more lasting joy than this world can ever offer. Having here no continuing city, dwelling in the pilgrim's tent, sinking no foundations in this terrestrial scene, they reach out for that which is to come. What a contrast to the time-serving trucklers to the present age, as well as to the faithless people and princes of the times of Jeremiah!

The Lord goes on to say that the words of Jonadab were performed by his descendants in all faithfulness; but although *He* had given His Word, "rising early and speaking," His people had not hearkened. Prophets, one after another, had been sent, bidding them refrain from their evil ways and amend their doings by turning truly to Himself from all their false gods. If they would thus obey His voice, He would prosper them still, and preserve them in their land. But there was no response. They inclined not the ear, nor hearkened to His entreaties.

Once more, therefore, it becomes the painful duty of the man who loved them so dearly that his heart was pained for them, to declare the doom that must soon be meted out to them. All the evil that the Lord had pronounced against them must shortly fall upon the city and the country, because, when He spake, they listened not; when He called, they answered not (vers. 16, 17). This is the opposite of what we get in Prov. 1: 28. There the wayward are warned of a time coming of which God says, "Then shall *they* call upon *Me*, but I will not answer; they shall seek Me early, but they shall not find Me." This is the fearful result of such a course as that pursued by treacherous Judah, and by an equally treacherous Christendom.

As to the house of the Rechabites, it was declared to them, by the authority of the Lord Himself, that because of their faithful adherence to the commandments of Jonadab their father, he should not want a man to stand before Jehovah forever (vers. 18, 19). The family of this devoted man has long since been lost to history, both sacred and profane, but we gather from this promise that somewhere in this world his descendants still exist; and, doubtless, in the Millennium, when all the prophecies regarding Israel and Judah are fulfilled, the house of Rechab will once more appear upon the scene, a testimony to the faithfulness of Him who is "not a man, that He should lie; neither the son of man, that He should repent: hath He said, and shall He not do it? or hath He spoken, and shall He not make it good?" (Num. 23: 19).

In that day the Rechabites shall drink the pure joys that flow through the scene of Immanuel's presence; nor will it appear as a hardship that they were denied the fruit of the vine while the curse rested upon the earth for man's sake.

CHAPTER XX

THE FIRST DESTRUCTIVE CRITIC ON RECORD

(Chap. 36.)

Among the host of latter-day evils which are sapping the very foundations of Christianity in the minds of the masses, none has been more audaciously impious in its assault upon the truth of God than the so-called Higher Criticism. Under the guise of reverent scholarship seeking to determine the authenticity of books that faith has never questioned, the advocates of this destructive school have not hesitated to cut in pieces the Scriptures of truth, and deliberately seek to falsify the very words of the Lord Jesus Christ. He, at least, who knew all things, had no doubts as to the divine authority of every jot and tittle of the Old Testament. It was to Him the inspired utterance of the Holy Ghost.

His apostles, likewise, accepted every part of it —the Law, and the Prophets, and the Psalms— as God's unerring message to His creatures. Nowhere is there the least hesitancy as to owning the full authority of any portion of what was in their day the accepted canon of Holy Scripture

It has remained for present-day theorists, bereft alike of sound judgment and true godliness, to challenge the genuineness and to impugn the veracity of what our Lord and His first followers (themselves inspired men) received without question as the "oracles of God."

Terrible indeed must be the judgment of those who seek thus to undermine faith in God's holy Word, and to turn the simple from the ways that be in Christ to paths of error and confusion. And what, alas, will be the eternal state of those who, in many instances, accept all too greedily the poisoned sweetness of these venders of religious confections, glad in heart to be released from a sense of responsibility to God and His Word that has been at least a check upon their consciences, when tempted to ways of utter ungodliness?

Rest assured, dear fellow-believer, ours is a faith founded upon an impregnable Rock. Men who refuse it do so to their own destruction. The wild vagaries of the destructive critics are only the precursors of the great apostasy that is now near at hand. But, thank God, ere that awful night of gloomy unbelief settles down upon the minds of the great mass of Christendom, the Church will have been caught away to be with the Lord in the Father's house. The Holy Spirit, with the Body of Christ, leaving this scene, Antichrist will quickly arise, to whom all the vaunted learning of the day, then Christless, will bow the knee; for "God shall send them strong delusion, that they should believe the lie: that they all may be judged because they obeyed not the truth, but had pleasure in unrighteousness" (2 Thess. 2: 11, 12).

These opponents of the important truth of the plenary inspiration of the Scriptures are but the John the Baptists of Antichrist—the preparers of his way.

No honest reader of the Old Testament can fail

to see that inspiration is stamped on every page. Jesus affirms it again and again; and when quoting Old Testament Scripture, does so as giving forth the last word on the subject, against which there can be no gainsaying. Note it in His temptation, where each passage quoted in defeat of Satan is taken from Deuteronomy, the book so much attacked by the critics. He who knew all things questioned neither its reputed authorship, nor its divine authority. Elsewhere He solemnly declares, "The Scripture cannot be broken," and that "not one jot or tittle shall pass from the Law until all be fulfilled." The Scriptures everywhere bear witness of Him, and He is seen as the fulfilment of Scripture. In the wilderness; in His life of service; in His passion on the tree—one thing after another is said or done "that it might be fulfilled which was written" in the Law, the Prophets and the Psalms concerning Him; and in resurrection it is still the same. To the two on the road to Emmaus He opens up the sacred volume, explaining in every scripture the things concerning Himself.

It is the same with the apostles: for Peter, Paul, James or Jude the testimony of Scripture is the end of controversy: "Well spake the Holy Ghost," "The Holy Ghost saith," "As it is written"—such are the expressions used to introduce passages from the three great divisions of the Old Testament. In reverence they received every word as direct from the living God.

As to the New Testament writings, the stamp of divine authority rests upon every page. The Lord Jesus said to His apostles, "Whoso heareth

you heareth Me." And John therefore writes,
"We are of God: he that knoweth God heareth
us; he that is not of God heareth not us. Hereby
know we the spirit of truth, and the spirit of error" (1 John 4: 6). In the most solemn way he
seals the authority of the book of Revelation,
testifying that "if any man shall add unto these
things, God shall add unto him the plagues that
are written in this book; and if any man shall
take away from the words of the book of this
prophecy, God shall take away his part out of the
book of life, and out of the holy city, and from
the things which are written in this book" (Rev.
22: 18, 19).

Peter, too, classes the letters of "our beloved
brother Paul" with "the other Scriptures," thus
attesting their divine source; and the great
apostle to the Gentiles asserts full inspiration in
unmistakable terms: "Which things also we
speak, not in the words which man's wisdom
teacheth, but which the Holy Ghost teacheth" (1
Cor. 2: 13). And in 1 Cor. 14: 37 he writes: "If
any man think himself to be a prophet, or spiritual, let him acknowledge that the things that I
write unto you are the commandments of the
Lord." To so acknowledge brings lasting blessing; to deny, brings shame and everlasting confusion, after the plaudits of the "liberal-minded"
have been hushed for aye!

It is sometimes stated there are portions of
Paul's epistles where he himself disclaims divine
authority, but gives his own private opinion. Because of the importance of the subject, and in
order to help any reader who may thus be troubled,

we will turn aside to notice these passages. In
1 Cor. 7 he writes, as to the relations of husbands
and wives, and in the opening verses gives them
their true place in the family. In ver. 5 he says:
"Defraud ye not one the other, except it be with
consent for a time, that you may give yourselves
to fasting and prayer; and come together again,
that Satan tempt you not for your incontinency."
Then he immediately adds : "But I speak this
by permission, and not by commandment." That
is, he does not command such times of separation,
which in some households might bring in confusion—he simply permits it in cases where it
would be profitable. The Revised Version reads:
"I speak this by way of permission." Only an
ungodly will could pervert this to teach that the
apostle was denying direct inspiration.

Ver. 12 is supposed to teach similarly. If compared with vers. 10 and 11 all is clear. "Unto
the married I command, yet not I, but the Lord,
Let not the wife depart from her husband: but
and if she depart, let her remain unmarried, or
be reconciled to her husband: and let not the
husband put away his wife." All this was directly commanded by the Lord in Matt. 19. Therefore he says, "Yet not I, but the Lord." *He* had
already spoken. Now look at the next verse:
"But to the rest speak I, not the Lord (that is,
the Lord had not heretofore spoken as to what
is to follow; the apostle himself declares the mind
of God regarding it) : "If any brother hath a wife
that believeth not, and she be pleased to dwell
with him," etc.; and here instruction is given for
varied cases as they might come up.

Notice the authoritative tone in ver. 17: "And so ordain I in all the churches." Here we have both conscious inspiration and authority.

In ver. 25 he writes: "Now concerning virgins I have no commandment of the Lord: yet I give my judgment, *as one that hath obtained mercy of the Lord to be faithful.*" The italicized portion negatives all thought of partial or non-inspiration. He gives an inspired judgment based on the place God has given him. The 40th verse is similar. His was a judgment guided by the Spirit of God. There is a difference between revelation and inspiration. Here we have the latter, but not necessarily the former.

As to the universality of his writings, or their application to all believers, the opening verses of the epistle we have been looking at state it most emphatically. He writes "unto the church of God which is at Corinth, to them that are sanctified in Christ Jesus, *with all that in every place call upon the name of Jesus Christ our Lord,* both theirs and ours" (ver. 2). Could words be plainer? Who, that is at all subject to the Scriptures, would limit the application of a letter so addressed?

Note, too, how he speaks of himself in the introduction to the Romans. "By whom we have received grace and apostleship, for *obedience to the faith among all nations,* for His name" (ver. 5).

And so one might go on from epistle to epistle and point out similar evidences of his consciousness that what he wrote was binding on the consciences of *all* saints, because inspired by the Holy Ghost.

Let us turn now to the chapter before us, which gives us the first recorded instance of this unhallowed mutilation and rejection of the written Word of God—now so common. The exceeding importance of the subject alone has made so long a digression permissible.

In the fourth year of Jehoiakim, Jeremiah was instructed by the Lord to take a roll of a book and to write all that He had spoken against both Israel and Judah and the surrounding nations, from the beginning of the prophet's ministry in the days of Josiah unto the time when so commanded (vers. 1, 2). We read of no writings of his prior to this; the letters of chap. 29 having been penned some years later. All his messages had been delivered orally. Now they are to be gathered together in the form of a book, so that the king and the house of Judah may the better consider what God had said. Jehovah adds, "It may be that the house of Judah will hear all the evil which I purpose to do unto them; that they may return every man from his evil way; that I may forgive their iniquity and their sin" (ver. 3). How God longed for their recovery! He had no delight in their judgment. Much more readily would He have granted forgiveness had there been any evidence of repentance and contrition of heart.

Accordingly, Baruch wrote "all the words of the Lord" at Jeremiah's dictation. The prophet himself was "shut up" (in what way we know not), and could not go to the house of the Lord, but Baruch is sent to read all that has been written to the assembled multitudes, upon the occasion of a fast which had been proclaimed because of the wretched conditions prevailing, when all the cities of Judah would be represented in Jerusalem. Gathered thus for humiliation and the afflicting of their souls, it might be they would give ear to the Word of God, and turn from their manifold iniquities when they knew the great anger of the Lord and what He had pronounced against them (vers. 6, 7).

This fast was to take place in the ninth month of Jehoiakim's fifth year. On that day the son of Neriah repaired to the temple and read in the book before all the people, at the door of the new gate of the Lord's house, standing in the entrance to the chamber of Gemariah the son of Shaphan the scribe.

The son of this Gemariah, Michaiah by name, seems to have been deeply affected by the words to which he had listened. His heart and mind full of them, he went down to the scribe's chamber, of the royal palace, where he found a company of the chief men assembled. Among them were his own father, and a scribe known as Elishama, together with other leaders of the people, and all the princes. To them the young man gave an outline of all he had heard from Baruch's reading of the roll. They were evidently concerned, for the time at least, for they sent at once to summon the servant of the prophet to bring the book and come to their council-hall; and having come, they said, "Sit down, and read it in our ears."

So for the second time that day Baruch read the solemn messages, with the result that they were afraid, and said to the reader, "We will surely tell the king of these words." They desired to be certain that the writing was indeed what it professed to be, a series of messages from Jehovah through Jeremiah; so they asked Baruch, "Tell us now, How didst thou write all these words at his mouth?" He replied, "He pronounced all these words unto me with his mouth, and I wrote them with ink in the book."

Evidently realizing something of the importance of the contents of the roll, yet fearing the king's wrath upon the promulgators of it, and being solicitous as to the prophet's welfare, the princes warned Baruch, saying, "Go, hide thee, thou and Jeremiah; and let no man know where ye be" (vers. 11-19).

Laying up the roll in the chamber of Elishama, the scribe, the princes and chief men hied themselves to the king's palace, and gave to Jehoiakim the gist of the words it contained. Jehudi is sent at once to fetch it, and began to read it in the presence of the king and of the princes who stood beside him. The reader had but gone over three or four leaves when the impatient monarch "cut it with a penknife," or a "scribe's knife," and deliberately cast it into the fire before him. In vain three of the princes besought the king not to burn the sacred roll. The king persisted in his impiety; neither did he nor his servants manifest any fear or concern for the affront offered to Jehovah. On the contrary, an order was issued for the arrest of both Baruch and Jeremiah, but the Lord cared for His servants, and "hid them" (vers. 20-26).

The king thus put himself on record as the first mutilator of the Word of God recorded in Scripture. Alas, how many have followed in his steps since that day, when, all unknown to himself and his foolhardy friends, he sealed his doom by his wilful rejection of the inspired message. The "scribe's knife" has often been used since to mutilate and destroy the Word of truth—aye, to the final sorrow of every one that does it! Heaven and earth may pass away; the Word of God, never! Truth cannot be destroyed; it is unalterable, and the will of impious "scholarship" can never set it aside. The emissaries of Rome, also, sought to make an end of it in the days of papal persecutions. Thousands of Bibles were consigned to the flames, but they became as the seed from which millions of copies sprang. Infidelity has raged and done its worst to discredit it. Still the Bible is triumphant. Any other book, so treated, would long ago have been but a memory, and have disappeared from the face of the earth: but *God* has cared for it.

It has remained for so-called Christian scholars to emulate Romanism and Atheism, under the guise of legitimate criticism, in knifing the sacred volume and consigning large portions of it to the fire of their cheap scorn and derision, as unreliable and uninspired; but they have yet to learn that the book they criticize is, itself, the supreme critic. "For the Word of God is quick and powerful, and sharper than any two-edged sword, piercing even to the dividing asunder of soul and spirit and of the joints and marrow, and is a *discerner* (literally, *critic*) of the thoughts and intents of the heart. Neither is there any creature that is not manifest in His sight; but all things are naked and opened unto the eyes of Him with whom we have to do" (Heb. 4: 12, 13). Of the Word of God, as of the person of Christ, it may be said: "Whosoever shall fall on this stone shall be broken; but on whomsoever it shall fall, it will grind him to powder" (Matt. 21: 44).

In that solemn day when the "books are opened" Jehoiakim will find, unharmed by the flames, the roll he wantonly sought to destroy brought out as a witness against his guilty soul; and those who now, whatever their profession, assail the truth, seeking to discredit the Scriptures as the very Word of God, will be judged then by the very portions they now refuse. Who can conceive the awful awakening of men in that day who have filled Christian pulpits and doled out veneered infidelity to the ignorant and the blind, to the destruction of themselves and their willing hearers—what an awakening, when they stand face to face with Him who sits upon "the great white throne," whose Word they have dared to impugn! They will behold in the glory the "mythical Abraham" who believed God; the "unknown" Isaiah, who testified to the coming of the Lord Jesus in terms so unmistakably clear; the very Jonah whose story they had laughed to scorn; and the Daniel whose experiences they had classed with fables: all these veritable, living men, in the abode of light and bliss; but themselves, who ridiculed their very existence, alas, cast into outer darkness forever, nevermore to doubt the Word of God!

Jehoiakim's effort to destroy the Scriptures, like all others since, could only be utterly futile. The Word of the Lord came again to Jeremiah to "take another roll, and write in it all the former words that were in the first roll, which Jehoiakim the king of Judah had burned" (vers. 27, 28). Not only would the prophecies which had been consigned to the flames be re-written and preserved forever, but much more was to be *added*.

As for the impious monarch, condign punishment must be meted out to him, that others might learn not to trifle with or reject the Word of God. "Then shalt thou say to Jehoiakim king of Judah, Thus saith the Lord: Thou hast burned this roll, saying, Why hast thou written therein, saying, The king of Babylon shall certainly come and destroy this land, and shall cause to cease from thence man and beast? Therefore thus saith the Lord of Jehoiakim king of Judah: He shall have none to sit upon the throne of David: and his dead body shall be cast out in the day to the heat, and in the night to the frost" (vers. 30, 31). It may have seemed to some that this declaration, so far as his having none to sit upon David's throne was concerned, had signally failed, when upon his captivity his son Jehoiakim, or Jeconiah, ascended that throne. But after an inglorious reign of but three months and ten days he was carried away to Babylon with a great number of the people, in accordance with the doom pronounced upon him by this same prophet, in chapter 22: 30.

Not one thing should fail of all that Jehovah had pronounced against Judah and Jerusalem. To refuse to read the roll and to destroy it in the fire did not in any sense annul it (ver. 31).

In accordance with this word, "Jeremiah took another roll, and gave it to Baruch the scribe, the son of Neriah, who wrote therein from the mouth of Jeremiah all the words of the book which Jehoiakim king of Judah had burned in the fire: and there were added besides unto them many like words" (ver. 32).

CHAPTER XXI

THE FALL OF JERUSALEM.

(Chaps. 37-39.)

We now enter upon what is more especially the historical part of the book. Jeremiah's admonitory ministry was drawing to a close. Faithfully and fervently he had, ever since Josiah's day (that is, for a period of some thirty years or more), warned and pleaded and entreated his backsliding and treacherous people; but there had been no true response. They had put Jehovah's word behind their backs and drifted further and further from His counsels. Now the judgment so long announced, while the Lord waited in long-suffering patience, can be no more delayed, but must fall with awful fury upon the devoted nation. The words spoken through Hosea two centuries earlier must at last be fulfilled. "I will go and return to My place till they acknowledge their offence" (or, till they be guilty; that is, confessedly so), "and seek My face: in their affliction they will seek Me early" (Hosea 5: 15).

In wondrous grace and mercy they had been spared the final blow thus far; but there is now no remedy. Nothing can turn aside Jehovah's indignation. They must learn in captivity what they would not be taught in their own land.

In the 37th and 38th chapters we have a detailed account of the temporary withdrawal of the Babylonian troops upon the occasion of the

Egyptian invasion. This for the moment raises the hopes of the people, as already noted in chap. 34. Jeremiah, having the secret of the Lord, assures them that the respite is but temporary, and that the Chaldeans will return shortly and utterly destroy Jerusalem.

Then we find this honored servant of God seeking to escape from the doomed city. It is apparently a mistake on his part: though we would not criticize. He was worn in body and mind. His testimony was rejected. He himself was hated and persecuted. What more natural than that, feeling his work is completed, he should seek quiet and respite in his old home in the land of Benjamin? It was indeed a *natural* thing, but not a *spiritual* one; hence we find the Lord does not permit him to carry out his purpose. His apprehension results in a false charge and imprisonment. From death he is marvelously delivered. Chap. 39 gives the fall of the city. The prophet is, however, favored by the conqueror. There was no need to flee to Benjamin. The hand of God is stretched forth to protect His servant in the woeful day. But we must look at all this more in detail, for it is of intense interest, and pregnant with instruction.

"And king Zedekiah the son of Josiah reigned instead of Coniah the son of Jehoiakim, whom Nebuchadrezzar king of Babylon made king in the land of Judah. But neither he, nor his servants, nor the people of the land, did hearken unto the words of the Lord which He spake by the prophet Jeremiah" (chap. 37: 1, 2). We have already noticed that no chronological order is followed in the arrangement of this book. Rather, we have prophecies and incidents grouped together, and narrated in such moral order as to give us an ever-increasing sense of the departure from God, which culminated at last in His rejection of His once-favored heritage, and the pouring out of condign judgment. In these two verses we have a succinct account of Zedekiah's whole reign. It was eleven years of indifference to the Word of the Lord. This king personally was not so daringly impious as some of his predecessors. He realized in some measure the claims of God upon him and his people, but he never earnestly set himself, like Hezekiah or his father Josiah, to seek His face and to do those things that were pleasing in His sight. He was supine and frivolous—almost incredibly so, at so serious a time.

In the next verse we read of his sending Jehucal and Zephaniah the priest (whose acquaintance we made in chaps. 21, 29) to Jeremiah with the request, "Pray now unto the Lord our God for us." It was a similar errand upon which Zephaniah had gone shortly before (chap. 21: 1, 2). There is no word of repentance; no confession, or grief for Judah's awful sin. Jehovah is owned in a certain sense, and His aid is sought, but all is selfish; there is no prostration of soul in His presence.

Pharaoh's army had essayed to come out of Egypt to the relief of the Hebrew king, who had sent ambassadors beseeching him to "give him horses and much people" (Ezek. 17: 15). Hearing of this move, the Chaldeans immediately

raised the siege of Jerusalem and departed to
give battle to this new enemy ere he could secure
any real advantage (ver. 5). This to the Jews
seemed a good omen and greatly revived their
hopes. Now, if their long-neglected God would
help them, they might achieve a decided victory,
and by union with Egypt throw off the hated
Babylonian yoke. This was not to be, however.

In answer to Zedekiah's request, the prophet
replies: "Thus shall ye say to the king of Judah,
that sent you unto me to inquire of me: Behold,
Pharaoh's army, which is come forth to help you,
shall return to Egypt, into their own land. And
the Chaldeans shall come again, and fight against
this city, and take it, and burn it with fire. Thus
saith the Lord: Deceive not yourselves, saying,
The Chaldeans shall surely depart from us: for
they shall not depart. For though ye had smitten the whole army of the Chaldeans that fight
against you, and there remained but wounded
men among them, yet should they rise up every
man in his tent, and burn this city with fire"
(vers. 6-10). Both in grace and in judgment
God will fulfil all His word. For stubborn, wilful Judah there can be no deliverance, because
there is no self-judgment nor humbling on their
part. It seemed as though some mad infatuation
possessed the people. They "knew not the time
of their visitation," as was the case with their
children in a later period.

How strikingly analogous was their condition
to that of Christendom, "whose judgment now
for a long time slumbereth not." Men still love
to deceive themselves with a vain optimism

founded on the desires of their own deceitful
hearts, ignoring the sure testimonies of Him who
hath said,"Vengeance is Mine; I will recompense."
Teachers and people, or clergy and laity, as
they are unscripturally designated, congratulate
themselves on the great strides being made, as
they affirm, by Christianity and civilization; but,
alas, in how large a measure is it a mere Christless religiousness and a culture that in no sense
affects the heart! The departure from God and
His Word plainly evidenced on every hand calls
forth no confession of sin, no repentance; but,
instead, men congratulate each other and boast
of large-mindedness and liberality, while despising the ways that be in Christ, and the paths of
scriptural simplicity. Church and world are
linked up in an unholy concubinage, and thus
God is dishonored and His claims ignored. Surely the prophetic Word points to dire judgment to
come upon the professing body, composed largely,
as it is, of mere earth-dwellers who are strangers
to the heavenly calling. It is a time when every
faithful minister of Christ needs both grace and
wisdom to "cry aloud and spare not," but to show
the people their sins. We know the end of
this empty profession, persistently dishonoring
Christ's holy name and Word, must be the subjection to spiritual Babylon, whose power is yet
to be supreme on earth in matters religious,
though but for a brief space, God having likewise
already pronounced her judgment (Rev. 17, 18).
What God had decreed concerning Israel and
Judah for their apostasy and forgetfulness of
His Word was fulfilled to the letter. His declara-

tions concerning a far guiltier Christendom shall likewise be carried out.

It was when Jeremiah saw that all hope of the people's repentance was past, and that sure and certain wrath awaited them, that he essayed to leave the city, where he had ministered so long, to go to the land of Benjamin: probably to his own home, for it is to be remembered he was a priest of Anathoth, a city belonging to that tribe. He was now considerably past middle life, possibly prematurely aged because of all that he had gone through, and his usefulness appeared to be over. It does not seem to be fear that actuates him. Through grace he is above that. It would rather seem to be a longing for rest after so arduous a life, with its sorrows and its disappointments. Accordingly, taking advantage of the withdrawal of the Chaldean army, he endeavors to make good his purpose (vers. 11, 12). However good and right that purpose might appear, it is a step in advance of the Lord. It is never safe to plan one's own way, or to seek an easier path for one's self. In this instance the prophet clearly is acting in the energy of nature. God has a service for him still, as will be manifested in due time, even after the rebellious city has been overthrown. Jeremiah, devoted servant as he was, erred in choosing for himself. Even a Paul went to Jerusalem against the plain testimony of the Holy Ghost, drawn by natural affection for his kinsmen after the flesh. So our prophet is for the moment turned aside from the path of implicit dependence upon God, led apparently by a desire for rest and quiet after his stormy life. He must learn, as every other, that it is not in man to direct his way. The Lord is not yet through with him. He has a ministry for the poor who are to be spared from the sword, and for all who are left in the land.

As a result of his effort to better his condition, he is misunderstood and brought into deeper distress. He was in the gate of Benjamin when a captain of the ward, Irijah, apprehended him, saying, "Thou fallest away to the Chaldeans" (ver. 13). In vain Jeremiah protested his innocence and the utter falsity of the charge. Irijah refused to credit his explanation, and carried him before the princes. It is hardly to be supposed that these men really believed him to be guilty, but it gave them an opportunity to vent their hatred upon the man who had so often reproved them. He was ignominiously smitten, and, apparently without a hearing, was cast into prison, in the house of Jonathan the scribe (ver. 15). From what befell Jeremiah we may learn it is always best to sit still when there is no command from God to move. The best of servants and the most faithful men blunder when they take things into their own hands. Little as one may realize it, or mean it to be so at the time, this acting for one's self really implies lack of confidence in God's love and care. Faith can wait upon Him, assured that He is far too much concerned about His children to overlook anything that is for their good; hence it is quiet and restful amid all changing circumstances. Unbelief forgets God and suggests that *we* must act; opportunities are slipping away—something

must be done, and at once. This looks, to the
natural mind, like sound judgment and common
sense; but, alas, how often, when acted upon, are
things made not better, but worse! It is far
preferable to wait quietly upon Him whose wisdom never fails, and who sees the end from the
beginning, than to rashly venture forth in the
energy of nature, only to be defeated in the very
purpose one seeks to achieve.

That the king knew the prophet was innocent
of the charge upon which Irijah had arrested him
is evident from the remaining verses of the chapter (16-21). Jeremiah was cast into the dungeon
and into the cells—probably underground apart-
ments, gloomy and damp. There he was allowed
to remain for many days, neglected, and with no
opportunity given to clear himself of the imputa-
tion of treachery. Eventually Zedekiah sent and
took him out for a secret conference in the palace, and asked him, "Is there any word from the
Lord?" What a picture is here presented for us:
the man on the throne and the man from the
dungeon confronting each other, and the former
is forced to own the superiority of the latter.
The falsely accused prisoner has the secret of the
Lord, and the haughty monarch is dependent on
the prisoner to learn of Jehovah's purpose.

In reply to the anxious question Jeremiah
gives the old answer. There is indeed a message
from the Lord: it is the same so often given before, and unheeded. "For," said he, "thou shalt
be delivered into the hand of the king of Babylon." There is no effort to palliate the terrible
truth; no endeavor to win the king's favor by

good words and fair speeches. The plain, unwelcome truth is declared; and then, with neither
apology nor flattery, he pleads his cause before
the king: "What have I offended against thee,
or against thy servants, or against this people,
that ye have put me in prison? Where are now
your prophets which prophesied unto you, saying, The king of Babylon shall not come against
you, nor against this land? Therefore hear now,
I pray thee, O my lord the king: let my supplication, I pray thee, be accepted before thee, that
thou cause me not to return to the house of
Jonathan the scribe, lest I die there."

Manifestly the army of the king of Babylon
had again invested the city; the word of Jeremiah had proved true, and the false prophets had
been put to shame. Convinced that injustice and
wrong had been done the man of God, Zedekiah
gives order that his circumstances be made more
endurable, though he does not release him nor
declare abroad his innocence. With the shame of
supposed crime against his country hanging over
him still, Jeremiah is taken from the dungeon
and given a place in the court of the prison, with
the allowance of "a daily piece of bread out of
the baker's street," so long as any bread remains
in the city. Famine rations are being served out
by weight. The end cannot be far away.

Among the king's ministers of state there were
many, however, who entertained for the pessi-
mistic prophet feelings far different to those of
the monarch himself. It was reported to a few
of these that Jeremiah had said to the people,
"Thus saith the Lord: He that remaineth in this

city shall die by the sword, by the famine, and by the pestilence: but he that goeth forth to the Chaldeans shall live; for he shall have his life for a prey, and shall live." It was also told them that he had declared, "Thus saith the Lord: This city shall surely be given into the hand of the king of Babylon's army, which shall take it" (38: 1-3. As we know, these prophecies had indeed been uttered. Almost the identical words are recorded in chap. 21: 9, when Pashur, the son of Malchiah (or Melchiah, as he is there called), was one of the messengers sent to him by king Zedekiah. He is now one of Jeremiah's accusers, with three others, Shephatiah, Gedaliah (the son of another Pashur), and Jucal. Again and again, on divers occasions, the fall of Jerusalem had been clearly foretold. Like his Lord, Jeremiah could say, "In secret have I said nothing." Openly, in the presence of the populace, nobles, priests, and the king, had he faithfully declared the truth of God regarding the doomed city. For this he was hated. His words seemed to put a premium upon what to the nobles and captains looked like treachery.

Burning with indignation against the man who so solemnly declared the utter futility of all their schemes and devices, they accused Jeremiah before the king, and urged that he be executed as a traitor. "We beseech thee," they pleaded, "let this man be put to death, for thus he weakeneth the hands of the men of war that remain in this city, and the hands of all the people, in speaking such words unto them, for this man seeketh not the welfare of this people, but the hurt" (ver. 4).

How little can worldly men understand that true
love for the people leads one faithfully to show
them their sins and their danger! Little indeed
could these four accusers enter into the deep sorrows and anguish of heart that the "weeping
prophet" had experienced on their account. Like
Paul, the more abundantly he loved them, the less
he was loved in return. It is one of the hardest
trials a devoted servant has to bear when his
good is thus evil spoken of, and his very affection mistaken for malice, because it makes it impossible for him to hold his peace and to permit
the people to sleep on in their sins without lifting a warning voice. Yet, in some measure, such
has been the cup that every truly godly soul has
had to drink; and none ever tasted it so deeply
and frequently as our blessed Lord Himself. It
is of the false prophets that the world speaks well.
The true are accounted as the offscouring of the
earth.

In this case Zedekiah, ever a weakling, suc-
cumbs to the demands of his ministers. He con-
sents to the death of Jeremiah in words that well
betray his impotency, but which, like Pilate's, in
no sense lessen his guilt. "Behold, he is in your
hand: for the king is not he that can do anything against you" (ver. 5). Having obtained the
royal consent, the four conspirators took Jeremiah and cast him into the dungeon of Malchiah,
which was in the court of the prison, letting him
down with cords—a filthy pit, with no water, but
offensive mire, in which Jeremiah sank, and was
heartlessly left in this wretched plight. The object, doubtless, was to let him die, unknown to

the populace, who might have had superstitious or conscientious scruples about making away with the man who professed to speak in the name of Jehovah. Shephatiah and his associates would allow him to starve to death, alone and unsought, in this abominable, miry dungeon.

God had other thoughts, however, and would not thus permit His servant's martyrdom. The suffering and shame were all part of the discipline His love saw to be necessary, and He would not allow him to be spared the humiliation and anguish they entailed; but, like Job, his life was inviolable. In the prophet's hour of need a friend is raised up of whom otherwise we might never have heard. He is a colored servant in the king's household, an Ethiopian eunuch, Ebed-melech— perhaps nameless, so far as our narrative is concerned; for Ebed-melech, translated, is simply "servant of the king," and may not be a proper name at all. In this dark-skinned servant's heart glowed a pity and a sympathy, as well as a recognition of the divine office of Jeremiah, to which the four accusers were strangers. Like the young man in Acts 23:16 used for Paul's deliverance, here also God had prepared this His servant for Jeremiah's deliverance. Hearing that the prophet had been left to perish in the filthy pit of the prison court, this Ethiopian went boldly to entreat the king's favor, who was "then sitting in the gate of Benjamin"—the professed representative of the law, in the gate to dispense justice, when this inexcusable injustice had been perpetrated with his consent (vers. 7, 8). Earnestly and faithfully the eunuch presents the cause of the man of God: "My lord the king," he pleads, "these men have done evil in all that they have done to Jeremiah the prophet, whom they have cast into the dungeon; and he is like to die for hunger in the place where he is: for there is no more bread in the city" (ver. 9).

Again, Zedekiah, a typical changeling, whose mind is controlled by the last man who gains his ear, reverses his judgment. Ebed-melech is commanded, "Take from hence thirty men with thee, and take up Jeremiah the prophet out of the dungeon, before he die" (ver. 10). The king makes no confession of sin in thus having treated Jehovah's messenger; nor is there a word of apology to the prophet for the indignities so unrighteously heaped upon him after his pledged word as to provision for his comfort!

It is enough for the Ethiopian that he has permission to relieve the loved prisoner's sufferings, and he hastens to deliver him. Thoughtfully and tenderly he provides from the house of the king, under the treasury, old clouts and rags, which he let down by cords into the dungeon to Jeremiah, with directions to put them under his armholes under the ropes (vers. 11, 12). Apparently a trifling thing this, but a loving heart directed it, and God has been pleased to place it on record where it will stand forever. In that day when every cup of cold water given in the name of the Lord shall not fail of reward, Ebed-melech's "old cast clouts and rotten rags" used to lessen the pain of the man of God will be remembered and duly taken into account.

Thus protected, the weak and emaciated proph-

et is gently lifted out of the miry dungeon by
the eunuch and his thirty helpers. Only once
again is Ebed-melech mentioned, in the next chapter, for the Lord's commendation, ere he dis-
appears from the scene until he takes his place
with the host of the redeemed, when his good
deeds will have their due reward.

Jerusalem's **case had become desperate, and in**
his distress Zedekiah once more sent for Jeremiah for a secret interview. Knowing in the
depths of his heart that this man, whom he had
so shamefully treated, had the mind of the Lord,
he said to him, "I will ask thee a thing; hide
nothing from me" (ver. 14). Fear now makes
him desire to know what God had revealed; but,
as his previous career had manifested, there was
no true bowing of heart to that word when made
known. A double-minded man was he, therefore
unstable in all his ways. Self and selfish interests ruled in his heart, not the glory of the God
of Israel.

The well-merited and withering reply comes to
him, "If I declare it unto thee, wilt thou not
surely put me to death? And if I give thee counsel, wilt thou not hearken unto me?" (ver. 15).
Thus boldly does the prophet answer him. Cruel
treatment had in no sense filled his soul with
slavish fear. As God's free man, he speaks to the
conscience of the king.

Secretly, the guilty monarch swore neither to
harm him himself, nor, as before, to give him
into the hand of the men who sought his life (ver.
16). Accepting the pledge, Jeremiah gives him
the word of the Lord, saying: "Thus saith the

Lord, the God of hosts, the God of Israel: If thou wilt assuredly go forth unto the king of Babylon's princes, then thy soul shall live, and this city shall not be burned with fire; and thou shalt live, and thy house; but if thou wilt not go forth to the king of Babylon's princes, then shall this city be given into the hand of the Chaldeans, and they shall burn it with fire, and thou shalt not escape out of their hand" (vers. 17, 18). For Zedekiah to accept the advice tendered so solemnly in the name of Jehovah would mean a complete and unconditional surrender. The victorious Chaldean army had once more spread its tents around Jerusalem, and was carrying on the siege with vigor; the Egyptian army having returned in discomfiture to their own land. This was in itself an evidence of the truth of Jeremiah's predictions. When the false prophets declared that Nebuchadrezzar's power was broken, he had insisted on the overthrow of Pharaoh's forces and the early return of the Babylonians to invest the capital once more. Zedekiah evidently feared him, and in a vague, uncertain kind of way realized that God was with him. But he was of the number of those who cannot stand the sneers or the anger of their fellows, though they can sin against their Creator unblushingly. It is natural to fallen man to be ashamed to do what is right, if contrary to public opinion, and to do evil with a certain kind of pride. Of this stamp was the unworthy son of Josiah. He "loved the praise of men more than the praise of God."

In his faltering reply to Jeremiah, he shows the smallness of his soul, as also the haughtiness of his heart. "I am afraid," he owned, "of the Jews that are fallen to the Chaldeans, lest they deliver me into their hand, and they mock me" (ver. 19). What gross unbelief, when the Lord had just given the word that he should be spared if he surrendered; and what wretched pride that made the thought of mockery so bitter to the already ruined man!

Faithfully, even tenderly, the prophet urged him to obedience, assuring him that they should not deliver him up as he feared. "Obey, I beseech thee," he entreated, "the voice of the Lord, which I speak unto thee: so it shall be well unto thee, and thy soul shall live" (ver. 20). On the other hand, he warned him solemnly that if he refused to go forth, he should be reduced to the degradation of seeing "all the women that are left in the king of Judah's house" brought forth in captivity to the princes of the king of Babylon, who should mock in their turn, and reproach him for his inglorious rebellion and its awful consequences. He, too, should be taken captive, and the city burned with fire; with himself alone to blame (vers. 22, 23).

The moody and well-nigh distraught king deigned no reply that would indicate whether he intended to bow to the authority of the Lord or not, but strictly commanded silence on the part of Jeremiah as to the purport of the conversation they had had together. If the princes importuned him as to what had taken place, he was to mention the matter of his request to be released from prison, but nothing more (vers. 24-26).

As anticipated, the princes did seek to know the drift of the conference, but he replied discreetly, as he had been bidden—the truth, though not all the truth—and they are satisfied to leave him in the court of the prison, where he remained until the fulfilment of his prophecies regarding the siege, for "he was there when Jerusalem was taken" (vers. 27, 28).

This terrible climax, to which all the previous portion of the book has been pointing, is reached in chap. 39. The long-suffering patience of God at last gives way to judgment; the glory departs, and Jerusalem, whose name means "the foundation of peace," or, "founded in peace," is delivered into the hands of the Gentiles. What other city on earth has had a history so full of pathos and tragedy, and which so dreadfully belies its name? Yet the prophetic Word assures us that it shall eventually be established in peace, no more to be overthrown.

Nebuchadrezzar's siege lasted eighteen months, save for the brief respite when he withdrew his troops to meet the king of Egypt. During this long period, how terrible the suffering of the inhabitants had been! Yet, in it all, there was callousness of conscience and hardness of heart, coupled with a complaisant self-righteousness most abhorrent in the eyes of the Lord. Trouble does not result in repentance, unless the soul sees in it the hand of God in government. Even in the awful days of the last great tribulation, when men shall be scorched with great heat, they will blaspheme the name of God and repent not to give Him glory; and when the kingdom of the beast (the Satan-inspired ruler of the ten kingdoms in that day) shall be full of darkness, they will gnaw their tongues for pain, and blaspheme the God of heaven, repenting not of their deeds (Rev. 16: 9, 11).

It is a fallacy, that has become very popular to-day, that punishment of necessity results in repentance. Upon this is based the "larger hope" of men who try to persuade themselves that, in the judgment to come after death, God will be better than His Word, and that it will not be eternal in its nature, because leading those who are the subjects of it to self-judgment. Scripture holds out no such hope. There is not a single ray of light to illumine the future of the Christ-rejecter throughout eternity's unending ages. "He that believeth not the Son *shall not see* life, but the wrath of God *abideth* on him" (John 3: 36). Even on earth, where the Holy Spirit pleads with men, suffering does not always result in men's turning to the Lord in confession and contrition of soul; neither will it when time has ceased to be, and the Spirit has ceased His striving.

In the case of the men of Judah and Jerusalem, the last act of the fearful tragedy found them as hard and unresponsive as ever. "In the eleventh year of Zedekiah, in the fourth month, the ninth day of the month, the city was broken up" (ver. 2). How definite the date, to be remembered by the Lord forever! His heritage turned over to strangers, the sheep of His pasture devoured by the wild beast of the nations! That ninth day of the fourth month of Zedekiah's eleventh year shall have its place in His heart evermore. Vainly had they sought to put far off the evil day. Long deferred in grace, while Jehovah waited for some sign of brokenness of spirit, it had to come at last. And how brief the account of the fall of the one-time metropolis of the world: "The city was broken up!" What a world of anguish and sorrow is wrapped up in these five words! The details are all omitted, save in regard to Zedekiah's vain effort to escape when redemption point* had been passed and it was too late.

The horrors of the sack of a great city by an Oriental army beggar all description. Neither age nor sex nor beauty avails to avert the cruel work of the blood-drunken conquerors. Death, shame and slavery tell the dreadful story.

Nebuchadrezzar was not present in person when Jerusalem fell, but his chief princes, "Nergal-sharezer, Samgar-nebo, Sarsechim (chief of the eunuchs), Nergal-sharezer (chief of the Mages), and all the rest of the heads of the king of Babylon," sat at the middle gate to direct the troops (ver. 3). We have used Dr. Young's translation of this verse. It will be noticed that Rab-saris and Rab-mag, left untranslated in the Authorized Version, are really not proper names,

---

* Many will remember that there is an insignificant headland in the Niagara river, just above the Falls, known as "Redemption Point," because no boat, once past, has ever been saved from destruction. In men's lives there is also a "Redemption Point."

but titles. This helps to distinguish the two princes who bear the name Nergal-sharezer. The second one was chief of the Magi, or the priests of the Babylonish mysteries. It is a similar title to the Roman Pontifex Maximus, and was sometimes borne by the kings of Babylon.

When Zedekiah and his men of war (their ranks sadly depleted by famine, pestilence, and battle) saw that all effort to save the city was vain, they fled, leaving Jerusalem under cover of darkness, "by the way of the king's garden, by the gate betwixt the two walls." It will be remembered that strong walls separated the royal city, or the city of David, from the lower portion of Jerusalem. The palace and its environs as yet remained intact, though it was clear that their overthrow was but a matter of a few days at most, with no hope of succor. Zedekiah defended the stronghold to the last, and fled only when to remain would have been madness and a needless act of bravado. Stealthily the little company took the way of the plain, hoping to avoid detection. But all their efforts were in vain, for the Chaldeans pursued them and brought them to bay in the plains of Jericho. Those who could, forsook the king and fled to the wilderness (2 Kings 25: 4-6). He himself was taken captive. The word of the Lord by Jeremiah had declared it; now it is fulfilled.

Nebuchadrezzar was at Riblah (where Pharaohnechoh had bound Jehoahaz thirty-four years earlier) when Jerusalem fell. Thither, Zedekiah was hurried, that the conqueror might wreak his vengeance upon the vassal who had rebelled against him, violated his oath, and occupied his army for a year and a half in accomplishing his overthrow. The wretched man who had lost his crown and sceptre by refusing to heed the words of Jeremiah had to endure the anguish of beholding his own sons slain before his eyes, and then, that no other scene might ever efface that one to the end of his life, his own eyes were put out. Then, ignominiously bound in chains, he is carried to Babylon. The word of the Lord through Ezekiel, concerning Zedekiah, though *he* may never have learned of it, had been, "My net also will I spread upon him, and he shall be taken in My snare: and I will bring him to Babylon, to the land of the Chaldeans; yet shall he not see it, though he shall die there" (Ezek. 12: 13). See, also, chap. 17: 12-21 of the same book, where what is related as history by Jeremiah is all foretold by the prophet of the dispersion. Thus minutely had the Holy Spirit made known, ere it came to pass, the evil that should befall Zedekiah, that when it had been literally fulfilled all might know that God had spoken.

The palatial residence of the kings of Judah was razed to the ground in the conflagration that followed the taking of the city: nor was the temple of Jehovah spared, as we learn from chap. 52: 13. The sack of the city was complete. The walls were broken down, and the gates consumed with fire. Well might the man who for so long had sought to turn his people's hearts back to the God of their fathers cry out in the bitter anguish of his soul, "How doth the city sit solitary that was full of people! How is she become as a

widow!" (Lam. 1: 1.) Her judgment had come,
because of her unfaithfulness to her Lord (ver.
8).

The remnant who were not put to death were
carried away captive into Babylon by Nebuzar-
adan, chief of the executioners. Those also who
had obeyed the voice of Jeremiah, and had gone
out to the Chaldean camp before the sack of the
city, were spared the pains of death, but sent
captive to the queen city on the Euphrates, as
the prophet had predicted. Step by step, down
to the smallest detail, the word through Jeremiah
was fulfilled (ver. 9).

Another prophet, Zephaniah the son of Cushi,
had declared that even at this time a few of the
lower class should be spared to dwell in the land.
This too must be carried out. He lived in the
days of Josiah, and may have known Jeremiah
personally. He had said, "I will also leave in the
midst of thee an afflicted and poor people, and
they shall trust in the name of the Lord" (Zeph.
3: 12). How brightly shines this instance of the
divine clemency in behalf of a few, and their true
piety, in a day so dark, when the mass of the nation was utterly apostate. In accordance with
this word, Nebuzar-adan, unconscious that he was
carrying out the declaration of the God of Israel,
left a few "of the poor of the people, *which had
nothing,* in the land of Judah, and gave them
vineyards and fields at the same time" (ver. 10).
Striking are the lessons here brought before us.
It is the poor in spirit who are blessed—those
who own their nothingness. These had nothing,
and did not seek to hide their poverty; and the

Lord gave them both vineyards and fields. The former tells of joy; the latter, of sustenance. Both were to be found in Himself, though all else had failed. He could still meet the need of any who would confide in Him. Such an one was the prophet Habakkuk, who, though at first greatly bewildered by God's governmental dealings with the people of His choice, learned the great lesson that the just shall live, not by sight, but faith, and could therefore sing, in view of the very destruction we have been considering, "Although the fig tree shall not blossom, neither shall fruit be in the vines; the labor of the olive shall fail, and the fields shall yield no meat; the flock shall be cut off from the fold, and there shall be no herd in the stalls: yet I will rejoice in the Lord, I will joy in the God of my salvation" (Hab. 3: 17, 18).

There is no day so dark but that the Lord will be the light of every soul that ceases from man and turns to Himself; no sorrow so great but that fellowship with Him will sweeten the bitter waters. In every trial He is near; in every hour of discouragement and gloom He abideth faithful still—"He cannot deny Himself." The little remnant left in the land might seem to be bereft of all that could make life worth living. But they had Himself, and they could call upon His name, knowing that if He had been faithful to His own holy character in chastening them for their sin, now bowels of mercy were moved for them when, in lowliness of mind and confession of their iniquities, they sought His face.

The Lord was looking out for the interests

likewise of the now aged man who had witnessed for Him so long in the midst of a gainsaying people. In so doing He made use of what men call natural causes, as He often does to carry out His purposes. It had evidently been reported to Nebuchadrezzar how Jeremiah had ever counseled submission to the Babylonian yoke, and reproved the kings of Judah for breaking their oaths of allegiance. He therefore sent a special message to Nebuzar-adan regarding the prophet, bidding him: "Take him, and look well to him, and do him no harm, but do unto him even as he shall say unto thee" (vers. 11, 12).

It was a pompous company who went down to seek out the man who was the subject of this communication from the king: composed of the chief captain himself, together with Nebushasban, another chief of the eunuchs, the pontifex Nergalsharezer, and all the princes of Babylon. They found Jeremiah in the court of the prison, where he still abode in confinement; none having, apparently, given him a thought when the city fell. Releasing him, they gave him to the care of a man whose father, on several occasions, had befriended him—Gedaliah the son of Ahikam—with instructions to carry him home and see to his welfare. Gedaliah had already been selected to fill the position of governor in the land. He gave Jeremiah liberty to go wherever he desired; "so he dwelt among the people"—evidently the poor who were left, as we have seen (vers. 13, 14).

He had already received a message for another man whom God had not forgotten. While still in the prison-court, the word of the Lord had come to him bidding him: "Go and speak to Ebed-melech the Ethiopian, saying, Thus saith the Lord of Hosts, the God of Israel: Behold, I will bring My words upon this city for evil, and not for good; and they shall be accomplished in that day before thee. But I will deliver thee in that day, saith the Lord . . . and thou shalt not fall by the sword, but thy life shall be for a prey unto thee; because thou hast put thy trust in Me, saith the Lord" (vers. 15-18). Thus was the service of the faithful Ethiopian rewarded. God will be no man's debtor. The last clause gives us the secret of Ebed-melech's devotion: he had put his trust in the Lord. Though a stranger to the commonwealth of Israel, he was a child of God through faith; and faith in his case worked by love.

Various have been the shifting scenes brought to our notice in this section. May grace be given to lay all to heart and find eternal profit from our meditations upon it.

CHAPTER XXII

ISHMAEL'S TREACHERY AND THE FLIGHT TO EGYPT

(Chaps. 40-44.)

Kaleidoscopic were the changes through which the remnant passed, while left in the land by the clemency of Nebuchadrezzar, in the year following the destruction of Jerusalem.

Gedaliah, the governor, was a truly pious man, of upright principles, but not at all the kind of a person to take the lead in the troublous times that had fallen upon his native land. Brave, honorable and unsuspicious, he yet lacked that genius for true leadership, and that necessary sternness in dealing with evil, which the times demanded. It was not long, therefore, ere he became the victim of a diabolical conspiracy which resulted in his assassination by one whom his too generous heart had implicitly trusted, and who owed his own preservation from death to the man he so basely murdered.

Nebuzar-adan having given him his liberty Jeremiah, as we have seen, attached himself to the governor. The Chaldean captain had given him free choice as to his abode; even offering him a safe and comfortable asylum in Babylon, had he desired it. How much this man really understood the ways of Jehovah in the chastening of His people, we know not; but he shows himself to be at least familiar with the words spoken by both Ezekiel and Jeremiah, alleging this in his interview with the latter : "The Lord thy God

hath pronounced this evil upon this place" (vers.
1. 2). He gives, too, the correct reason for this
strange dealing. Because Judah had sinned, and
not obeyed His voice, their God had brought these
afflictions upon them. Sad it is to note that this
heathen conqueror had a clearer sense of the
truth than the majority of the leaders among the
Jews.

Loosing Jeremiah from his chains, he gave him
the king's message: "If it seem good unto thee
to come with me into Babylon, come; and I will
look well unto thee: but if it seem ill unto thee
to come with me into Babylon, forbear: behold,
all the land is before thee: whither it seemeth
good and convenient for thee to go, thither go"
(ver. 4). Then, apparently divining the prophet's mind, and courteously seeking to relieve him
of the embarrassment of refusing his well-meant
offer to go to the imperial city, which, after all,
represented the power of the oppressor of his people, Nebuzar-adan added, "Go back also to Gedaliah the son of Ahikam the son of Shaphan, whom
the king of Babylon hath made governor over the
cities of Judah, and dwell with him among the
people: or go wheresoever it seemeth convenient
unto thee to go." This offer Jeremiah accepted,
and departed to seek the governor, receiving both
victuals and a reward from the captain of the
guard. He found Gedaliah at Mizpah, a historic
trysting-place never to be forgotten by lovers of
Israel. Many and varied had been the scenes
enacted there, both in the unsettled days of the
judges and the early days of the kings. Here
Gedaliah kept his simple and unostentatious

court, and here Jeremiah dwelt with him, "among
the people left in the land" (vers. 5, 6).

It was the choice of a man who walked with
God, and could view things in the light of His
presence. To many it might have been considered a fine thing to be invited to the conqueror's
capital, there to be honored as a sage and a seer,
and to receive various tokens of the king's appre-
ciation because of his steady opposition to the
policy of resistance to Babylon and dependence
upon Egypt. But in all this, Jeremiah had been
in no sense the servant or tool of the Chaldean
emperor. He had remained to the last the simple
prophet of Jehovah. If he counseled submission
to Babylon, it was because the Word of the Lord
so directed. If he warned the princes and the
people of the folly of counting upon the Egyptian alliance, he did so because he had the mind
of the Lord regarding it. This did not alter his
personal abhorrence of all that Babylon stood for.
None knew better than he its abominable pag-
anism and its cruel tyranny. None knew more
clearly, too, the doom soon to fall upon it. In
God's government He had used it to chastise His
erring people. Soon *it* also must pass under the
rod of His vengeance. Consequently the city by
the Euphrates had no charms for the man of
God. Far better a small place among "the poor
of the flock" in Immanuel's land, than a large
place in the Gentile oppressor's palace. He desired not the world's patronage, as he feared not
its wrath. In this he is the consistent type of
the man of God still—"*in* the world, but not
of the world"—perchance even serving the world;

as Abraham long before had, in delivering Lot,
really served Sodom; but looking for no recognition from the world: leaving all that to the judgment-seat of Christ.

Self-interest would surely have taken Jeremiah
to Babylon. Providence, too, might have seemed
to favor such a move; for, how useful to his people might he not have been in the councils of the
empire—as in the cases of Mordecai and Nehemiah at the court of Medo-Persia some years
later. Faith, however, kept him in the desolated
land of Canaan, among the poor and distressed
remnant who called upon the name of the Lord.
Like Moses, he chose rather to suffer affliction
with the people of God than to enjoy the temporary prosperity that an abode in the royal city
might have brought him. Faith ever runs counter
to the mere pleadings of nature.

We shall see something very different to this
disinterested and unselfish devotion to the Lord
and His people as we now turn to consider the
captains of the roving bands of the Jews, concerning which the next part of the chapter treats.

Jerusalem being destroyed, several companies
of unsubdued warriors remained, or fled to mountain fastnesses and wilderness hiding-places, thus
safely eluding the Chaldean armies. These bands,
formed in what we call "guerrilla corps," officered
by daring, impetuous leaders, were determined
not to own the sway of the king of Babylon.
Hearing that Gedaliah, one of their number, had
been appointed governor, and that he had established himself at Mizpah, these outlawed bands
now gathered about him, hoping doubtless to find

independence and rebellion. Ishmael, two sons of Koreah (Johanan and Jonathan by name), Seraiah, Jezaniah, together with the sons of Ephai, with their companies, were the ones who repaired thither (vers. 7, 8). If they expected Gedaliah to break his plighted word, and assist in him one who would further their schemes of them in throwing off the yoke of Chaldea, they soon learned their mistake. He faithfully counseled submission, bidding them: "Fear not to serve the Chaldeans: dwell in the land, and serve the king of Babylon, and it shall be well with you" (ver. 9). As for himself, he declared his full determination to dwell at Mizpah, and to render service to the nation into whose power God had given them. He also counseled them to cease from warfare, and to seek to reap the fruits of peace and quietness, bidding them gather wine, and summer fruits and oil, and dwell in the cities they had taken (ver. 10). We read of no dissenting voice on the part of the guerrilla captains or their men; but it is plain from what follows that they were thoroughly opposed to what must have seemed to them a peace-at-any-price policy. Resentment burned fiercely in the heart of one at least, Ishmael, though he was politic enough to hide his feelings for the time.

Hearing the cruel war was over—even if disastrously ended—numbers of Jews who had fled to Moab, Ammon, and Edom, also returned to their land and gathered to Mizpah, owning the gentle sway of the pious Gedaliah. These quietly followed the advice given, and proceeded to harvest the summer fruits and wines, thus making provision for the approaching winter (vers. 11, 12). A people not strong were they, but they prepared their meat in the summer (Prov. 30: 25).

Meantime Ishmael, returning from the country of the Ammonites, was secretly plotting the assassination of Gedaliah. We gather from the context he had pledged himself to Baalis, the king of Ammon, before he left, to do this, if Gedaliah was not prepared to be a tool in his hands. The too confiding governor was warned of the foul errand upon which the captain of the sinister name had come, for there was jealousy and treachery among the various outlawed chiefs, leading Johanan and the rest of the captains at last to inform upon the traitor. They told Gedaliah the errand upon which he had come, sent by Baalis the Ammonite. Simple and honest himself, the governor discredits the tale of Ishmael's depravity, and takes no measures to protect his life, so valuable to his compatriots at this dark period. Johanan accordingly sought another, and this time a private, interview with him, assuring him of the truth of the former report, and pleaded for commission to forestall the murder, by himself taking the life of Ishmael in secret, so that no man should know it, pleading that in no other way could the death of, not only the governor, but all the Jews that were gathered with him, be averted. The noble-hearted Gedaliah replied, "Thou shalt not do this thing: for thou speakest falsely of Ishmael" (vers. 13-16). The sequel shows how ill-placed his confidence was.

Very shortly after this, and only three months after the sack of Jerusalem, Ishmael (who we now learn was of the seed royal, which accounts in large measure for his hatred of Gedaliah), and ten princes came again to the house of the governor at Mizpah, and all ate bread together—a complete expression of fellowship according to Eastern custom. But, alas, it was like the feasting of Judas at the last passover. Those who ate bread with Gedaliah lifted up the heel against him. At Ishmael's signal, he and the ten princes rose up against their gracious host, slew him in cold blood, and then massacred the Jews and the Chaldeans that were in Mizpah (41:2).

None of those connected with Gedaliah had escaped to carry to other parts the awful tale of carnage and bloodshed. On the morrow, four-score men from Shechem, from Shiloh, and from Samaria, came to bring an offering to the house of the Lord. How they had corrupted the way of approach to God, and taken up with heathen manners, is evident by their shaven beards, and rent clothes, and gashes upon their flesh, as were commonly made by the worshipers of Baal. Yet offerings and incense were in their hand, and however ignorant, they felt the need of seeking the face of the Lord.

Ishmael's abominable hypocrisy and horrid treachery stalk out again. Assuming the air of one sorely grieved over the desolations of the land, he goes out weeping and lamenting, and offers to be their guide to Gedaliah the governor. Having led the doomed men into the midst of the city, he suddenly threw off the mask, and, with his associates, slew these unsuspecting men, as he had the others before, and cast their bodies into a pit—sparing ten of them for the hidden stores of wheat, barley, oil and honey which they were to reveal (vers. 5-8).

The pit into which the slain had been cast was a subterranean chamber, built by order of Asa, king of Judah, as a hiding-place in case Baasha king of Israel should besiege him during the re-building of Mizpah, nearly four centuries earlier (1 Kings 15: 22). It now became the tomb for the guileless Gedaliah and his attached followers, as also for the seventy visitors (ver. 9). Having thus disposed of the dead, Ishmael beat a hasty retreat to the land of the Ammonites, carrying with him the king's daughters and all the people (probably the poor) who dwelt in Mizpah that had not been included in the massacre.

As was to be expected, the awful news of his bloody acts soon got abroad. Johanan and the other captains being apprised thereof, at once pursue the fleeing traitor, and overtake him by "the great waters that are in Gibeon"—the old battlefield where Joab and Abner contended—pitching on either side of the pool (2 Sam. 2: 12-17), and near the historic spot where Joshua achieved his great victory over the allied armies of the Canaanites, when he went to the defence of the men of Gibeon.

The freebooters who followed Ishmael made no attempt to stand against the men of Johanan, but fled with their leader, while all the people they were carrying away "cast about and returned" (vers. 13-15).

Johanan was unquestionably a brave and a pa-triotic man, but lacked the piety of Gedaliah; a

man of action, but not one who waited upon God
for his path. Without hesitation, or inquiring of
the Lord, he leads his confederates and the delivered company to Chimham, near Bethlehem, the
route to Egypt, determined to leave the land of
Palestine, fearing the wrath of the Chaldeans because of Ishmael's assassination of the governor
deputed by Nebuzar-adan, and the Babylonian
guard (vers. 16-18).

Having thus determined upon their path, like
multitudes before and since, they make a pretence of seeking the mind of the Lord. Jeremiah
being among the number carried away from
Mizpah, the representatives of the people now
turned to him. Their words were very fair and
well-spoken: "Let, we beseech thee, our supplication be accepted before thee," they said, "and
pray for us unto the Lord thy God, even for all
this remnant (for we are left but a few of many,
as thine eyes do behold us); that the Lord thy
God may show us the way wherein we may walk,
and the thing that we may do" (chap. 42: 1-3).
One is reminded of Jehoshaphat professedly seeking the mind of God after the alliance with the
king of Israel had already been made and his
word pledged. Alas, this is but trifling with God;
yet, dear reader, are *we* altogether clear of this?
How many a saint has set his heart upon a certain course without asking counsel of the Lord;
and then, actuated by a feeling of unrest and anxiety, has sought to get the divine approbation for
his self-concocted plans! Notice here that the
people do not say, "The Lord our God," but "The
Lord thy God." There is a sense of distance.

They do not feel they can approach Him with confidence, hence they turn to Jeremiah, and would fain have him act the part of a go-between, or a mediator. It is always a bad sign when there is diffidence in approaching God; when the petitioner has more confidence in the prayers of a ministering servant than in his own. Unmistakably, it reveals the lack of communion with God which inspires confidence in the hour of need. If the eye is single, the whole body is full of light, having no part dark. If the desire to glorify God be supreme in the soul, one can turn to Him for guidance without fear. But when some cherished aim or selfish object is controlling the heart, there is and must be a lack of confidence towards Him.

Such was the present state of the spared remnant. Jeremiah makes no comment upon it, but quietly replies, "I have heard you; behold, I will pray unto the Lord your God according to your words; and it shall come to pass, that whatsoever thing the Lord shall answer you, I will declare it unto you; I will keep nothing back from you" (ver. 4). Note how he throws them back on their own responsibility. He says, "The Lord *your* God," and speaks of what "the Lord shall answer *you*." He will be the spokesman for them, but not the go-between.

In the most solemn way they declare that they will abide by the Word of the Lord, whatever it may be; and no doubt, like many another in a similar place, they really thought they would. But they had settled it in their hearts to go into Egypt, and they counted upon the Lord's endorsement of their fleshly determination. They replied,

"The Lord be a true and faithful witness between us, if we do not even according to all things for the which the Lord thy God shall send thee to us" (ver. 5). Then growing bolder, they use the term, "The Lord our God," declaring, "Whether it be good, or whether it be evil, we will obey the voice of the Lord our God, to whom we send thee; that it may be well with us, when we obey the voice of the Lord our God" (ver. 6). This certainly sounded well. Alas, that "good words and fair speeches" can be so cheap and so meaningless!

A significant ten days was allowed to elapse ere the Lord communicated His mind to His servant—a number suggesting man's responsibility Godward and manward, as set forth in the Ten Commandments given at Sinai. On that ground the remnant could claim nothing. The delay in answering indicates the distance at which they were from God. They had failed grievously, and yet there was no repentance (ver. 7).

Before all the people, Jeremiah declared the word of Jehovah: "Thus saith the Lord, the God of Israel, unto whom ye sent me to present your supplication before Him: If ye will still abide in this land, then will I build you, and not pull you down; and I will plant you, and not pluck you up: for I repent Me of the evil that I have done unto you" (vers. 8-10). What riches of grace are here unfolded! On their part, no adequate sense of guilt; yet on His, such amazing compassion and loving-kindness. If they will but trust Him now in their weak, broken state—if they will rely upon His mighty arm and thus dwell in the land

He had given them—if they will accept the chastisement, and bow to His Word, then He will build them up and care for them as a husband-man cares for his vintage.

Obeying His voice, they need have no fear of the wrath of Babylon's king. "For I," says God, "am with you to save you and to deliver you from his hand. And I will show mercies unto you, that he may have mercy upon you, and cause you to return to your own land" (vers. 11, 12). Restoration and blessing, under the divine protection, would be the happy result of subjection to Himself. On the other hand, it were worse than folly for them to seek relief in Egypt. Nought but dire distress and judgment could result. To go back to Egypt was like a Christian going back to the world for help. The Lord Jesus "gave Himself for our sins, that He might deliver us from this present evil world, according to the will of God and our Father" (Gal. 1:4). This is the antitype of the deliverance from Egypt of old.

Pharaoh's land, for the redeemed of the Lord, was a land of bondage—it could never be their home. To settle there in peace and happiness was absolutely impossible. To attempt to do so was to ignore the blood of the passover and the parting of the Red Sea. For the Christian this would be to forget that he is purged from his old sins through the shedding of the precious blood of Christ, and separated from this world by the death of that blessed One. The Cross of Christ has come in between the believer and the world, enabling him to say, "God forbid that I should glory, save in the Cross of our Lord Jesus Christ, by whom the world is crucified unto me, and I unto the world" (Gal. 6:14). As the Red Sea rolled between Egypt and the place of Israel's blessing, so the death of Christ has cut me off from this world if I am a child of God. I cannot get back to it now, save by, for the time being, ignoring that solemn fact and acting as though the Cross to me were nothing! Alas, alas, how often, dear fellow-believer, have we so acted! Oh, the shame that it ever should be so! Yet what need there is that we own before God with confusion of face our wretched failures in this connection! But of one thing there can be no question: no truly converted soul was ever able to find rest in this world after being delivered from it once.

The history of the remnant here is, like all Scripture, "written for our admonition," and should speak loudly to our consciences. To go back to Egypt, for them, must mean increased sorrow and disaster. They might try to persuade themselves that they would there find a land of plenty and quietness, where, undistracted by war and the sound of the trumpet, they could eat bread to the full and dwell in peace; but this was a delusion (vers. 13, 14). The sword from which they sought to flee should pursue them there, and the famine of which they were afraid should follow close after them, and Egypt should be to them but a graveyard, because of the anger of the Lord which should be poured out upon them (vers. 15-18).

The Egyptians might indeed dwell securely in their own land, but not so with the remnant of

Israel. The worldling may occupy himself in this scene in comparative quietness and peace, but the child of God is spoiled for the world and can never be happy in it.

That the captains and the people had in no sense deceived the Lord with their fair words is evident in what follows. He admonished them faithfully not to go into Egypt, and then makes bare their hearts: "For ye have used deceit against your souls," the prophet declares, "when ye sent me unto the Lord your God, saying, Pray for us unto the Lord our God; and according unto all that the Lord our God shall say, so declare unto us, and we will do it" (vers. 19, 20— *margin*). It was in vain to seek to deceive Him whose eyes as a flame of fire penetrate the inmost secrets of the being. They were not upright before Him. He knew it well, and yet condescended in grace to point out the path of blessing, and warn of the road to ruin. The word had been set before them. Already their downcast faces gave the answer. Jeremiah waits for no reply, but announces: "Now I have this day declared it to you; but ye have not obeyed the voice of the Lord your God, nor anything for the which He hath sent me unto you. Now therefore know certainly that ye shall die by the sword, by the famine, and the pestilence, in the place whither ye desire to go and to sojourn" (vers. 21, 22).

Indignation filled the hearts of "the proud men" of Judah at these words. Angrily, Azariah and the captain, Johanan, exclaimed, "Thou speakest falsely: the Lord our God hath not sent thee to say, Go not into Egypt to sojourn

there. But Baruch the son of Neriah setteth thee
on against us, for to deliver us into the hand of
the Chaldeans, that they might put us to death,
and carry us away captives to Babylon" (chap.
43: 1-3). It was a case of the wish being father
to the thought. They were determined to go
down to Egypt. They would not believe that God
had forbidden them to do so. Nor did they have
the effrontery, after all their humble speeches before, to charge *Jeremiah* with deliberately seeking to deceive them by palming off his own
thoughts as a divine revelation; but *Baruch* was
made the scapegoat, and upon him the blame was
laid. This man had faithfully stood in the breach
with his master, and on several occasions had put
his life in jeopardy by his boldness in carrying
out commissions entrusted to him. But it was
sheer folly to suppose the prophet to be a mere
puppet moved by his servant. Only gross unbelief and determinate self-will could so conclude.

Forthwith Johanan and the captains gathered
all the remnant together, forcing both Jeremiah
and Baruch to be of the number, and set out for
Egypt in direct opposition to the Word of the
Lord. We read of no further delay until they
arrived at Tahpanhes, where they concluded to
settle (vers. 4-7). This city was located in north-
eastern Egypt, some twenty miles from the historic treasure city of Pithon, the scene and reminder of Israel's former degradation, as built by
their fathers in the days of their slavery. It
was in the land of Goshen, and was dedicated to
a heathen goddess.

Here the emigrants sought a home, hoping that

they had left far behind them the awful trinity of destruction that had harassed them for so long—war, pestilence, and famine. This could not be, however, for they were bent on a course of rebellion against the Lord. They could never be at home in the land from which He had once delivered them, when He separated them to Himself.

Jeremiah is again commissioned to warn them of the impending storm of divine wrath. He may be in a sense a prisoner, but "the Word of the Lord is not bound," and he is bidden to instruct the people both by an object-lesson and by word of mouth. At Jehovah's bidding, he took great stones in his hand, which he hid in the brick-kiln at the entry of Pharaoh's house in the city, in the sight of the men of Judah. From this it would appear that the king of Egypt sometimes resided in Tahpanhes (vers. 8, 9), if at this time it was not, indeed, his capital.

Having thus attracted the attention of the people, he declared in the name of the Lord of hosts that He was about to send Nebuchadrezzar, who is again designated "My servant," and all the land of Egypt should be given into his hands. His throne was to be set upon the stones thus hidden, and his royal pavilion spread over them. Like a shepherd (as the shepherd kings had done before, in the days of the patriarchs), he should "array himself with the land of Egypt" as with a garment. Egypt's gods and their people would be destroyed in that day, and it would be vain for the men of Judah to seek relief from his vengeance (vers. 10-13).

With more fulness of detail the same theme is taken up in the next chapter. Again the Word of the Lord came to His servant "concerning all the Jews which dwelt in the land of Egypt, at Migdol, at Tahpanhes, and at Noph, and in the country of Pathros" (ver. 1). Migdol was a royal fortress, not far from the place where the Red Sea was parted for the deliverance of the redeemed host under Moses. Noph is supposed to be the same as Memphis, the ancient capital of Upper Egypt. The general term Pathros covered a considerable district in Upper Egypt, inhabited originally by the Pathrusim. It will be seen from the mention of these various localities that the Jews had in a very short time, a few months at most, spread themselves over a large part of the country; though there may have been several earlier colonies planted there prior to the movement we have been considering.

The Lord's expostulation is recorded in verses 2 to 14. He bids them consider the evil which He brought upon Jerusalem and all the cities of Judah because of the frightful wickedness there perpetrated. "Rising early," He had sought their good, sending prophets saying, "Oh, do not this abominable thing that I hate!" It was idolatry that provoked His special abhorrence. But they would neither give heed to the warnings and entreaties of the prophets nor turn from their iniquitous ways. Therefore His fury had been poured forth and the land now lay waste and desolate. Their present course was but an aggravation of the evil, and would, if persisted in, result in national suicide. In Egypt they were fast relapsing into idolatry. Unless they repented, He could but cut them off from the face of the earth. Yea, by their folly, they were cutting themselves off.

How short their memory! Had they already forgotten the wickedness of their fathers, and the wickedness of the kings of Judah, and their own wickedness, and the wickedness of their wives in the land of Judah, which had drawn down so awful a punishment? They were not humbled, even after all the past; nor was there any evidence of godly fear; neither had they walked in His law, nor in His statutes, which He had set before them and their fathers. Because of this persistency in wrongdoing, He would set His face against them for evil, to cut them all off. From the least to the greatest, all the men of Judah who dwelt in Egypt should be consumed—those, of course, who had gone there of their own volition. Jeremiah and Baruch, together with many of Gedaliah's former followers, were there by force, and hence could not be included with the self-willed captains and their retainers. Even should the latter desire to return, they would not be permitted so to do. "None shall return but such as shall escape" (vers. 11-14).

Open and unblushing defiance greeted this serious warning and earnest expostulation. The true state of the people was at once made manifest, and the hypocritical nature of their former protestations became clearly apparent. Idolatry of the most degrading character had already been secretly practised by them; the women leading, and the men abetting, as formerly in the land (ver. 15). The latter boldly declared, "As for the word that thou hast spoken to us in the name of the Lord, we will not hearken unto thee" (ver. 16). It was wilful, deliberate, high-handed opposition to the truth!

The reasons given illustrate the grave danger of trusting in experience rather than going to the Word of God, in spite of all outward appearances. Walking by sight, not faith, they reasoned that when, in the cities of Judah, they ignored Jehovah's word and burned incense unto the queen of heaven, and poured out drink offerings unto her, they had a measure of prosperity; at least they had "plenty of victuals, and were well, and saw no evil." On the other hand, since they had left off so to do, they "have wanted all things, and have been consumed by the sword and by the famine" (vers. 17-19). Therefore they argue, it is clear that the blessings of the gods of the heathen were theirs while they thus served the queen of heaven. This blessing had been withdrawn when they gave up the outward symbols of idolatry and professed to worship Jehovah. How plausible and specious was their sophistry! Yet are there not many who reason in similar ways now? It was the appeal to a momentary experience, instead of to the Word of God—the only safe guide.

Jeremiah's answer is ready and convincing, whether they will own it or not. It was their idolatrous practices which brought down the wrath of the Lord upon them. He stood it until He could no longer bear it; then His judgment fell. For this very cause all the evil they complained of had come upon them (vers. 20-23).

For the women He had a special word. Because they were the leaders in thus dishonoring His Name, that Holy Name should "no more be named in the mouth of any man of Judah in all the land of Egypt, saying, The Lord God liveth" (ver. 26). He would give them up to destruction, watching over them for evil, and not for good, until they should all be consumed, save a small number, who, escaping the sword, should return unto the land of Judah. Thus "all the remnant of Judah, that are gone into the land of Egypt to sojourn there, shall know whose words shall stand, Mine, or theirs" (vers. 27, 28).

A sign of the coming destruction was also given, that, when it came to pass, they might know the hour of their judgment was no more to be delayed. Pharaoh-hophra, the king of Egypt, was to be given into the hand of his enemies. Thus the bruised reed upon which they leaned should be broken (vers. 29, 30).

How vain the effort of man to withstand his Maker! What folly to strive with Him! Truly, "The fear of the Lord is the beginning of wisdom, and to depart from evil, that is understanding."

CHAPTER XXIII

A WORD FOR BARUCH AND FOR US ALL

(Chap. 45.)

This beautiful though brief chapter of just five verses is pregnant with instruction for the children of God in all ages, and particularly for any who essay to serve the Lord in any public or official capacity.

Chronologically, it follows chapter 36, as the first verse makes plain: "The word that Jeremiah the prophet spake unto Baruch the son of Neriah, when he had written these words in a book at the mouth of Jeremiah, in the fourth year of Jehoiakim the son of Josiah king of Judah." The expression "these words" refers to the words penned by Baruch, at the prophet's dictation, in the roll that was read before the king and his counselors, only to be contemptuously cast into the fire. Another copy, with added words, was then written by the same scribe.

Baruch had thus been an instrument, used of God to communicate His mind to others. His own soul must not be neglected, however; hence the message given him, as narrated in this portion of the Scriptures. It is of the greatest moment that those who minister to others be in a right state of soul themselves. Nothing is more dangerous than to go on giving out the truth of God, as suited to saint or sinner, while the heart is set upon self-seeking, or the private life of the servant is accompanied with unholiness and lack of humility before the Lord. It is this that leads to what another has most solemnly denounced as "trafficking in unfelt truth." Only as the truth has power over one's own heart and conscience can it be safely ministered to others.

In Baruch's case, it would seem that he felt the king's rejection of the Word of God as an insult aimed at himself and his master, rather than at the Lord who inspired the writing that was in the roll. The result was sore discouragement. Therefore the prophet's message: "Thus saith the Lord, the God of Israel, unto thee, O Baruch: Thou didst say, Woe is me now! for the Lord hath added grief to my sorrow; I fainted in my sighing, and I find no rest" (vers. 2, 3). It was quite right that the son of Neriah should feel, and feel keenly, the wretched state of his people, and their departure from holiness and truth. Every godly soul must of necessity have thus felt. Jeremiah did, as we know; and Ezekiel, in vision, saw a mark placed upon the foreheads of the men who sighed and cried because of Jerusalem's abominations (Ezek. 9). This was pleasing to God, and indicated a chastened spirit and divine sensibilities. But the grief of Baruch is more personal, like that which threatened to consume the prophet himself, in chapter 15. It was prompted in large measure by disappointment. He had not received the recognition as Jehovah's servant and the amanuensis of Jeremiah that he looked for. Hence he faints in the day of adversity, because his strength is small. He has not yet learned to deny himself, which is

quite another thing to merely being self-denying.
This latter thing he knew: the former he has not
yet reached. Perhaps almost unknown to himself,
and unseen heretofore even by Jeremiah, Baruch
was seeking a measure of recognition from man.

It is so easy to slip into this, especially if one
is serving the Lord in the gospel, or in teaching
the children of God. There is the secret desire,
often, to be accorded a place, with the corresponding grief when that place is refused and one's
ministry is unacknowledged. Frequently this may
be mistaken for sorrow because of the rejection
of the Word of God; but in that case the soul
finds refuge in the Author of that Word; and
though tried, is not cast down, knowing that when
the truth is proclaimed "we are unto God a sweet
savor of Christ, in them that are saved, and in
them that perish: to the one we are the savor of
death unto death; and to the other the savor of
life unto life" (2 Cor. 2: 15, 16).

It was not in this way that Baruch seemed
to be affected. He felt the personal slight, the
setting at nought, the despising of his ministry
—always so hard for a sensitive soul to bear, if
out of the presence of God. Therefore he fainted,
and could find no rest.

But the Lord has been graciously considering
his case, and has for him a needed word, both of
admonition and of comfort. His is no harsh, un-
kind rebuke; no hard and severe scourging.
Knowing full well that Baruch was, after all,
seeking to honor Him, however he might have,
well-nigh unconsciously, permitted self to have a
place, He ministers a needed word in tenderness

and love. "Thus shalt thou say unto him," He says to Jeremiah, "The Lord saith thus: Behold, that which I have built will I break down, and that which I have planted I will pluck up, even this whole land" (ver. 4). Surely, when all was so obnoxious to God, it was a specially improper scene for personal ambition. When the times were so evil, it was a specially improper season for self-seeking. One is reminded of Elisha's words to Gehazi after he had profited in a material way by his deception of Naaman: "Is it a time to receive money, and to receive garments, and oliveyards, and vineyards, and sheep, and oxen, and menservants, and maidservants?" (2 Kings 5:26). Poor, wretched Gehazi had been planning for his own comfort in a day when judgment, like a destroying angel, was stalking through the land. How awful to be so engaged at such a time! In a similar way the apostle Paul also speaks to the Corinthians when he writes: "But this I say, brethren, the time is short: it remaineth, that both they that have wives be as though they had none; and they that weep, as though they wept not; and they that rejoice as though they rejoiced not; and they that buy, as though they possessed not; and they that use this world, as not abusing it: for the fashion of this world passeth away" (1 Cor. 7:29-31).

This was what, in his measure, Baruch needed to learn. God was about to bring the then present order of things to an end in judgment, as He will soon bring the age in which we live to a close by the coming of our Lord Jesus Christ and our gathering together unto Him, to be followed by the opening of the seven-sealed book of His indignation, when wrath to the uttermost must fall on apostate Christendom. For Baruch it was no time to be occupied with self-seeking, or to be troubled because he failed to gain the respect of a people who had so grievously departed from their God. And what shall be thought of a professed servant of Christ, sent to testify against the unspeakable corruptions of this age, expecting to be honored by the unspiritual for so doing? Such an one has quite failed to appreciate the call of God, and the condition of the world fast ripening for the judgment about to fall upon it.

But the Lord goes on to give His servant a watchword that may well be kept in mind by all who endeavor in any way to contend for the faith once delivered. *"And seekest thou great things for thyself? Seek them not"* (ver. 5). A suited motto this for each of us. How apt is the heart to crave "great things;" but in doing so, how unlike the servant becomes to the Master who "pleased not Himself," but could say, "I do always those things that please Him;" and again, "I came not to do Mine own will, but the will of Him that sent Me." And does not the position He took when down here determine our only proper one? What was it, then, as to the world? Alas, He was ever the Rejected One! For *Him* there was "no room in the inn" at His birth; no place among the great in His life; and when dead, only room in a borrowed tomb. He was always the outside One—always getting wrongs instead of His rights; as one has said, always in a different path from that of the "dwellers on the earth" in His day of humiliation. And yet it might have been so different—if one dare allow the thought. He need not have taken the place of rejection they gave Him. He could justly have claimed and acted upon the rights that were truly His. Had there been in Him an atom of self-seeking (which there was not, for He was the Holy One of the Father), He might have claimed a place among the mighty here, as others did. All the kingdoms of earth and the glory of them were offered Him; but on what conditions? Conditions which involved some violation of the Word of God. How utterly abhorrent, this, to the Holy One of God! (Oh that we were more like Him!) And so, faithfulness to God kept Him ever the Rejected One, till at last He suffered outside the gate.

Let us ever remind ourselves that this is the One to whom we owe everything for eternity, whose loving-kindness is better than life, and who "also suffered for us, leaving us an example, that we should follow His steps: who did no sin, neither was guile found in His mouth: who, when He was reviled, reviled not again; when He suffered, He threatened not; but committed Himself to Him that judgeth righteously: who His own self bare our sins in His own body on the tree, that we, being dead to sin, should live unto righteousness" (1 Pet. 2: 21-24). Do we, then, desire a place where He had none? Can we desire it so much that we will have it despite the fact that we must disobey His Word and grieve His Holy Spirit to get it; and knowing that if, like Him, we seek only to be faithful to God, we

never can obtain it? Is it really worth so much
to be thought well of by sinful men and foolish
saints? Will it appear so when we stand at His
judgment-seat and gaze upon His face? Ah, better, far better, to be poor and despised here and
have His approval than to seek great things for
ourselves and lose His smile of approbation! Our
"great things" are coming by and by. Let our
faith lay firm hold of *these*. Till then may we
have grace to truly say,

> "We'd not have joy where He had woe,
> Be rich where He was poor."

If tempted to turn aside from the narrow path
of subjection to the truth for an easier path, or
to be better thought of in a world like this, let
us remember these words to Baruch; if "great
things" attract and would lure us on, remember
the words—"Seek them *not*."

The Lord adds, "For, behold, I will bring evil
upon all flesh; . . . but thy life will I give unto
thee for a prey in all places whither thou goest"
(ver. 5). No harm could come to Baruch, let men
rage as they might, while God was His protector.
Famine, sword and pestilence may destroy, but
he should be preserved. He lived in a dispensation when temporal blessing was a sign of the
divine favor. With us, in this spiritual dispensation, our blessings are of a different character.
Precious it is to know that even though the body
might be destroyed, yet nothing can touch the
eternal life of the Christian; and even as to the
body,

"Not a single shaft can hit
Till the God of love sees fit."

He who bids us not to seek great things for
ourselves undertakes to carry us on, and has declared, "I will never leave thee nor forsake thee."
So that we may boldly say, "I will trust and not
be afraid."

CHAPTER XXIV

Egypt, Philistia, Moab, Ammon, Edom, Syria, Arabia, Elam, and Babylon.

(Chaps. 46-49.)

Jeremiah's ministry to the rebellious men of Judah is now over. He is commissioned to announce the judgment soon to fall upon the Gentiles. When called of God to the prophetic office, he was appointed to be a prophet unto the nations (chap. 1:5). Accordingly, the Word of the Lord is now given through him concerning the various peoples surrounding the land of Palestine. Nine different nations are brought before us: we take them up briefly in the order given.

EGYPT.

The entire forty-sixth chapter, with the exception of the last two verses, is devoted to declaring the judgments foreseen by the prophet, which have fallen upon this once rich and populous country. In Scripture, Egypt is invariably a type of the world, either as the oppressor or the would-be patron of the people of God. As such, its judgment speaks of that which is yet to fall upon the present guilty order of things, which first crucified our Lord and persecuted His followers to the death, but now seeks to take them under its protecting wing; thus nullifying that separation from its vanities which should have charac-

terized the Church while waiting for an absent
Lord.

In the chapter before us we have two distinct
prophecies, uttered about eighteen years apart.
The occasion of the first was the attempt made
by Pharaoh-nechoh to invade the provinces of the
king of Babylon, and to break his rising power.
This is set forth in vers. 2-12. It is a vivid
apocalyptic description of the overthrow of the
Egyptian forces by Nebuchadrezzar and his in-
vincible armies. The date given is the same as
for the preceding chapter. The Egyptians, "dis-
couraged and turned away back," were "beaten
down, and fled apace," not looking back, "for
fear was round about" (vers. 4, 5). Like the
waters of a raging flood, the forces of Cush, Put,
and Lydia (the various provinces subject to Pharaoh), led by the trained Egyptian troops, had
thought to overflow the land of the Chaldeans;
but they knew not that the Lord had raised up
Nebuchadrezzar, and that the day of His vengeance upon Egypt had come, when, as a great
sacrifice, they were to be offered up on the banks
of the Euphrates (vers. 6-10). Hope of relief
was vain. "Many medicines" would fail to effect
a cure. Egypt's hour of doom had struck. Her
manifold iniquities had called down Jehovah's
vengeance (vers. 11, 12). All this was literally
fulfilled in the overthrow of Pharaoh-nechoh's
magnificent army.

The next section refers to a later judgment;
and although no date is given, we gather, by a
comparison with chaps. 43 and 44, that it was
uttered by Jeremiah during the time when the

remnant abode in Egypt, after the fall of Jerusalem. It sets forth prophetically the complete
devastation of the land of Mizraim upon the defeat of Pharaoh-hophra, second after Pharaoh-
nechoh, the last Pharaoh mentioned in the Bible.
He is known to have been a man of ignoble spirit,
foolhardy and deceitful. In vain he sought to
stand against the rising power of Nebuchadrezzar. His valiant men were to be swept away.
"They stood not, because the Lord did drive
them" (ver. 15). It should not be the might of
Nebuchadrezzar that would insure him the victory, neither the pusillanimity of Pharaoh-hophra
that would determine his defeat. The Lord of
hosts, the God of battles, was about to destroy
the Egyptians because of their impiety and idolatry. He it is who puts down one nation and
exalts another. "The most high ruleth in the
kingdoms of men." This the victorious Nebuchadrezzar had also to learn for himself in due time.

Hence for Egypt, her gods and her kings, there
could be no quarter. They had defied the living
and true God. They must be brought low till
they learn His power. Such was the sentence;
and it has been fulfilled to the letter, as the centuries witness. Egypt, however, has not fallen
to rise no more. In the last days grace shall be
shown to it. "Afterward it shall be inhabited, as
in the days of old, saith the Lord" (ver. 26).

In that day Judah also, together with the ten
tribes denominated Israel, shall be delivered; and
"Jacob shall return, and be in rest and at ease,
and none shall make him afraid" (ver. 27).

Jehovah has never forgotten His chosen. He may make a full end of the nations whither He has driven them to correct them, but He will not utterly destroy *them*. They must be corrected; His holiness demands that they be not wholly unpunished, but His grace will yet secure their reestablishment in the land, and the enjoyment of His covenanted mercies.

Having pronounced the mind of the Lord as to Egypt, Jeremiah next gives His word in regard to

PHILISTIA.

The Philistines dwelt on the western borders of the land of Canaan. They were originally of Egypt, and therefore, typically, would speak of unconverted men of the world taking a place as dwellers in the land of blessing and privilege— mere unsaved professors, who, while pretending to be children of God, are in reality the enemies of His truth and of His people. Their temporal judgment predicted by Jeremiah, and literally fulfilled shortly afterwards, would set forth symbolically the more terrible judgment soon to fall upon the apostate class in Christendom of whom they are the type.

The seven verses of chap. 47 are devoted to this subject. The date when first uttered is not definitely stated, but ver. 1 informs us that it was "before that Pharaoh smote Gaza," which would place it about the time of the first prophecy regarding Egypt.

From the north "waters should rise up;" that is, the Babylonian armies should overwhelm them; while the power of Egypt in the south was also to be turned against them. Even the world hates a hypocrite. Fear and anguish should take hold upon them; fathers and sons should be overwhelmed in the dreadful carnage. Tyrus and Zidon, Phœnician cities of Philistine origin, would have no power to help. It was the Lord who was about to destroy Philistia. The cup of the iniquity of this warlike and aggressive people was full. They must know the power of Jehovah's anger. "The country of Caphtor" is a general name for the entire strip of country which they had occupied since the days of Abraham and Lot. Caphtor is an Egyptian word, and plainly indicates the ancient home and lineage of these intruders in the land of promise.

"Baldness is come upon Gaza" indicates that this ancient city, for long in possession of Judah (Josh. 10: 41; Judges 1: 18; 1 Kings 4: 24), had again fallen into the hands of its original occupants. It was devoted to destruction—so complete that it could be described as shaving city and people off the face of the ground; a figure frequently used by the prophets to signify utter desolation (Isa. 7: 20; Ezek. 5: 1, 2; Amos 8: 10, etc.). As hair symbolizes the strength of dependence upon God (as in the example of Samson), and glory (as in the woman's case), baldness indicates the absence of both. Philistia should be weak and helpless before her foes; her glory a mere memory, and her power departed.

Ashkelon, likewise, was to be cut off "with the remnant of their valley" (ver. 5). This, too, was one of the five cities of the lords of the Philistines in the days of Joshua. For location and the fertility of the surrounding country it was unexcelled. No doubt the desolations of Judah had permitted the Philistines once more to occupy it, but their season of repose should be brief. They must be broken and fall before the might of the armies sent against them by Jehovah whom they had defied.

"The sword of the Lord" could not be quiet until its charge against Ashkelon had been fulfilled. That accomplished, it should be put into its scabbard. It is not that God authorized the numberless cruelties perpetrated by the armies of Pharaoh and Nebuchadrezzar, but He used them, in spite of all that was contrary to His mind, to wreak summary vengeance upon those who had so long been the oppressors and the enemies of His people. He is the Governor of the world, ruling among the nations; and it was true then, and it is true now, that "righteousness exalteth a nation, but sin is a reproach to any people."

The burden of Philistia ended, the prophet abruptly turns to

MOAB.

The somewhat lengthy forty-eighth chapter is taken up with the Word of the Lord to these descendants of inglorious Lot and his wretched first-born daughter; as the next chapter deals in part with the woes to come upon the children of the younger.

Typically, these Moabites picture that large and careless class to-day who "have a name that they live, and are dead," called in Heb. 12: 8 "bast-

ards, and not sons." Illegitimately born, Moab
was without claim to an inheritance in Israel,
yet a near neighbor, dwelling upon the eastern
shores of the Dead Sea. Lifeless, easy going profession is thus set forth. Such may glide on care-
lessly throughout life, partaking not of the
chastisement of the Lord, which is for His own
children; but judgment must come eventually.

The way of address to Moab in the opening
verse is noticeable: "Against Moab thus saith the
Lord of hosts, the God of Israel." This brings
out the close relationship of Moab and Israel. To
none of the others in this group of nations does
He introduce Himself as "the God of Israel."

Woes are pronounced upon Nebo, the mountain
of Moab from whose summit Moses viewed the
promised land; Kiriathaim, called in Numbers
32:37 Kirjathaim; and Misgab, a fortified city
of which little is known.

In Heshbon, the city of "*devices*," as its name
means, "they have devised evil against it." Mad-
men, that is, "dunghill," shall become a scene of
carnage. Horonaim and Luhith shall be spoiled
likewise. "There shall be no more praise of
Moab" (vers. 1-5).

The inhabitants are warned to flee and save
their lives; to be "like the heath in the wilderness" (ver. 6), as it is not God's purpose to utterly destroy them. The heath (literally, "the
naked tree") referred to, is a desert shrub, having an abundance of vitality; so much so, that
if a part be torn from the parent bush and carried away by the wind, it will take root where
it may fall. The application of the figure to the

remnant of Moab is plain. Their seed abides to-
day, and shall remain even in the Millennium.
In chap. 17: 6 the same figure is applied to the
one who trusts in man, though there it is the
nakedness of the plant to which attention is
drawn.

Chemosh, the patron deity of Moab, was to be
put to shame. He should go into captivity with
his priests and his princes together. Upon every
city the spoiler should come; for so the Lord had
spoken (vers. 7, 8).

The only safety is in flight; for Jehovah's curse
rested upon him who should do the Lord's work
of judgment negligently. It must be unsparing,
and he who held back his sword from blood
should be devoted to judgment himself (vers. 9,
10).

For a long season Moab had been permitted
to go unpunished. The result was a settling down
in haughty carelessness, with utter indifference
to the abominations everywhere practised. "Moab
hath been at ease from his youth, and he hath
settled on his lees, and hath not been emptied
from vessel to vessel, neither hath he gone into
captivity: therefore his taste remained in him,
and his scent is not changed" (ver. 11). This
condition can be no longer tolerated. The Lord
is about to "send unto him wanderers, that shall
cause him to wander, and shall empty his vessels
and break their bottles" (ver. 12). The result
shall be to destroy their confidence in Chemosh
and to make them ashamed "as the house of
Israel was ashamed of Bethel their confidence"—
that is, of the calves set up by Jeroboam (ver.

13). It is evident that Moab's destruction was not to be forever. Like Israel, they were to be punished in measure; but the discipline would eventually prove corrective.

In vers. 14 to 25 the prophet sees in vision the advancing armies of the spoiler, and graphically portrays the alarm and final rout of the inhabitants of the cities of this interesting people. "The horn of Moab is cut off" signifies that all his power was to be broken. In his pride he had "magnified himself against the Lord," and gloried over Israel when their affliction came. "He shall wallow in his vomit, and be himself in derision" (vers. 26, 27). Ere the besom of wrath shall come upon them, the dwellers in the cities are warned to flee to "the rocks" for safety. A remnant would thus be preserved. They are exhorted to "be like the dove that maketh her nest in the sides of the hole's mouth" (ver. 28).

Pride ever goes before destruction, and a haughty spirit before a fall. It was this abominable trait that particularly characterized these descendants of Lot. "We have heard the pride of Moab—he is exceeding proud!—his loftiness, and his arrogancy, and his pride, and the haughtiness of his heart" (ver. 29). Because he will not humble himself, he must be humbled—in the case of individuals as well as nations who fail to acknowledge Heaven's rule. Upon all the land the hand of God shall fall; for it *is* His hand, though a heathen army be the instrument used. How fitting that he who prophesies such dire sorrow should do so with weeping and strong crying (vers. 30-34).

Idolatry will be made to cease in their cities, and "There shall be lamentation generally upon all the housetops of Moab, and in the streets thereof," when the Lord has "broken Moab like a vessel wherein is no pleasure" (vers. 35-41). It is the same simile of the potter and the clay, used long before in regard to Israel (chap. 18). "And Moab shall be destroyed from being a people, because he hath magnified himself against the Lord." This was his awful sin. How many, alas, have followed in his steps! For such, judgment is certain at last, though it may for a long time seem to slumber. When it falls, there shall be no escape. "Fear, and the pit, and the snare," shall devour them all (vers. 42-46). Thus Balaam's prophecy was to be at length fulfilled, when the Lord should "smite the corners of Moab" (Num. 24 : 17). "Yet will I bring again the captivity of Moab in the latter days, saith the Lord. Thus far is the judgment of Moab" (ver. 47). In the Millennium, when the Lord, in His own times, shall show who is that blessed and only Potentate, the King of kings and Lord of lords, Moab shall rejoice with His people, a remnant being spared to enter into the world-kingdom of our God and His Christ.

The burden of the neighboring kingdom of the

AMMONITES

is much briefer, the six opening verses of the next chapter giving it all. As before noted, they descended from the younger daughter of Lot, and typically speak of practically the same thing as

Moab, only that they might also suggest those who prey upon the true Church of God, like Simon Magus and his numberless kin. They ever seem to have been a warlike people, and possibly had thus been considerably decimated, as we never find them occupying as large a place as the nation we have just been considering. Restless, predatory and nomadic, they did not possess the number of fenced cities, neither did they enjoy the high state of civilization characteristic of the Moabites. From the first they were the enemies of Israel, even though Moses sought to placate them, and directed the people to "distress them not" (Deut. 2 : 19), as in the case of Moab also.

In the times of Jeremiah they dwelt in several of the cities of Gad, and possibly also of Reuben and Benjamin; their own capital being Rabbath as of old, which was just across the border from Gad. Bold and fearless, but with no great cities, they could not be characterized by the pride of national glory that we have seen in Moab; but the indictment here brought against them is that she "trusted in her treasures, saying, Who shall come unto me?" They were thus independent of God equally with their more cultured neighbors.

In verse 1 the Lord asks, "Hath Israel no sons? Hath he no heir? Why then doth their king inherit Gad, and his people dwell in his cities?" The Ammonites had taken advantage of the captivity of Israel and their manifold afflictions to enrich themselves, and to occupy the territory contiguous to their own land. "Therefore, behold, the days come, saith the Lord, that I will cause an alarm of war to be heard in Rabbah of the

Ammonites; and it shall be a desolate heap, and her daughters shall be burned with fire: then shall Israel be heir unto them that were his heirs, saith the Lord" (ver. 2): that is, the power of Ammon was soon to be broken, and Israel made once more to occupy the cities that had been wrested from them. This has already had a partial fulfilment. It will have a more complete one in the Millennium, when Israel shall dwell in his own land, with none to make him afraid.

Lamentation and mourning, the prophet declared, should take the place of Ammon's proud boasting and conceit; for her king should go into captivity with the princes and priests, and their whole people that were spared from the sword should be driven out of their land, with none to "gather up him that wandereth." Afterward, when the chastisement shall have been productive of blessing, the children of Ammon will be restored, as in the case of Moab (vers. 3-6).

Somewhat more lengthy is the prophetic word concerning

EDOM.

The descendants of "Esau, which is Edom," had ever been the enemies of the descendants of his brother Jacob. By comparing the short prophecy of Obadiah with the passage before us, the reader will get a full account of the sin and the doom of this high-handed race. In type, we have the flesh symbolized—ever lusting against the Spirit. Hence there is no restoration for Edom. They were to be utterly cut off. Human wisdom could not avail to save this proud nation. All their counsels were in vain. "The calamity of Edom" was near at hand. God had decreed it. None of the men should be spared. Grape-gatherers leave some gleaning grapes upon the vines. Midnight robbers do not utterly despoil those whom they wrong. But in the case of the children of Esau they would be utterly destroyed, so far as nationality is concerned (vers. 7-10).

It is touching to find in this connection the precious message that has been a source of untold comfort to many a tried saint in later days. "Leave thy fatherless children, I will preserve them alive; and let thy widows trust in Me" (ver. 11). This was God's gracious provision for the helpless and feeble even of Edom. How blessedly it tells out the real compassion of His heart! Judgment is His strange work. His holiness demands that sin be dealt with. In His righteous government the nations that have practised iniquity must perish. But He forgets not the cry of the lowly; He ever remembers the poor and the needy. The widow and the fatherless have a special claim upon His love and mercy. Never was that claim pleaded in vain.

This is the only bright light in the dark picture of Edom's woes. They could not go unpunished, but must assuredly drink of the cup of Jehovah's wrath. The surrounding nations were to be the instruments used to bring this about. Though Edom should make his nest as high as the eagle, the Lord would bring him down from thence, giving up his cities and fortresses to desolation. The ruin was to be as complete as that of Sodom and Gomorrah and the cities of the plains. Like a lion coming out from the swellings of Jordan, the enemy would rise up against the habitation of the strong till the heart of his mighty men became as the heart of a woman in her pangs (vers. 12-22). With this the prophet abruptly concludes. There is no word of recovery. It is a ruin complete and irrevocable, as Obadiah also testifies.

DAMASCUS

is next told of her impending doom. Already this once great city was being bereft of her glory, the Syrian empire paling before Nebuchadrezzar's rising sun. Hamath and Arpad, famous in their day, were confounded. Evil tidings had reached them of the overthrow of the Syrian armies. "There is sorrow on the sea; it cannot be quiet." The restlessness of the sobbing surf was but a picture of the state of their inhabitants. Damascus, waxing feeble, sought to flee; but "anguish and sorrows have taken her, as a woman in travail" (vers. 23, 24). It is too late to escape. The conqueror is at the door. "Therefore her young men shall fall in her streets, and all the men of war shall be cut off in that day, saith the Lord of hosts." The city was to be burned, and the palaces of Ben-hadad, Israel's old enemy, destroyed (vers. 25-27). Thus briefly, in the space of five verses, does the prophet portray the downfall of one of the greatest powers of ancient times.

ARABIA,

with its various tribes, is likewise apprised of

Nebuchadrezzar's purpose and ultimate victory. Kedar and Hazor are to be smitten. Fear shall be on every side. The flocks and herds of these pastoral people shall feed the conqueror's armies. All their treasures shall be seized for a spoil: "And Hazor shall be a dwelling for dragons, and a desolation forever: there shall no man abide there, nor any son of man dwell in it" (vers. 28-33). (The word for "dragons" might better be rendered "jackals.")

These fierce Arabian tribes' father was Ishmael, Abraham's first-born, by Hagar. As outlined in Galatians, they picture those who, born after the flesh, seek to obtain a place of blessing through legal works, only to find that "the son of the bondwoman shall not be heir with the son of the free woman" (Gal. 4: 30).

ELAM.

In the beginning of the reign of the unstable Zedekiah, the Word of the Lord had come to Jeremiah against the rising power of Elam, destined to play an important part in the history of nations, as an ally of the mighty kingdom of Persia, afterwards allied with Media, assuming an imperial place under Cyrus (ver. 34). It was at this time a Babylonian province (Dan. 8: 2), though in years gone by it had flourished as an independent kingdom (Gen. 14: 1-12). As being part of the prophet's testimony to the nations, the burden of Elam is introduced here in connection with the preceding kingdoms and tribes.

The Lord was to "break the bow of Elam, the

chief of their might;" and by means of the four winds He should scatter them toward every quarter of heaven, so that there should "be no nation whither the outcasts of Elam" should not come.

Dismayed before their enemies, they should know the fierce anger of the Lord, who would send a sword after them until He had consumed them. His throne should be set in Elam, when their king and princes should be destroyed. It is the same thing as in the case of Nebuchadrezzar; they should know that "the heavens do rule" (vers. 35-38). This was fulfilled when the victorious Macedonians and their allies drove the luxurious Persian armies before them, under Alexander the Great. Yet between this time and the time when the prophecy was uttered, Elam rose from the position of an insignificant kingdom to an integral part of one of the mightiest empires the world had known, overthrowing the Babylonians and ruling the entire known world, with the exception of the feeble states of Europe. In God's appointed time all her power availed nothing, and she became but another witness to the truth of prophecy.

There is hope in her latter end however, for the Lord has pledged Himself to bring again her captivity. So we see the very same people existing to-day, despite the changes of the centuries; and in the coming kingdom of our Lord the remnant of Elam shall have a place, when the nations that are spared shall own Messiah's benignant yet righteous sway (ver. 39).

Thus God had revealed "things to come" concerning the Gentile nations surrounding Immanuel's land. From one to another the cup of His vengeance should be passed. Judgment began at the house of God, when Israel and Judah were given up to captivity. Their heathen neighbors rejoiced in their discomfiture. But they too must drink of that cup, and learn that "those that walk in pride He is able to abase." Egypt and her daughter Philistia; together with Moab, Ammon and Edom, so closely related to Israel; as also Syria, Arabia and Elam, must all alike be swept with the besom of His wrath. Jeremiah foretold it long before it became a matter of history, as it has become since.

For one more nation He has a similar word —for the very power used to chastise Judah when she departed from the living God: Babylon must be destroyed when her iniquity has come to the full. But we reserve this for another chapter.

CHAPTER XXV

THE DOOM OF BABYLON AND THE DELIVERANCE OF THE REMNANT

(Chaps. 50, 51.)

In the New Testament two solemn chapters are devoted to an account of the worldly glory and the awful overthrow of mystical, or spiritual, Babylon (Rev. 17, 18). In our prophet, two chapters give in detail the splendor and ruin of literal Babylon, the city by the Euphrates, which answers to the Babylon of the Apocalypse as type to antitype.

It has been a question with many as to whether or no the literal city in the plain of Shinar is again to be built, and destined to become the queen city of the world. Those who think so consider the Babylon of Revelation to refer, not to Rome and its unholy politico-religious system, but to the actual Chaldean city, when it has awakened from the slumber of centuries. Such point to the fact that Babylon as well as Rome was built upon seven hills, or mounds; and as the prophecy of Jeremiah so closely connects Israel's restoration with Babylon's ruin, they hold that it is essential to prophetic exactness that this city shall once more become the wonder of the world.

On the other hand, the opponents of this view consider the resurrection of literal Babylon to be an idle dream, utterly opposed to the teaching of these chapters now before us. They hold that any plain man, reading Jeremiah's vivid description of the downfall of Shinar's capital, could but gather from it that it was cast down forever. Unless one has a theory to uphold, this would be the plain sense of the passage, in their judgment. There seems to them to be no proper reason for supposing the apocalyptic Babylon to be other than Rome, as held by the majority of Christians of all ages. The description so exactly tallies with papal and pagan Rome in the past, as well as with what one may so readily expect the papacy to develop in the future, when the Church has been caught up—and this view seems so thoroughly in accord with the predictions of Daniel and other prophets of both the Old and New Testaments—that one finds it difficult to believe in the necessity for the rebuilding of the literal city in order to carry out the "sure word of prophecy." Without desiring to be offensively dogmatic, the writer finds himself in this class, and is compelled, in what follows, to view the present portion of Jeremiah from this standpoint. Let the reader carefully seek to "prove all things, and hold fast that which is good." Because of these conflicting views, we shall not glance as cursorily at these chapters as we have done in regard to the others that give the prophecies of the nations; but we shall look at them verse by verse, seeking to point out the general trend of the teaching as we go along.

"The Word that the Lord spake against Babylon and against the land of the Chaldeans by Jeremiah the prophet" (chap. 50:1). It is noteworthy that the same man who had previously predicted the ascendancy of Babylon now foretells its doom. He who had counseled submission to its authority now exhorts the remnant of Israel to flee from it, that they be not partakers of its sins and its judgment. This is all perfectly consistent. Jeremiah was no politician, no courtier, no man-pleaser. He spake "as pleasing God that trieth the heart." When the Lord would chasten Judah, He chose Nebuchadrezzar to be His rod, When Babylon lifted up herself against Him, she too must fall, and fall lower far than Judah, never to rise again.

"Declare ye among the nations, and publish, and set up a standard; publish, and conceal not: say, Babylon is taken, Bel is confounded, Merodach is broken in pieces; her idols are confounded, her images are broken in pieces" (ver. 2). God speaks of the things that are not as though they were. Vividly He describes the downfall of the special form of idolatry that characterized Babylon, together with the taking of the city by the monotheistic armies of Cyrus. Bel was the sun-god worshiped under the names of Baal, Zeus, Jupiter, Osiris, etc., by various nations. Merodach is but another name for the same demon-deity. He is called Marduk in the Babylonian inscriptions. Often the two names are joined together, as Bel-Marduk. Bel was the name under which he was worshiped among the old Accadians. He is sometimes called Bel of Nippur. Before the power of Jehovah's might he is to be put to shame, and all the images broken to pieces.

"For out of the north there cometh up a nation against her, which shall make her land desolate, and none shall dwell therein: they shall remove, they shall depart, both man and beast" (ver. 3). The northern nation was the Medo-Persian confederacy, whose end we have noted in chapter 49. The Persians generally were believers in one unseen God, whom they worshiped under the symbol of fire. They abhorred idolatry with a relentless hatred, and were a nation of iconoclasts. It was fitting that such a people should be used to overthrow the mother of all idolatrous practices—Babylon, with her powerful secret priest-caste. By this means should the way be opened for the return of the captivity of Israel and Judah to the land of their nativity.

"In those days, and in that time, saith the Lord, the children of Israel shall come, they and the children of Judah together, going and weeping: they shall go, and seek the Lord their God. They shall ask the way to Zion with their faces thitherward, saying, Come, and let us join ourselves to the Lord in a perpetual covenant that shall not be forgotten" (vers. 4, 5). We know that it was a mere handful that thus responded to the opportunity given by Cyrus. Nevertheless they were prospered on their way, and were settled in their land when Messiah appeared. The perpetual covenant, however, shall not be truly entered into until their future return. The *first* was but a picture of the *final* restoration, when they shall be brought into millennial blessing.

Touchingly, Jehovah describes the afflicted state of His people under Babylon's rule: "My people hath been lost sheep; their shepherds have caused them to go astray, they have turned them away on the mountains: they have gone from mountain to hill, they have forgotten their resting place. All that found them have devoured them: and their adversaries said, We offend not, because they have sinned against the Lord, the habitation of justice, even the Lord, the hope of their fathers" (vers. 6, 7). Thus had the nations combined to heap ignominy and reproach upon the failed nation that had enjoyed blessing above every other. But though the Lord permitted all this for their discipline, He had not failed to note the hatred manifested toward them by the haughty Gentile powers. The time was near when He was to awake for the deliverance of His own, and the judgment of their oppressors. To the leaders among the captivity He sends the word, "Flee" (or, remove) "out of the midst of Babylon, and go forth out of the land of the Chaldeans, and be as the he goats before the flocks" (ver. 8). His wandering sheep are to be restored to their own fold under the guidance and care of the "Shepherd of Israel."

"For, lo, I will raise and cause to come up against Babylon an assembly of great nations from the north country: and they shall set themselves in array against her; from thence she shall be taken; their arrows shall be as of a mighty expert man; none shall return in vain. And Chaldea shall be a spoil: all that spoil her shall be satisfied, saith the Lord" (vers. 9, 10). The "assembly of great nations from the north" under Cyrus consisted of the Persians and Medes, together with the Elamites and the surrounding nations which had become tributary to the mighty conqueror, whose triumph Daniel had plainly predicted in the very court of the kings of Babylon.

The reason for the desolation of this once glorious city is given in the next two verses, as also a summary of her destruction. "Because ye were glad, because ye rejoiced, O ye destroyers of My heritage, because ye are grown fat as the heifer at grass" ("that treadeth out the corn," R. V.), "and bellow as bulls; your mother shall be sore confounded; she that bare you shall be ashamed: behold, the hindermost of the nations shall be a wilderness, a dry land, and a desert" (vers. 11, 12).

Only genuine faith in the Word of God could have led any one to credit a prophecy so unlikely of fulfilment to the mind of the natural man. When Jeremiah spoke, or wrote, the words Babylon was the greatest city in the world, with apparently impregnable defences. Her massive walls, with their hundred gates, seemed calculated to withstand the siege of centuries; especially as the vast space within, suitable for cultivation, apparently provided against all possibility of famine. But God had spoken; and though her inhabitants knew it not, the doom of proud, luxurious, idolatrous Babylon was sealed. Where the city once stood, now all is desert, as foretold by both Jeremiah and Isaiah (see Isa. 47). It was with great difficulty that archaeologists were even able to find its site, buried deep beneath the rubbish of ages. It shall never be rebuilt; for He who cannot lie hath declared, "Because of the wrath of the Lord it shall not be inhabited, but it shall be wholly desolate: every one that goeth by Babylon shall be astonished, and hiss at all her plagues" (ver. 13).

In the light of this verse, if there were no other corroborative, we cannot conceive of any room for the notion that the city is yet to be rebuilt in order to be thrown down once more. No one, without a theory to maintain, could gather from these words other than that, once destroyed, it should rise no more forever. Jeremiah's hearers must have so understood it. There was no hint that he referred to another destruction than that begun under Cyrus. It is useless to urge against this that the desolation was not accomplished at once, when Belshazzar was conquered and slain by the armies of Cyrus. The prophet does not predict a sudden blotting out. She is to become first the "hindermost of the nations;" then, eventually, "a wilderness." This is exactly what took place. God's word was fulfilled to the letter, for "the Scripture cannot be broken."

As though beholding the invading army surrounding the city, Jeremiah vividly describes the onslaught of the Persian cohorts. "Put yourselves in array against Babylon round about: all ye that bend the bow, shoot at her, spare no arrows; for she hath sinned against the Lord. Shout against her round about: she hath given her hand: her foundations are fallen, her walls are thrown down: for it is the vengeance of the Lord: take vengeance upon her; as she hath done, do unto her. Cut off the sower from Babylon, and him that handleth the sickle in time of harvest: for fear of the oppressing sword they shall turn every one to his people, and they shall flee every one to his own land" (vers. 14-16). It is the undeviating law of God's government that "whatsoever a man soweth, that shall he also reap"—and a nation in like manner. According as Babylon had done to others, so was it done to her. The New Testament seer uses language very similar in referring to mystical Babylon. (See Rev. 18:6.) Retribution may be long delayed, but it is as certain as the fixed stars. "God is not mocked." He still sits on the throne as the moral Governor of the universe. How important, then, for the nations, as well as individuals, to remember and act upon the words of our Lord Jesus: "As ye would that men should do to you, do ye even so to them."

Again the prophet turns to Israel to declare God's unfailing promises. They have sinned, and sinned most grievously, but His Word cannot be thus made void. "Israel is a scattered sheep; the lions have driven him away: first the king of Assyria hath devoured him; and last this Nebuchadrezzar king of Babylon hath broken his bones. Therefore thus saith the Lord of hosts, the God of Israel: Behold, I will punish the king of Babylon and his land, as I have punished the king of Assyria. And I will bring Israel again to his habitation, and he shall feed on Carmel and Bashan, and his soul shall be satisfied upon mount Ephraim and Gilead" (vers. 17-19). As surely as Assyria's haughty power had been broken, so should Babylon fall; and as surely as this seemingly impossible event should take place, so should Israel be brought back to the home of their fathers. Nor was it the merely temporary return under Ezra and Zerubbabel that is here referred to, for, "In those days, and in that time, saith the Lord, the iniquity of Israel shall be sought for, and there shall be none; and the sins of Judah, and they shall not be found: for I will pardon them whom I reserve" (ver. 20). This will only be when "they shall look upon Him whom they have pierced:" and the remnant of Judah, as later the remnant of the ten tribes, shall say, "Come, and let us return unto the Lord: for He hath torn, and He will heal us; He hath smitten, and He will bind us up" (Hosea 6: 1).

Reverting again to the main theme, Jeremiah goes on to picture, as in vision, the desolation of Babylon. "Go up against the land of Merathaim, even against it, and against the inhabitants of Pekod: waste and utterly destroy after them, saith the Lord, and do according to all that I have commanded thee" (ver. 21). Merathaim means "double rebellion," according to the best authorities, and seems here to be symbolically applied to Chaldea. Pekod is said by some to mean "Visitation;" and by reference to Ezek. 23: 23 it would appear to indicate a tributary city to the capital. If so, it is now impossible to find any trace of it. Some have thought it might simply refer to a certain quarter or suburb of the imperial city.

"A sound of battle is in the land, and of great destruction. How is the hammer of the whole earth cut asunder and broken! How is Babylon become a desolation among the nations! I have laid a snare for thee, and thou art also taken, O Babylon, and thou wast not aware: thou art found, and also caught, because thou hast striven against the Lord" (vers. 22-24). It was in this that her great offence consisted. She had lifted herself up against the Most High. In no other city did idolatry assume so fearful a form and so dreadful an aspect as in the great city Babylon. She was, as before pointed out, the mother of almost every heathen system. From her, too, mystical Babylon borrowed far more than many have any conception. Almost every unscriptural practice in the great Romish apostasy can be traced back to the Babylonish rites and ceremonies.

Because of her dreadful impiety, "The Lord hath opened His armory, and hath brought forth the weapons of His indignation: for this is the work of the Lord God of hosts in the land of the Chaldeans" (ver. 25). Not the superior strategy of Cyrus, nor yet the hardihood of his northern troops, nor the carelessness of her defenders, overcame Babylon. It was *the hand of God* that subverted that mighty empire when its iniquity had come to the full. Though the Medo-Persian legions knew Him not, He it was who summoned them, saying, "Come against her from the utmost border, open her storehouses: cast her up as heaps, and destroy her utterly: let nothing of her be left. Slay all her bullocks; let them go down to the slaughter: woe unto them! for their day is come, the time of their visitation" (vers. 26, 27).

The prophetic ear, made quick to hear things yet to come, catches the sound borne down from the years of the future, of "the voice of them that flee and escape out of the land of Babylon, to declare in Zion the vengeance of the Lord our God, the vengeance of His temple" (ver. 28). That temple had been despoiled and burned with fire by the ruthless armies of Chaldea. Its sacred vessels had been carried to Babylon; and, later, we learn from the book of Daniel that the crowning act of Belshazzar's impiety was reached when he caused these holy vessels to be desecrated at his idolatrous feasts by pouring out in them drink offerings to his false gods, and using them for the awful revels of his last great affront to the God of Israel. "The vengeance of the temple" was certain. No hand could stay it. Even as the feast went on, the wretched monarch's doom was sealed. Weighed in the balances, he was found wanting; his kingdom, numbered and finished, was given to the Medes and Persians.

"Call together the archers against Babylon: all ye that bend the bow, camp against it round about; let none thereof escape: recompense her according to her work; according to all that she hath done, do unto her: for she hath been proud against the Lord, against the Holy One of Israel" (ver. 29). It was not ignorance on her part. Testimony after testimony had been given to the true and living God, but she deliberately refused them all and rushed madly upon "the thick bosses of the Almighty." "Therefore shall her young men fall in the streets, and all her men of war shall be cut off in that day, saith the Lord" (ver. 30). Falling into the hands of the God of judgment, she learns His awful power, when repentance is forever too late.

"Behold, I am against thee, O thou most proud, saith the Lord God of hosts: for thy day is come, the time that I will visit thee. And the most proud shall stumble and fall, and none shall raise him up: and I will kindle a fire in his cities, and it shall devour all round about him" (vers. 31, 32.) Do not the words, "The most proud shall stumble and fall, and none shall raise him up," clearly indicate that there can be no future rebuilding of this abhorred city? She had her day of opportunity. Blindly she refused the things that belonged to her peace. When her time of visitation came, her fall was complete and final.

Precious is the word that follows for the remnant of Israel and for us. "Thus saith the Lord of hosts: The children of Israel and the children of Judah were oppressed together: and all that took them captive held them fast; they refused to let them go. Their Redeemer is strong; The Lord of hosts is His name: He shall thoroughly plead their cause, that He may give rest to the land, and disquiet the inhabitants of Babylon" (vers. 33, 34). Israel and Judah should yet know Him as a Saviour-God, delivering them from all that oppressed them. In His love and in His pity He had redeemed them of old, He would never give them up, but in His own appointed time He should arise to their deliverance. His loving-kindness endureth forever. His grace must have its full display, however unworthy the objects of it may be.

But if we read of mercy and compassion for
His own, we find His sword of wrath unsheathed
for the punishment of His enemies. "A sword is
upon the Chaldeans, saith the Lord, and upon the
inhabitants of Babylon, and upon her princes,
and upon her wise men. A sword is upon the
liars" (or, boasters) ; "and they shall dote" (*i. e.*,
utter nonsense) : "a sword is upon her mighty
men; and they shall be dismayed. A sword is
upon their horses, and upon their chariots, and
upon all the mingled people that are in the midst
of her; and they shall become as women: a sword
is upon her treasures; and they shall be robbed"
(vers. 35-37). It is a graphic delineation of unsparing judgment. No words of ours are needed
as to what is in itself so plain.

The next verse clearly tells the reason for so
frightful a catastrophe. "A drought is upon her
waters; and they shall be dried up: *for it is the
land of graven images, and they are mad upon
their idols.*" The Lord's controversy was not
with the people of Babylon and Chaldea alone,
but with the whole demoniacal system which,
from the days of Nimrod, had its centre in the
plains of Shinar. "Therefore the wild beasts of
the desert with the wild beasts of the islands
shall dwell there, and the owls shall dwell therein; and *it shall be no more inhabited forever;
neither shall it be dwelt in from generation to
generation*" (vers. 38, 39). This is surely con-
clusive. To look for a resurrection of Babylon
only that she may be again destroyed is, in our
judgment, an idle dream. She has been blotted
off from the face of the earth, and shall be so

forever. "As God overthrew Sodom and Gomorrah and the neighbor cities thereof, saith the Lord, so shall no man abide there, neither shall any son of man dwell therein" (ver. 40). The ruin is complete and irremediable. The silent mounds by the Euphrates are as distinct witness to the holiness of God as the salt plains by the Dead Sea.

Verses 41 and 42 are a vivid description of the Persian cavalry, with their allies advancing to the siege of the luxurious city. "Behold, a people shall come from the north, and a great nation, and many kings shall be raised up from the coasts" (or, uttermost parts) "of the earth. They shall hold the bow and the lance: they are cruel, and will not show mercy: their voice shall roar like the sea, and they shall ride upon horses, every one put in array, like a man to the battle, against thee, O daughter of Babylon." One can almost see the advancing armies, with the forest of lances and standards, as they draw near the city that proudly boasted of being impregnable. "The king of Babylon hath heard the report of them, and his hands waxed feeble: anguish took hold of him, and pangs as of a woman in travail" (ver. 43). All the might of Chaldea's armies, the ingenuity of her officers, and the walls and bastions around her capital, could avail nothing to turn aside the dire calamity. Babylon had lifted herself up against Jehovah. She sought to measure her strength with the Almighty. She must be crushed to the dust never again to lift up her head.

Cyrus, God's chosen, whom Isaiah had called

by name long before (Isa. 45: 1-4), is described
as a lion coming up from the swelling of Jordan, driven into the inhabited country from the
wilderness because of the rising waters. "Behold, he shall come up like a lion from the swelling of Jordan unto the habitation of the strong:
but I will make them suddenly run away from
her: and who is a chosen man, that I may appoint over her? for who is like Me? and who
will appoint Me the time? and who is that shepherd that will stand before Me?" (ver. 44). Almost the same words are used in chap. 49: 19 to
describe the enemy of Edom. No strong habitation could withstand the assault of an army sent
by God as a punishment for national iniquity.

"Therefore hear ye the counsel of the Lord,
that He hath taken against Babylon; and His
purposes, that He hath purposed against the land
of the Chaldeans. Surely the least of the flock
shall draw them out: surely He shall make their
habitation desolate with them" (ver. 45). Even
the feeblest could overcome the mighty, when
fighting the battles of the Lord. He had but to
give the word, and all the defences of Babylon
became as the toppling walls of Jericho. The
astonishment of the nations is expressed in the
closing verse of this chapter. "At the noise of
the taking of Babylon the earth is moved, and the
cry is heard among the nations" (ver. 46).

The following chapter, which closes the series,
continues the same general subject. "Thus saith
the Lord: Behold, I will raise up against Babylon, and against them that dwell in the midst of
them that rise up against Me, a destroying wind;

and I will send unto Babylon fanners, that shall
fan her, and shall empty her land: for in the
day of trouble they shall be against her round
about" (vers. 1, 2). As grain is winnowed and
the chaff carried off by the wind, so should the
inhabitants of Babylon be swept away by the
"destroying wind" of the Lord's indignation.
The only wheat to be found therein was the
feeble remnant of Israel and Judah—scattered
because of their sins though they were.

"Against him that bendeth let the archer bend
his bow, and against him that lifteth himself up
in his brigandine: and spare ye not her young
men; destroy ye utterly all her host. Thus the
slain shall fall in the land of the Chaldeans, and
they that are thrust through in her streets"
(vers. 3, 4). All attempts at defensive warfare
were destined to be in vain. Neither archers nor
strategy could avail anything to save the city
when Jehovah had devoted it to destruction.

"For Israel hath not been forsaken, nor Judah
of his God, of the Lord of hosts; though their
land was filled with sin against the Holy One of
Israel" (ver. 5). Israel and Judah were under
the rod of the Lord's chastening because of their
sins, but nothing could alter His covenanted
mercies to them. It was the Holy One with whom
they had to do; one who is of purer eyes than
to behold iniquity; but even their failure could
not change the word of His grace and the love
of His heart. He was for them still, and therefore more than all that could be against them.
Accordingly, He apprises them of the judgments
before they fall, and warns them to depart from

the doomed city. "Flee out of the midst of Babylon, and deliver every man his soul: be not cut
off in her iniquity; for this is the time of the
Lord's vengeance; He will render unto her a
recompense" (ver. 6). So also, in the days when
the apocalyptic vials are being poured out upon
the earth, the call will go forth to the Jewish
remnant of that fearful time, "Come out of her,
My people, that ye be not partakers of her sins,
and that ye receive not of her plagues" (Rev.
18: 4). As righteous Lot was delivered from
Sodom ere fire from heaven fell, so the opportunity was given for the men of Judah and Israel
to flee out of Babylon in time to escape the visitation of Jehovah's wrath. It was the same before Jerusalem was taken by Titus, when the
Christians in accordance with the word of the
Lord Jesus, were permitted to retire from the
city prior to the final assault. The same principle holds good in regard to the Church in this
dispensation, which is to be caught away to be
with the Lord before the seven-sealed book is
opened and the trumpet and vial judgments are
meted out to this guilty, Christ-rejecting world.
"Because thou hast kept the word of My patience, I also will keep thee from the hour of
temptation which shall come upon all the world"
(Rev. 3: 10).

"Babylon hath been a golden cup in the Lord's
hand, that made all the earth drunken: the nations have drunken of her wine; therefore the
nations are mad" (ver. 7). It is the wine of
idolatry that was passed from one nation to another, but which had its origin in Babylon. Her

mystical antitype has in her hand a golden cup, with which she too makes drunk the nations "with the wine of her fornication" (Rev. 17: 1-6). There, the wine speaks of spiritual adultery, which is the union of the Church and the world. It will be observed how closely the New Testament Babylon is likened to that of the older revelation.

"Babylon is suddenly fallen and destroyed: howl for her; take balm for her pain, if so be she may be healed." Though her fall is so sudden, yet, as remarked in our study of the preceding chapter, she was not instantaneously blotted out. Here, after her fall, her admirers have remedies to offer for her recovery. But it is too late. Her end is decreed. So the remnant declares: "We would have healed Babylon, but she is not healed: forsake her, and let us go every one into his own country: for her judgment reacheth unto heaven, and is lifted up even to the skies. The Lord hath brought forth our righteousness: come, and let us declare in Zion the work of the Lord our God" (vers. 8-10).

May we not make an application of this solemn word to present conditions in Christendom? Not yet have the Roman and Protestant communions fully developed into Babylon the Great. But is it not patent, even now, that there is no healing for the professing body? The Word of God is rejected, and its inspiration called in question. The Holy Spirit is quenched and resisted. The Lordship of Christ, the Church's Head, is denied practically. What remains for those who value the favor and the truth of God in such a time as

this but to forsake every company where these
conditions prevail? And, like Judah and Israel returning to Zion, ask once more for the old paths
and gather in simplicity to the name of the Lord
Jesus, refusing, in any sense, to go on with that
which dishonors Him through whose precious
blood we have been redeemed to God. "We would
have healed Babylon, but she is not healed: forsake her!" It is useless to go on seeking to purify
what will never be purified. When evil can no
longer be purged out (as in accordance with 1
Cor. 5), the only other resource is to purge one's
self out of all that is in opposition to God and
His Word, as in 2 Tim. 2:15-21. When men who
take the place of Christian teachers make it manifest that they have but a form of godliness and
deny the power thereof, the only course left for
those who would be faithful to God and His truth
is implicit obedience to the injunction, "From
such turn away" (2 Tim. 3:5).

Turning again to the words of Jeremiah, we
note the realistic description of the march upon
Babylon. "Make bright the arrows; gather the
shields: the Lord hath raised up the spirit of
the kings of the Medes: for His device is against
Babylon, to destroy it; because it is the vengeance of the Lord, the vengeance of His temple. [See chap. 50:28.] Set up the standard
upon the walls of Babylon, make the watch
strong, set up the watchmen, prepare the am-
bushes: for the Lord hath both devised and
done that which He spake against the inhabitants of Babylon" (vers. 11, 12). With the vivid-
ness of an eyewitness, the prophet depicts the ad-

vancing army of the enemy, led, be it noted, not
by Cyrus in person, though he directed it all, but
by "the kings of the Medes." That part of the
army which was sent against Babylon was, according to Dan. 5:31, under the command of
"Darius the Median;" and although contemporary history does not use the actual name Darius,
it does assure us that it was a Median chief and
not the mighty Cyrus himself who had charge of
the troops that besieged and sacked the capital
city. Scripture is ever exact. How could it be
otherwise, when it is the very breathing of the
living God? Not only does Jeremiah vividly portray the assembling of the Median troops, but
with a few master-strokes he presents the confi-
dent activity of the imperial guard. Every pre-
caution was taken to insure the safety of Babylon; but they knew not that the hour of Jehovah's vengeance had struck, the vengeance of His
insulted and wasted temple.

Though they dwelt in apparent security "upon
many waters," and flattered themselves that they
were "abundant in treasures," the Lord had decreed, "Thine end is come, and the measure of
thy covetousness." He had therefore sworn by
Himself, saying, "Surely I will fill thee with men,
as with caterpillars; and they shall lift up a
shout against thee" (vers. 13, 14). As the destruction of a field of green herbs by that most
common of all tropical plagues—an onslaught of
ravenous, crawling creatures—so should be the
destruction of haughty Babylon, the queen city of
the ancient world, whose gardens were numbered
among its seven wonders.

He with whom they had to do was not as the powerless idols of the nations, nor yet as the malignant demons behind them. "He hath made the earth by His power, He hath established the world by His wisdom, and hath stretched out the heaven by His understanding" (ver. 15). Against the Mighty One who controls the vapors, the lightnings and the rain, had the Chaldean girded on his armor. Made brutish by idolatry, confounded because of confidence in breathless images, they must learn the vanity of their hope; for "in the time of their visitation they shall perish" (vers. 16-18).

How different the "portion of Jacob." "He is the Former of all things: and Israel is the rod of His inheritance: The Lord of hosts is His name" (ver. 19). He, the omnipotent Creator of all things, had deigned to take up the seed of poor, failing Jacob—surnamed, in grace, Israel. This people He had formed for Himself. He would use them as His battle-axe and weapon of war. With them He would break in pieces the nations and destroy the kingdoms of their oppressors. All classes must learn that the Lord hath chosen Jacob; for with them, not the warrior only, but the people in every walk of life, must be broken, and His word fulfilled which declared, "And I will render unto Babylon and to all the inhabitants of Chaldea all their evil that they have done in Zion in your sight, saith the Lord" (vers. 21-24). How deeply significant it was, in view of all this, that in the last night of the Chaldean kingdom, it was a Jewish captive, Daniel, who read the mystic letters of doom upon the wall of Belshazzar's palace and gave the terrified king the interpretation!

"Behold, I am against thee, O destroying mountain, saith the Lord, which destroyest all the earth: and I will stretch out My hand upon thee, and roll thee down from the rocks, and will make thee a burnt mountain. And they shall not take of thee a stone for a corner, nor a stone for foundations; but thou shalt be desolate forever, saith the Lord" (vers. 25, 26). Words could not be plainer to declare Babylon's absolute destruction. Not only shall the city itself never be rebuilt, but the very stones should not be used, as in the case of many another fallen capital, for the building of any other place. As an accursed thing, her foundations should be held in perpetual abhorrence and her site given up to continual desolation. Nor can the words, by any process of reasoning, be legitimately made to refer to a future overthrow immediately before the Millennium. For over two millenniums already the wastes of Babylon have been a testimony to the sure Word of God. It will be so forever.

Verses 27 and 28 emphasize what we have been going over by recapitulation, with additional details. The kingdoms of Ararat, Minni and Ashkenaz are found under the Median standard. "And the land shall tremble and sorrow: for every purpose of the Lord shall be performed against Babylon, to make the land of Babylon a desolation without an inhabitant" (ver. 29).

The final entry into the city "at either end," and the demoralization of its defenders, are described before the actual event in language only possible to the pen of inspiration. "The mighty men of Babylon have forborne to fight, they have remained in their holds: their might hath failed; they became as women: they have burned her dwelling-places; her bars are broken. One post shall run to meet another, and one messenger to meet another, to show the king of Babylon that his city is taken at one end" (properly, "at either end;" or, as in the R. V., "on every quarter"), "and that the passages are stopped, and the reeds they have burned with fire. and the men of war are affrighted" (vers. 30-32). The waters of the Euphrates, which flowed directly through Babylon, having been, as described by Herodotus, turned out of their course through the city, left an entry way at each end for the warriors of Darius to enter, under the walls, in the dry river bed. Thus they were able to appear suddenly in the streets at a time when the people were given up to frivolity and merry-making, and a thousand of their lords were reveling in the palace of the effeminate Belshazzar.

Having thus pictured the consummation, the prophet goes back to continue the recital of Jehovah's grievance against this impious city. As a ripe field, ready for the threshing-floor, Babylon's harvest was near, when judgment without mercy should be meted out to her because of Nebuchadrezzar's severity to the inhabitants of Zion and Jerusalem. The violence done to Israel should be upon Babylon, and the blood shed be upon the inhabitants of Chaldea (vers. 33-35). Jehovah would plead the cause of His downtrodden people. He it was, not Darius merely, who would "dry up her sea, and make her springs dry." As a result, "Babylon shall become heaps, a dwelling-place for jackals" (R. V.), "an astonishment, and a hissing, without an inhabitant. They shall roar together like lions, they shall yell as lions' whelps" (vers. 36-38). It is to be noted that this utter desolation is to follow, not some future overthrow, but the sack of the city resulting upon the turning aside of the waters in which her inhabitants trusted. They are doomed to "sleep a perpetual sleep, and not wake, saith the Lord" (ver. 39).

From the bed of her river her enemies should arise and come upon her like the sea while her defenders were feasting and drunken. In that very hour they should be given up "as lambs to the slaughter, like rams with he goats." Thus should Sheshach be taken, and Babylon become a desolation among the nations (vers. 40-42). Sheshach is used symbolically for Babylon. The name is said to be derived from the goddess Shach.

"Her cities are a desolation, a dry land, and a wilderness, a land wherein no man dwelleth, neither doth any son of man pass thereby" (ver. 43). Such is the present state of the once prosperous land of Chaldea. Even in the Millennium Babylon's judgment will be the perpetual reminder of God's abhorrence of idolatry.

"And I will punish Bel in Babylon, and I will bring forth out of his mouth that which he hath swallowed up: and the nations shall not flow together any more unto him; yea, the wall of Babylon shall fall" (ver. 44). It was against the

demon symbolized by Bel that the wrath of the
only true God was vented. He it was who had
instigated Nebuchadrezzar and the Chaldeans to
persecute Judah. Because of their sins the Lord
had given them into the hands of the Babylonians; but now He was about to visit their cruelties and wickedness upon their own heads. By
this means would Judah's deliverance be effected.
To them He says, "My people, go ye out of the
midst of her, and deliver ye every man his soul
from the fierce anger of the Lord. And lest your
heart faint, and ye fear for the rumor that shall
be heard in the land; a rumor shall both come
one year, and after that in another year shall
come a rumor, and violence in the land, ruler
against ruler" (vers. 45, 46). He would have
His own little flock delivered from the strife of
tongues, dependent upon Himself and resting on
His Word. Whatever might come, He would not
forget them. The warring nations should but
work out His counsels; for "He maketh the wrath
of man to praise Him, and the remainder of
wrath He doth restrain." The disquieting rumors
of approaching disaster, that might be calculated
to strike terror to their hearts, but pointed to
the overthrow of the power of their oppressors
and the judgment of "the graven images of
Babylon," when "her whole land shall be confounded, and all her slain shall fall in the midst
of her. Then the heaven and the earth, and all
that is therein, shall sing for [joy over] Babylon: for the spoilers shall come unto her from
the north, saith the Lord. As Babylon hath
caused the slain of Israel to fall, so at Babylon

shall fall the slain of all the earth" (vers. 47-49).

Pointedly the remnant are told to count upon God when this awful period of judgment should arrive. It was but the precursor of their deliverance. "Ye that have escaped the sword, go away, stand not still: remember the Lord afar off, and let Jerusalem come into your mind" (ver. 50). In perfect accord with this, we find the Lord stirring up the spirit of Cyrus, in his first year as world-ruler, to permit the rebuilding of the temple and the return of the Jewish remnant to the land of their fathers.

The 51st verse is the suited expression of their hearts as they turn again to their God. "We are confounded, because we have heard reproach: shame hath covered our faces; for strangers are come into the sanctuaries of the Lord's house." This might be taken as the key to the attitude of the returned company, as told in the book of Ezra.

Because of the insult to Jehovah's house, the days were near when He would pour judgment upon the idols of Babylon, and cause her wounded to groan through all the land. "Though Babylon should mount up to heaven, and though she should fortify the height of her strength, yet from Me shall spoilers come unto her, saith the Lord" (vers. 52, 53). He was about to arise in His might to avenge His own elect. Therefore "the sound of a cry cometh from Babylon, and great destruction from the land of the Chaldeans: because the Lord hath spoiled Babylon, and destroyed out of her the great voice; when her waves do roar like great waters, a noise of their voice is uttered: because the spoiler is come upon her, even upon Babylon, and her mighty men are taken, every one of their bows is broken: for the Lord God of recompenses shall surely requite. And I will make drunk her princes, and her wise men, her captains, and her rulers, and her mighty men: and they shall sleep a perpetual sleep, and not wake, saith the King, whose name is The Lord of hosts" (vers. 54-57).

Solemn indeed is the title taken by the offended God of despised Jacob in this section: "The Lord God of recompenses." How seldom do men in general think of Him in this character! In the 24th verse He had declared that He would do unto Babylon and Chaldea "all their evil that they had done to Zion." Here He reveals Himself in a special way as the God of vengeance. In Ps. 94: 1 the remnant of Israel are heard addressing Him in this way: "O Lord God, to whom vengeance belongeth, show Thyself." And in the New Testament the apostle Paul reminds us that He has said, "Vengeance is Mine, I will repay [or, recompense], saith the Lord" (Rom. 12: 19; Heb. 10: 30; Deut. 32: 35). Because of this he entreats the suffering Christians to avenge not themselves, but rather give place unto wrath. It is never necessary for the child of God to be occupied with the thought of self-preservation, or self-vindication. He can afford to leave all in the hands of "the Lord God of recompenses." No power can turn aside His governmental dealings; none can stay His hand, or hinder the activities of His righteousness. "It is a righteous thing with God," we are told, "to recompense tribulation to them that trouble you" (2 Thess. 1:6). This being the case, the Christian can well afford to leave his affairs entirely in the hands of infinite wisdom, knowing that "he that doeth wrong shall receive for the wrong he hath done; and there is no respect of persons with God."

It was because of this principle that Jeremiah had ever counseled submission and obedience to the king of Babylon. He would have His people accept the affliction as from the Lord, and leave with Him the matter of dealing with the oppressing power in His own way and time. It was given to the same prophet to set forth that judgment, and to make known the nature of the recompense that had been decreed: "Thus saith the Lord of hosts: The broad walls of Babylon shall be utterly broken, and her high gates shall be burned with fire; and the people shall labor in vain, and the nations for the fire [R.V.], and they shall be weary" (ver. 58). With these words he concludes the burden of Babylon.

This, then, was to be the end of all her splendor and haughty independence of God. Her broad walls, upon which several chariots could be driven abreast of each other, if Herodotus is to be believed, were to be utterly thrown down, and her massive gates consumed by the flames. The labor of the people to make it the grandest city in all the world would thus end in vanity. They had been building *for the fire.* How significant the words, as given by the Revisers! May not the same be said of man's vaunted energy in this progressive age? He fancies he is building what shall be the lasting admiration of generations yet unborn. But, though he realizes it not, "the coming of the Lord draweth nigh," and it soon shall be manifested that he has but been building for the fire!

Having concluded this series of messages to the nations, thus making known the future of the Gentiles surrounding Palestine, Jeremiah wrote in a book "all the evil that should come upon Babylon," and gave it into the hand of Seraiah, chief chamberlain of Zedekiah. These prophecies were uttered a number of years before this prince was taken captive; it is plain, therefore, there was a moral reason for placing them where they are in the book which we have been considering. Seraiah was going down to Babylon on behalf of the Jewish monarch, as an ambassador to the court of Nebuchadrezzar, in the fourth year of Zedekiah's reign (vers. 59, 60). We thus learn that during much of the time that Jeremiah was urging submission to Babylon, he was aware of its impending doom.

Seraiah was commanded to read the book when he reached his destination; and having done so, he was to say, "O Lord, Thou hast spoken against this place, to cut it off, that none shall remain in it, neither man nor beast, but that it shall be desolate for ever" (vers. 61, 62). Having so said, he was instructed to bind a stone to the roll and cast it into the midst of the Euphrates, crying, "Thus shall Babylon sink, and *shall not rise again,* because of the evil that I will bring upon her: and they shall be weary" (vers. 63, 64, R.V.). Clearly and unequivocally the finality of her overthrow was thus attested in the mouth of two witnesses.

"Thus far are the words of Jeremiah." We have now gone briefly over the varied messages of this honored, yet persecuted servant of Jehovah, embracing a very wide range of prophetic ministry, commencing with his early appeals to Judah in the revival days of Josiah, and closing with his words to the nations. As to the actual order of his prophecies, the words of chapter 44 are the latest; but it was morally fitting that the messages to Judah and Israel should be given first, then those to the Gentiles. The order in the Septuagint varies considerably from that followed in the Hebrew, but it seems plain that in the Greek translation we have but a sample of man's meddling, attempting to improve upon the divine order. The words with which the chapter closes are, in our judgment, meant to inform us that Jeremiah was his own editor. He, by the direct guidance of the Holy Spirit, arranged his books in the order we have in our Bibles. A later hand, equally inspired by God, added the Historical Appendix that follows.

CHAPTER XXVI

THE HISTORICAL APPENDIX

(Chap. 52.)

We have no means of knowing to whom, under God, we are indebted for the historical account of Zedekiah's captivity here narrated. It has pleased God not to reveal the name of the man whom He chose for this. The chapter is practically a duplication of 2 Kings 24: 18-20 and 25 *et. al.* Doubtless the Holy Spirit was pleased to have it transcribed from the other record in order that the prophecy and the record of its literal fulfilment might thus appear together. It is not necessary that we know exactly who the writers of the various Old Testament books were, in order to be sure of their divine inspiration. Our Lord has settled that beyond the peradventure of a doubt by declaring that "the Scripture cannot be broken;" thus setting His seal upon every portion of the Law, the Prophets, and the Psalms, as we know them. The Holy Ghost has likewise told us, through the apostle Paul, that "all Scripture is God-breathed;" and it is to be remembered that the present portion was accepted as a part of the Scripture at the time the words were written.

False prophets had predicted the ultimate triumph of Zedekiah over Nebuchadrezzar. Jeremiah had proclaimed the unpopular truth of his crushing overthrow. History attests the reliability of his words. Zedekiah reigned eleven years in all. He was a brother of both Jehoahaz and Jehoiakim, and therefore a son of the pious Josiah; his mother being identical with the mother of the former king, namely, Hamutal the daughter of another Jeremiah, whose ancestral home was in Libnah (ver. 1). We have already noted that this Zedekiah, like his two immediate predecessors, forsook the ways of his father, and "did that which was evil in the sight of the Lord." He had been placed upon the throne as a kind of vice-king by Nebuchadrezzar after the carrying away of his brother to Babylon, having pledged himself to serve the Chaldean. Treacherous, and in every sense untrustworthy, he shortly after added to his manifold iniquities that of rebellion against his liege lord, in violation of his oath of fealty (vers. 2, 3), seeking an alliance with Egypt. This it was that brought the armies of the king of Babylon once more to the gates of Jerusalem.

The siege was begun on the tenth day of the tenth month, in the ninth year of Zedekiah. Upon the ninth day of the fourth month, in the eleventh year, the garrison became so weakened by means of war, pestilence, and eventually by famine in the city, that a breach was made in the wall, and all the men of war fled "by night by the way of the gate, between the two walls, which is by the king's garden." Zedekiah himself essayed to go with them, as before noted in chapter 39, only to be apprehended in the plains of Jericho, by the Chaldeans. Taken to Riblah, where Nebuchadrezzar was at the time, he was most severely dealt with. His two sons slain and his own eyes put

out, he was carried in fetters to Babylon and
kept in prison until the day of his death (vers.
4-11). Thus he had to learn that it was an evil
thing and bitter to have forsaken the Lord his
God. Jerusalem was burned to the ground (including the temple built by Solomon) and the
walls broken down; it doubtless being the in-
tention of the conqueror that it should be ruined
beyond repair (vers. 12-14). This was not God's
mind, however; *He* had decreed as to Babylon
what its king thought to do to the capital of
Judah.

Nebuzar-adan, the captain of the guard, transported the bulk of the surviving population to
Babylon, leaving a few of the poorest of the people to be vinedressers and husbandmen. Even in
this he was fulfilling the Word of the Lord,
though he probably knew it not (ver. 15).

With the captives, he carried away the temple
furniture, and even its pillars, thus despoiling
the house of Jehovah and dedicating its sacred
things to idols. The various pieces are mentioned
in detail, recorded in God's book, and are precious
as setting forth in various aspects the Person or
work of His beloved Son (vers. 17-23); and
when the impious Belshazzar defiantly used them
in honor of his false deities in his revelry, how
fitting that the predicted judgment should fall on
that night of culminative blasphemy!*

---

* Shortly after this, by order of Cyrus, they were
brought out from the idol temples where Nebuchadrezzar
had placed them; and, carefully numbered, were returned to Jerusalem with the returning remnant. (See
Ezra 1: 7-11.)

A number of priests, as well as officers and princes, besides threescore men of the city, were taken to Riblah and slain before the haughty tyrant who there held court. Thus, without mercy, was Judah devoured by the wild beast of the nations (vers. 24-28).

Three separate times the king of Babylon carried away a portion of the people. In his seventh year he deported over three thousand Jews (2 Kings 24:12). In his eighteenth year over eight hundred and thirty more were enslaved. This is the occasion here referred to. Later, in his twenty-third year, he was responsible for the carrying away of seven hundred and forty-five persons, making thus three distinct deportations (vers. 28-30).

Thus had Judah been ruined; her cities destroyed; her fields trodden down; and her people slain or brought into captivity. Such had been the awful result of forgetting the law of her God.

But He had thoughts of compassion for her still, and would yet grant a deliverance from her cruel enemy. Accordingly, the book closes by giving a hint of better days coming. In the thirty-seventh year of Jehoiachin's captivity, Evil-merodach (who came to the throne of Babylon 561 B. C.) conferred signal honor upon the deposed king of Judah by taking him out of the prison and speaking kindly to him: giving him a throne and a position of honor above other vassal kings in Babylon, he changed his prison garments and gave him to eat of the royal fare (vers. 31-34). Thus a measure of prosperity was restored to him, through the favor of Evil-merodach, who

appointed him a regular allowance till the day of
his death. Zedekiah had died in prison. His predecessor on the throne was advanced to a position
of honor. Jerusalem still lay a ruined heap amid
the desolations of Immanuel's land; but God's
heart was toward His people, and the year of her
release drew on.

THE LAMENTATIONS OF JEREMIAH

CHAPTER XXVII

THE DESOLATIONS OF JERUSALEM

(Lam. 1.)

It should be a matter of deep interest for the child of God, in any dispensation, to know that there is One above who notes with compassion all of his sorrows, and is afflicted in all his afflictions. Nothing could demonstrate this more clearly than the incorporation, as a part of the Holy Scriptures, of the expressions of the heart-sorrows of Jeremiah as he beheld the overwhelming woes of his people, and the desolations of the Holy City. These feelings were right and proper—nay, produced by the Spirit of God in the heart of His servant Jeremiah. He, the God of Israel, was no cold, indifferent spectator of the anguish, humiliation and pains of the people of His choice. His holiness demanded that He chasten them for their iniquities; and He had used the king of Babylon to that end, but His heart was grieved for them still, as a loving father is sorely pained in his own correction of a wayward son. He greatly valued, therefore, the soul-exercises of His grief-stricken prophet, and has seen fit to place his lamentations on record for our instruction and comfort. In a certain sense Jeremiah speaks for the godly ones left in the land—their mouth-piece, as it were.

The peculiar structure of this elegiac poem is worthy of note. In their original form, the first four chapters are acrostic, after the pattern of a number of the psalms. Chapters 1, 2 and 4 consist of twenty-two verses each; every verse commencing with a different letter of the Hebrew alphabet, in regular order. Chapter 3, in which the fullest confession of their sin and grief is found, consists of sixty-six verses; and here *three* verses are given to each letter. That is, each of the first three verses begins with *Aleph,* the first letter of the alphabet; and the next three verses, each begins with *Beth,* the second letter; and so on to the end of the alphabet.

In Ps. 119 we have twenty-two divisions of *eight* verses each, similarly arranged, as even the ordinary English Bible shows. There, every letter of the alphabet (which represents the whole compass of man's speech) is used in the praise of the perfect law of the Lord. In Lamentations every letter is required to express the sorrows following upon the neglect and breaking of that law.

Chapter 5 is an exception to the acrostic style, though containing the same number of verses as the first, second, and fourth.

In this first chapter the remnant of Judah confess the righteousness of the Lord in permitting their afflictions, though they are filled with sorrow as they behold the sad results. They acknowledge their own sinfulness and extol the holiness of God, while calling for judgment upon the instrument of His wrath.

In the opening verses the ruined city, where once Jehovah had set His name, is contemplated with broken heart and tearful eye. "How doth the city sit solitary, that was full of people!" exclaims the prophet; "How is she become as a widow! She that was great among the nations, and princess among the provinces, how is she become tributary!" (ver. 1). To a faithful Israelite it was indeed a sorrowful spectacle. What joy and gladness had once filled that now deserted city, in the happy, festive days when the law of the land was honored and His name exalted! How dreadful the change—the awful result of departure from God, manifested in pride, self-will, and idolatry! How could Jerusalem remain the acknowledged wife of Jehovah, when so faithless and wanton? Alas, she is left to sit in solitude in her widow's weeds until the day when God shall grant repentance.

"She weepeth sore in the night, and her tears are on her cheeks: among all her lovers she hath none to comfort her: all her friends have dealt treacherously with her, they are become her enemies" (ver. 2). The false gods in whom she trusted when she proved recreant to the covenant of Jehovah are unable to mitigate in any way her present sorrows. The powers upon which she sought to lean when she forsook the Word of her God, are all indifferent to her present plight. He, the "eternal Lover" whom she has despised, is the only One who loves her still.

Yet He had given her into the hand of her enemies, and had apparently hidden His face from her. "Judah is gone into captivity because of affliction, and because of great servitude: she dwelleth among the heathen, she findeth no rest: all her persecutors overtook her between the straits" (ver. 3). In this Judah becomes a warning beacon for saints of all time. Failing to maintain the place of separation to which God had called her, mingling promiscuously among her heathen neighbors, she soon proved, as all do who follow her steps, that "evil communications corrupt good manners." Walking with idolators, she learned their ways; and as a result God gave her up to wander among the nations until she sickened of their practices. Has not this been the repeated history of every company which God separated from the world and owned as His people? How soon the apostolic Church corrupted itself. The dense darkness of the Middle Ages was the governmental recompense. In even shorter time did the movement begun in the glorious Reformation of the sixteenth century become vitiated by conformity to the world; so that one has well asked, "Where is the Church?" and replied, "In the world!" Again, "Where is the world?" and answered, "In the Church."

From this mixed multitude, at various times, God has been pleased to separate little remnant companies to Himself; only to become, in their turn, enamored of the world they once professed to forsake. Has it been otherwise with those, enlightened above many, who in these last days were called out from human systems to be a testi-

mony to the unity and heavenly calling of the
Church? Alas, my brethren, "how are the mighty
fallen!" How unspeakably sad has been the
checkered history of that movement which began
so auspiciously, and once promised so much!
Worldliness, like a canker, is eating out the very
life. Pride, haughtiness and self-sufficiency are
everywhere apparent. In judgment God has sent
division following division until we are like to
be utterly destroyed; and yet how much preten-
sion; how little brokenness before Him; how
many indifferent hearts and calloused consciences!

Shall it be said of us as of Judah in the past,
"The ways of Zion do mourn, because none come
to the solemn feasts: all her gates are desolate:
her priests sigh, her virgins are afflicted, and she
is in bitterness. Her adversaries are the chief,
her enemies prosper; for the Lord hath afflicted
her for the multitude of her transgressions: her
children are gone into captivity before the enemy.
And from the daughter of Zion all her beauty
is departed: her princes are become like harts
that find no pasture, and they are gone without
strength before the pursuer" (vers. 4-6). Nor is
it possible to avoid so sad a result by "daubing
with untempered mortar," seeking to heal divisions by glossing over the evils that led to them,
and thus failing to hear the voice of God in them.
One course, and one alone, would have saved
Judah. That was genuine self-judgment and
brokenness of spirit before the Lord, causing
the people to "tremble at His Word." This is
what is needed everywhere to-day. It is not so

much looking for and learning new truth that will bless and deliver the saints of God, as testing our ways by the truth already committed to us, and seeking to walk in the reality of it. Because of failure so to do, Judah went into captivity, a Christian Church lost her candlestick of testimony, and the world was allowed to prevail against the people of the Lord.

Sad indeed it is to have to look back to blessings, once delighted in, when all is but a memory. "Jerusalem remembered in the days of her affliction and of her miseries all her pleasant things that she had in the days of old, when her people fell into the hand of the enemy, and none did help her: the adversaries saw her, and did mock at her sabbaths (or, her desolations, R. V., ver. 7)." A quiet like the rest of the sabbath lay over all the city, but it was the quiet of desolation and death. There was no longer anything to hinder her rest. The work of the Lord had often been a burden. She was delivered from it all now; but at how frightful a cost! Set aside as "a vessel wherein is no pleasure," Jerusalem was left in undisturbed repose.

Touchingly the prophet acknowledges the justice of all this in the four verses that follow (vers. 8-11). Jerusalem had grievously sinned. It is because of this that she "is removed," or "has become as an unclean thing," unfit to be used of God any more. Because of this, those who once honored, now despise her. Her nakedness had been openly manifested. Her filthiness is apparent to all. She forgot her latter end—forgot God's purpose in delivering her from Egyptian bondage." "Therefore is she come down wonderfully," until she has no comforter." Yet, in her season of dire shame and distress, there are some faithful hearts left to cry, "O Lord, behold my affliction, for the enemy hath magnified himself." Her adversary had triumphed over her, even defiling her sanctuary; the charge of which had been committed to Judah when they were commanded that no uncircumcised should enter into the congregation of the Lord. Having failed to guard her precious things, they were given up to the unclean of the nations. It is ever thus. If God's people do not value what He entrusts them with, He will teach them its worth by taking it from them, even to making it the sport of their enemies.

Left without bread, sighing for food to refresh the soul, the remnant cry, "See, O Lord, and consider; for I am become vile." These are precious and needful exercises. Would that they had characterized them in days of grace now gone by! Ah, brethren, may the spirit of humiliation and confession before God be found in us also. The Holy Spirit will associate Himself with this, and still comfort and bless such.

The Spirit of Christ speaks loudly through Jeremiah and the remnant of Judah in the next few verses. Primarily, the words refer unquestionably to what we have had under consideration, the chastisement meted out to the inhabitants of Jerusalem and the land. The query, "Is it nothing to you?" is addressed to the nations who had no sympathy for, but rather gloried over them in their deep anguish. But as all Scripture points to Christ, one must be blind indeed not to see here the suffering Saviour entering to the full into the griefs of the spared company, left like grape-gleanings in the vineyard.

What a pathetic interest attaches itself to every word as we thus look at them. "Is it nothing to you, all ye that pass by? Behold, and see if there be any sorrow like unto My sorrow, which is done unto Me, wherewith the Lord hath afflicted Me in the day of His fierce anger" (ver. 12). The sins of Judah drew down that fierce anger upon their heads. It was the just recompense for their departure from the Lord. But when He, the holy Sufferer of Calvary, bowed His head beneath the overwhelming flood of God's wrath, it was for sins not His own; but He who knew no sin was made sin for us, that we might become the righteousness of God in Him. He was incomparably "the Man of Sorrows," having full acquaintance with grief, that our joy might be full, as we enter into fellowship with the God we had so terribly offended.

Can it be that any one reading these lines would reply to the heart rending question of the dying Lamb, and honestly confess, "It is nothing, all nothing to *me?*" Nothing to you that He was wounded for our transgressions and bruised for our iniquities! Nothing to you that God manifest in flesh so gave Himself to save guilty rebels against His outraged majesty! Nothing to you that the dreaded cup of wrath was pressed to His parched lips in order that the cup of salvation might be offered to you! *Can* it really be that it is *nothing* to you?

Alas! there was a day when it was so with us all: when, even though our emotions might be stirred as we heard or read the story of the Cross, yet, so far as apprehending that it was to meet the need of our sinful souls, it was all nothing to us. How well has the saintly McCheyne expressed what many more could say:

> "I oft read with pleasure, to soothe or engage,
> Isaiah's wild measure, or John's simple page:
> But e'en when they pictured the blood-sprinkled tree,
> Jehovah Tsidkenu was nothing to me.

> "Like tears from the daughters of Zion that roll,
> I wept when the waters went over His soul;
> Yet thought not that *my sins* had nailed to the tree
> Jehovah Tsidkenu: 'twas nothing to me."

And this might be our condition still—if not yet in the pit of the lost, forever beyond the reach of mercy—had it not been for the sovereign grace of God that led Him by His Spirit to show us our needy, lost estate, and to cause us to flee to Him (so long and coldly neglected) for mercy and pardon.

Thus we can join with the same poet-preacher and sing:

> "When free grace awoke me by light from on high,
> Then legal fears shook me—I trembled to die.
> No refuge, no safety in self could I see;
> Jehovah Tsidkenu my Saviour must be.

> "My terrors all vanished before that sweet name;
> My guilty fears banished, with boldness I came,
> To drink at the fountain, life-giving and free;
> Jehovah Tsidkenu *is all things to me*."

In the joy of assured redemption we can look up into His face, once marred more than any man's, and cry from full hearts, "Yea, Lord, it *is* something, it is everything to me, that Thou didst so suffer and die!" And our souls are filled with holy awe as we turn aside to see this great sight, and hear Him cry, "From above hath He sent fire into My bones, and it prevaileth against them. He hath spread a net for My feet, He hath turned Me back: He hath made Me desolate and faint all the day" (ver. 13).

But we rejoice to know that nevermore shall He suffer thus. His sorrows and pains are now forever past; and with gladness unutterable "He shall see of the travail of His soul, and shall be satisfied" (Isa. 53: 11). How expressive is the use of that word "travail" in this connection! Two women were once overheard speaking of their sons. The one had adopted a boy from an orphan-house ; the other was the mother of a child by birth. "I am sure," said the first, "my love for my child is as deep as though he had actually been born into the family. I do not believe I could love him more than I do." "Ah," replied the other, "you do not really know mother-love yet. You never *suffered* for your son as I did for mine!"

O beloved, how *He* has suffered for us! What pangs He endured! What tears He shed! What drops of blood He sweat! How dreadful the travail He had to experience in order that we might be eternally saved! "Fire from above" descended upon Him that we might find a refuge where the fire has been, and thus be forever safe from the eternal fire to come for all who spurn His matchless grace. Precious and holy theme for devout meditation!

Not in the same sense could the next two verses be applied to the Lord Jesus. It involves the consciousness of guilt, and He was the guiltless One; but the words were most fitting in the mouth of the people of Judah. They confess that the yoke of their transgressions is bound by His hand. Like a wreath they are twined about the neck. Because of this, their strength failed, and they were unable to deliver themselves out of their enemies' hands. The Lord Himself it was who had destroyed their mighty men and summoned the Chaldeans for their ruin. As grapes are trodden in a wine-press, so had He cast the daughter of Judah into the press of His wrath because of her manifold transgressions (vers. 14, 15).

On account of these things the prophet weeps, as he had wept, before they came to pass, in foretelling them. There is no comforter; for Judah's children are desolate. Zion spreadeth forth her hands, but there is no helper, nor any to sympathize. She is as a separated, unclean woman, because of the Lord's anger (vers. 16, 17).

In verse 18 there is the unreserved acknowledgment, "The Lord is righteous; for I have rebelled against His commandments." This is an evidence of true godly exercise. They received but the due reward of their deeds; and they own it in contrition of heart and abasement of soul. They had been deceived by other lovers (ver. 19), and were left in great distress; but they humbly confess, "I have grievously rebelled." This is what makes it all so bitter: they realize they deserve all that they have been called upon to endure.

Their enemies had heard of their sighs. They rejoiced in their affliction, glad that the Lord had so dealt with them. Their time of woe was coming. God should bring the appointed day when they too should know His indignation because of their sins (ver. 21). So the prayer goes up that the time may be hastened when all their wretchedness shall come before Him and He will do as He has said (ver. 22). It is a cry for vengeance not consistent with Christian light and privilege and the grace of this dispensation, but thoroughly in keeping with the character of Jewish blessing. Their deliverance being an earthly one, it therefore requires the judgment of their oppressors.

In a certain sense these last two verses might also be looked upon as setting forth the doom of those who refuse to own the Lordship of Jesus. He too could say of such, "Thou wilt bring the day that Thou hast called, and they shall be like unto Me." Despising His sufferings, men who reject His grace must know for themselves the awful power of divine wrath.

CHAPTER XXVIII

THE DAY OF THE LORD'S ANGER

(Lam. 2.)

It is the city of Jerusalem in a very particular sense that is under contemplation in this chapter. That city, once famed as the dwelling-place of the great King, was now a waste of blackened ruins. Throughout, it is recognized that not an enemy from the outside acting of his own volition, but the Lord Himself, who had so long dwelt in the midst of the city, had devoted it to destruction.

This the very first verse brings out. "How hath the Lord covered the daughter of Zion with a cloud in His anger, and cast down from heaven unto the earth the beauty of Israel, and remembered not His footstool in the day of His anger!" It was sorrowful to contemplate that the city once called "the holy" should have become so vile and apostate that Jehovah could no longer endure it. It is noticeable, however, that the beauty of Israel is "cast down from heaven to earth;" not "to hell" (sheol, or hades, the place of the dead), as in the case of privileged Capernaum (Matt. 11: 23). There, the Lord Jesus had done many mighty works, and given a testimony beyond anything enjoyed by Jerusalem of old. But He and His words had been utterly rejected. Therefore Capernaum, "exalted to heaven," should be "brought down to hell." Its day was over forever. Not so was it with Jerusalem. "Cast down to earth," treated like a city of the nations; yea, trodden down of the Gentiles; still it is destined yet to occupy a place of glory such as it never knew in the past. It must be disciplined by adversity, but was not forsaken in perpetuity. In His indignation against idolatry, the Lord had "swallowed up all the habitation of Jacob," not pitying, because of the hardness of their hearts. He had "thrown down in His wrath the strongholds of the daughter of Judah," bringing them down to the ground and polluting the kingdom and princes. It was all because of sin. He loved them truly, but could not permit them to go in peace while in so dreadful a moral state. Therefore had He, "in His fierce anger," cut off the horn of Israel, and caused their right arms to fail before the enemy (vers. 2, 3).

Three times in verses 4 and 5 He is said to have acted as though He were their enemy. First, we read, "He hath bent His bow *like* an enemy." Second, "He stood with His right hand *as* an adversary;" and, third, "The Lord was *as* an enemy." But it is well to notice the qualifying expressions "like" and "as." An *enemy* He never was; though their conduct compelled Him to act as if He were. How many a Christian has had to know Him in a similar way! How often has He seemed to become an enemy! But faith looks beyond all that the eye can see, and knows that He is unchanged in His love and tenderness. It is sin in His children that has broken in on the fellowship He delights to have them enjoy. He is "of purer eyes than to behold iniquity;" and while He will never give up one of His redeemed, He will not countenance looseness of walk and an unbridled tongue in any, simply because He has saved them. In fact, it is just the contrary, for "whom the Lord *loveth* He chasteneth, and scourgeth every son whom He receiveth." This was the lesson the remnant of Judah had to learn; bitter as it must have been.

In verse 6, "tabernacle" should be as in the margin, "hedge." By turning to Ps. 80, we find the same metaphor employed. Israel is likened to vine brought out of Egypt and planted in a land from which the heathen had been cast out. Hedged in and tended by the divine Husbandman, it should have borne fruit for Himself, but we know His verdict (Isa. 5: 1-7): "It brought forth wild grapes." Because of this He allows it to be overrun by the heathen, as we read in Ps. 80: 12-16, "Why hast Thou broken down our hedges, so that all they which pass by the way do pluck her? The boar out of the wood doth waste it, and the wild beast of the field doth devour it. Return, we beseech Thee, O God of hosts: look down from heaven, and behold, and visit this vine; and the vineyard which Thy right hand hath planted, and the branch which Thou madest strong for Thyself. It is burned with fire, it is cut down; they perish at the rebuke of Thy countenance." It is the same thought that we have expressed here: the enclosure which in the past had separated the garden of the Lord from the Gentiles around was broken down by the Lord Himself, and "the places of the assembly" destroyed, so that the solemn feasts and sabbaths had been caused to cease in Zion.

His altar He had cast off, and abhorred His sanctuary; permitting the unclean to pollute it, because of the unfaithfulness of His people. The walls of the city, with the gates and bars, were leveled to the ground; the king and princes were captive among the Gentiles; the very law (so long despised) was no more; and the prophets (to whom the deaf ear had been turned for years) had no vision from the Lord. Zion's elders were girded in sackcloth, and sat upon the ground with dust upon their heads in speechless grief as they beheld the desolations on every hand (vers. 7-10). It was complete and overwhelming ruin, brought about by Jehovah because they had neglected His Word and followed in the ways of the heathen.

In deep-toned notes of woe Jeremiah cries: "Mine eyes do fail with tears, my bowels are troubled, my liver is poured upon the earth, for the destruction of the daughter of my people; because the children and the sucklings swoon in the streets of the city. They say to their mothers, Where is corn and wine? when they swooned as the wounded in the streets of the city, when their soul was poured out into their mothers' bosom" (vers. 11, 12). Only in fellowship with God do His people find peace and plenty. Away from Him unrest and famine must result. Is not this the reason why there are so many swooning babes and fainting children among the assemblies of God's saints to-day? Surely it is time to consider our ways and turn again to the Lord. Something is radically wrong when the gathering of believers is not a nursery where babes in Christ receive needed nourishment, and help for their upbuilding and establishment in the things of God. When it is otherwise, it augurs a fallen state and testimony.

Zion had been overwhelmed as by the waves of the sea, so that there was no healing of her breach, humanly speaking (ver. 13). Her prophets had seen vain and foolish things for her (as in the case of Hananiah, recorded in chap. 28), prophesying smooth things, but not discovering her iniquity. True peace there could not be with unjudged sin upon her (ver. 14). Thus Jerusalem had become the sport of the passer-by, who scornfully asked, "Is this the city that men call The perfection of beauty, the joy of the whole earth?" (ver. 15). Both these titles are found applied to it in the Psalms: the former in Ps. 50:2; the latter in Ps. 48:2.

Her enemies exulted in her ruin, and gloried in having "swallowed her up." This they had long desired, and now attributed it to their own prowess, not knowing of the Lord's controversy with her (ver. 16). It was not the might of their arms that had caused them to triumph over her. Her offended Lord had but done that which He had devised, and fulfilled His Word given in the days of Moses (ver. 17). To Him, therefore, the remnant turns, crying out in the bitterness of their souls and giving themselves no rest day nor night, but incessantly lifting up their hands toward Him for the life of their fainting children (vers. 18, 19). This was as it should be, and argued a returning in heart to their God. The last three verses (20-22) form a prayer, and set forth their pitiable condition "in the day of the Lord's anger." He had said, "Call upon Me in the day of trouble: I will deliver thee, and thou shalt glorify Me." To Him, therefore, they turn, bewailing their wretchedness, the result of their own evil ways, and beseeching His favor. They shall yet prove that His ear is not dull of hearing, neither is His eye blinded to their misery.

CHAPTER XXIX

"LET US SEARCH AND TRY OUR WAYS"

(Lam. 3.)

In the sixty-six verses of this chapter, arranged in a triple alphabetic acrostic, as before mentioned, Jeremiah speaks for the remnant, describing his and their affliction, but manifesting unfailing faith in the goodness of God and calling upon all to search and try their ways and return to Him. Bearing upon his own heart the bitter woes of his people, as did the Lord Jesus, he recites his sorrows in a way that plainly indicates the utterance of the Spirit of Christ, who, as remarked in our introduction to Chap. I., was afflicted in all their griefs, passing through all in spirit with them. Jeremiah here may almost be looked upon as a type of that Blessed One; for to him also, as to no other prophet, could the title be applied, "A man of sorrows."

"I am the man," he says, "that hath seen affliction by the rod of His wrath" (ver. 1). And he goes on to tell how he has been brought into darkness, but not into light: how God is turned against him, His hand being upon him in judgment every day. Under the weight of the divine displeasure, vigor and elasticity departed, and his bones were as broken (vers. 2-4). It is the expression of one who, himself well-pleasing to God, entered to the full into the sorrows of his people.

Verses 5 to 17 continue his wail in view of the dire calamities which had fallen upon them. Compassed with gall and travail, set in dark places as in the tombs of the dead, hedged about and weighted with a heavy chain, he cried and shouted, only to feel that God shut out his prayer. Nothing could be more mournful than the gloomy estate thus pictured to the mind's eye. The Lord had apparently forgotten, or was even become as an enemy. He had enclosed the ways of His servant, made his paths crooked, and been unto him as a bear or a lion waiting to take the prey. Made desolate and set as a mark for the arrow, Jehovah caused the darts of His quiver to enter into His servant's reins.

Thus had he become a derision to all his people and their song all the day. In this how like Him who became the song of the drunkards! (Ps. 69:12). Filled with bitterness and drunken with wormwood, his teeth were as broken with gravelstones, and he himself rolled in ashes. His soul was removed far off from peace, so that prosperity had been forgotten. It is a doleful recital of a man entering into the sense of God's displeasure because of sin.

But, though fallen, he was not completely cast down. True he said, "My strength and my hope is perished from the Lord" (ver. 18). Yet, as he remembered the wormwood and the gall, his soul was humbled within him, and he could say, "This I recall to my mind; therefore have I hope" (vers. 19-21).

Accordingly, an entirely different note is struck in ver. 22, and an exalted strain of joyous confidence is sustained down to ver. 36. In place of complaining that his woes were greater than he had deserved, he justifies God, and gratefully acknowledges that justice has been tempered with grace. "It is of the Lord's mercies," he owns, "that we are not consumed, because His compassions fail not. They are new every morning: great is Thy faithfulness" (vers. 22, 23). How precious the faith that, at such a time, could so speak! And what tried saint can truthfully say otherwise? Only when the soul is out of the presence of God does it seem as if His chastisements were too severe, and in part undeserved. No self-judged believer ever yet failed to own that he was far from receiving the full reward of his deeds. Rather, it seems as though God's grace leads Him to overlook even serious failure, and to correct but in part. "His compassions fail not." The rod is never directed by a cold, indifferent heart. He feels as no other can for the people of His choice, the children He loves. Every morning witnesses fresh evidences of His loving-kindness.

In contemplation of these precious truths the inspired seer can declare, "The Lord is my portion, saith my soul ; therefore will I hope in Him" (ver. 24). All else might fail, but He will abide. It is the confidence of Habakkuk (Hab. 3: 17, 18), and the abiding contentment of Paul (Phil. 4: 11). Thus is one enabled to rejoice *in the Lord,* even when no other source of joy is left. He becomes the soul's portion, as in Ps. 16: 5, where we read, "The Lord is the portion of my inheritance, and *my cup.*" Little wonder that Ps.

23 : 5 asserts, "My cup runneth over." How could it be otherwise, when He it is who fills it?

"The Lord is good *unto them that wait for Him,* to the soul that seeketh Him. It is good that a man should both hope and quietly wait for the salvation of the Lord" (vers. 25, 26). The reason the truths here taught are so little entered into is simply because waiting upon God is largely a "lost art" among Christians nowadays. The rush and hurry of the age; "the lust of other things;" in a word, the worldliness so characteristic of the present momentous period in the Church's history, effectually shuts out all inclination to wait upon God, it is to be feared, for a large number of those who confess the name of Jesus as Saviour and Lord. Consequently, little or nothing is known, in a practical way, of His goodness in meeting felt need, and of His ability to satisfy the soul that seeks His face.

It is perhaps needless to say that when Jeremiah wrote, "It is good that a man both hope and quietly wait for the salvation of the Lord," he was not referring to soul-salvation, but to deliverance from the troubles and perplexities of the way. Nowhere in Scripture is the eternal salvation of the soul put before us as something to be waited for in patience and quietness. Again and again the contrary is distinctly stated. The prophet is not speaking of salvation in that sense. For light as to the salvation of the soul, we turn to the New Testament, especially the Gospel of John and the epistles of Paul, John, and Peter. These two aspects of salvation must be clearly distinguished. The Lord has nowhere promised immediate relief from sorrow and suffering. When in His righteous government He permits His people to be the subjects of affliction, it is well that they at once seek His face, and wait upon Him. It may not be His will to extract every thorn in the flesh; but if not, He will give to the waiting soul grace to endure, and that with joyfulness.

There is a "ministry of suffering" which all believers have to learn in a greater or lesser degree. "It is good for a man," we are told, "to bear the yoke in his youth" (ver. 27). The result, if he is before God about it, will be to sober and humble him, and thus work out ultimate blessing. He may be called upon to sit alone and keep silence, to put his mouth in the dust, and, like his Saviour, to give his cheek to the smiters, but he can be assured of this: "The Lord will not cast off forever" (vers. 28-31).

As in Judah's case, God may cause grief—deep and heartrending; but He will still "have compassion according to the multitude of His mercies. For He doth not afflict willingly (or, from His heart), nor grieve the children of men" (vers. 32, 33). Not for His own pleasure does He chasten, but that we may be partakers of His holiness. He is too loving to lay upon us one unnecessary burden: He is too holy to omit one needed stroke. Unrighteousness He cannot tolerate. "To crush under His feet all the princes of the earth, to turn aside the right of a man before the face of the Most High, to subvert a man in His cause, the Lord approveth not" (vers. 34-36). All His ways are equal. It is only man's defective vision that makes it appear otherwise. When at last He takes us by the hand, and goes over all the path with us, letting the light of His own glory shine upon every step, we shall understand, as we cannot now, how just and true were all His ways as He led us through this scene.

Nothing can by any means assail His people apart from His permission, for "Who is he that saith, and it cometh to pass, when the Lord approveth not?" (ver. 37). It is a simple and elementary principle, yet which many are long years in comprehending. Once let it be clear before the soul that God is immediately concerned in every detail of life, and one is delivered from being engrossed with the instrumentalities acting. This comes out strikingly in the case of David when cursed by Shimei. He will not permit the ardent Abishai to touch the offender, for he realizes that "the Lord hath said unto him, Curse David," and he can therefore leave all in His hands, trusting that He will change the curse into a blessing. Job too, in the early period of his testing, is a fine example of submission to the will of God; and, refusing to consider second causes, "Shall we receive good at the hand of the Lord," he asks, "and shall we not also receive evil?" It is blessedly true, and most comforting to the soul to know, that, "Out of the mouth of the Most High proceedeth not evil and good" (ver. 38); but, on the other hand, He allows evil for our chastening; even, as in the case just cited, using Satan as an instrument to accomplish His gracious purposes.

In view of His holy and righteous government, "Wherefore doth a living man complain—a man, for the punishment of his sins?" Surely it is far more becoming to say from the heart, "Let us search and try our ways, and turn again to the Lord" (vers. 39, 40). This indicates that the discipline is having its desired effect. "No chastening for the present seemeth to be joyous, but grievous: nevertheless, *afterward* it yieldeth the peaceable fruit of righteousness (not necessarily in the case of every saint, but) unto *them which are exercised thereby"* (Heb. 12:11). It is this godly exercise that is so sadly lacking. Afflictions come, and souls faint under them; or else they are despised, and a stoical, self-confident air is assumed, that ill befits the state of one under God's hand. With most of us, it is to be feared, the first object is to get out of the place of discipline in any way that we can, apart from that breaking down before God which leads to the searching and trying of our ways. It was here that Judah so lamentably failed. When God sent the king of Babylon against them because of their sins, they turned to the king of Egypt for help, and that in plain defiance of the word of the Lord. But they had to learn in a practical way the bitterness of departure from God.

Thus, humbled in His presence, every false hope gone, the remnant search and try their ways, and the end of the Lord is reached. In brokenness of spirit they cry, "Let us lift up our heart with our hands unto God in the heavens. We have transgressed and have rebelled: Thou hast not pardoned. Thou hast covered with anger, and persecuted us: Thou hast slain, Thou hast not pitied. Thou hast covered Thyself with a cloud, that our prayer should not pass through" (vers. 41-44). There is an important lesson here. It is useless to pray while persisting in sin. The man who does not seek to walk with God has no right to expect anything from Him. "Delight thyself also in the Lord; and He shall give thee the desires of thy heart." "If ye abide in Me, and My words abide in you, ye shall ask what ye will, and it shall be done unto you" (Ps. 37: 4; John 15: 7). This is the key to answered prayer. Obedience gives confidence. It is impossible to ask in faith when clinging to something that is grieving the Holy Spirit and dishonoring the Lord Jesus Christ. If prayer is not answered, if the heavens seem as brass, it is a solemn indication of a wrong state of soul, and should lead to self-judgment and the forsaking of every evil way.

Because of the lack of this, Judah was brought very low. They were made "as the offscouring and refuse in the midst of the people, so that their enemies rejoiced over them. Fear and a snare had come upon them. Desolation and destruction were their portion" (vers. 45-47).

Hard indeed must have been the heart that could contemplate their sorrows without being deeply touched. Jeremiah says, "Mine eye runneth down with rivers of water for the destruction of the daughter of my people. Mine eye trickleth down, and ceaseth not, without any intermission, till the Lord look down, and behold from heaven. Mine eye affecteth my heart, because of all the daughters of my city" (vers. 48-

51). It was the manly grief of one who was not
ashamed of tears when his people were under the
chastening hand of the Lord. Censurable indeed
would insensibility to it all have been.

Identifying himself with the erring ones, he
continues to plead their cause, and invokes a recompense upon their persecutors. He was like a
bird chased by the hunters without cause. He
does not in this ignore the righteousness of God
in visiting His people with judgment. On that
side there was cause enough. But Babylon's oppression of Judah was quite unwarrantable from
the standpoint of human equity. Her wars were
dictated by the greed of dominion and the lust of
power. It often occurs that God permits sorrows to come upon His own by way of discipline,
which, so far as the actual troubles are concerned,
were not really deserved. For instance, a saint
may be falsely accused, and thereby caused ex-
treme mental grief, while all the time he frets
under the knowledge that he is guiltless of the
cruel charge, and feels that he is wickedly treated. But this, when rightly viewed, would be seen
to be but an opportunity to be a partaker of
Christ's sufferings. For was not He hated "without a cause," and did not false witnesses rise
up against Him? Such circumstances, therefore,
painful as they are to flesh and blood, are often
a necessary part of the education of the soul.
And if, at the time, we are conscious of having
failed in personal dealings with God, it is used
as chastisement, that we may be partakers of His
holiness.

As one cast into a pit and left to die, the remnant call upon Jehovah "out of the low dungeon," and faith can say, "Thou hast heard my voice," and "Thou drewest near in the day that I called upon Thee: Thou saidst, Fear not" (vers. 52-57). How comforting this is! God is quick to respond to the first cry of a troubled soul when there is integrity of heart before Him.

So the following verses celebrate His response in the hour of need. He has pleaded the cause of the soul of His afflicted one. He has redeemed his life. His eye has been upon all the wrong, and with confidence He is implored to judge the matter (vers. 58, 59). Into His sympathetic ear the story of the enemy's heartlessness is told out, and to Him the whole case is committed. Recompense upon the oppressor is also invoked, which, as we have already seen, is not the spirit of the Christian dispensation, but of the law, where the principle of "an eye for an eye" prevailed (vers. 60-66). To us who live in this dispensation of grace, our Lord's instruction is to "pray for them that despitefully use us and persecute us," even as He, the Lord of all, could pray, "Father, forgive them; for they know not what they do."

Grace is reigning; and having been taken up in grace we are responsible to manifest that same grace to others. But what we have here was quite in keeping with the dispensation of law, and will yet be suited language in the lips of another remnant, in "the time of Jacob's trouble," whose earthly deliverance can only be through judgment upon their enemies.

CHAPTER XXX

THE FINE GOLD BECOME DIM

(Lam. 4.)

Of a deeply spiritual character is the grief expressed in the lament of the fourth chapter. It is not now the temporal sorrows of the people of Judah and Jerusalem that occupy the prophet's mind, but their unhappy estate as away from God and no longer a testimony for Him in the earth. The past and the present stand out in vivid contrast. In days gone by, what grace has been manifested in them! Now, alas, how utterly fallen have they become!

"How is the gold become dim! How is the most fine gold changed! The stones of the sanctuary are poured out in the top of every street. The precious sons of Zion, comparable to fine gold, how are they esteemed as earthen pitchers, the work of the hands of the potter!" (vers. 1, 2). Failure has characterized every dispensation since Eve reached forth her hand and took of that which God had forbidden. "Man being in honor, abideth not, but is as the beasts that perish." Every fresh trial vouchsafed by God to man has but given occasion for the further manifestation of the incurable evil of his heart. Under conscience, from Adam to Noah, corruption and violence filled the earth. Under government, from Noah to Abraham, he forsook the true Governor of the universe; and not liking to retain God in his knowledge, worshiped and served the creature more than the Creator. Under promise and law, from Abraham to Christ, he violated every precept and broke every pledge; and at last, his awful course of wilfulness and rebellion culminated in the crucifixion of the Prince of Life. Under grace, the present dispensation of the Holy Spirit, he has turned that very grace into lasciviousness, and corrupted every truth committed to the Church.

If the long period from Abraham to Christ be subdivided into the numerous sections into which it readily falls, then each of them becomes a witness to the same sad failure. The days of the patriarchs witnessed the treachery of the sons of Jacob, and the resultant descent into Egypt. The wilderness was a forty years' record of God's faithfulness and man's unreliability. The days of the Judges but confirmed the same story; while the history of the kingdoms of Judah and Israel emphasized still more the deceitfulness of the human heart. From time to time God wrought in power and grace, giving revival and blessing; but soon the people wearied of His law, and gave themselves up to doing their own pleasure, "till there was no remedy," and Assyria and Babylon swallowed up the favored people.

"Whatsoever things were written aforetime were written for our admonition." Israel's history has often been duplicated by that of the professing Church; for "as in water face answereth to face, so the heart of man to man." Only, in Christendom, the corruption has been even more detestable and the departure from God even more glaring. He, blessed be His name, has never left Himself without witness; and, as in the past dispensation, so in this, has ever and anon worked in power bringing about special awakenings, thus rousing those who were sleeping among the dead to renewed activity and true-hearted judgment of what they saw His Word condemned. But how soon the manifested energy of the Spirit declines, because of a settling back into the old ways, or worse ones, of the next generation. What is predicted of Israel in Josh. 24:13 has had its counterpart again and again down through the centuries since the ascension of the Lord Jesus and the descent of the Holy Spirit. "And Israel served the Lord all the days of Joshua, and all the days of the elders that outlived Joshua, and which had known all the works of the Lord that He had done for Israel." But the generations following soon relapse into formality and worldliness. The fine gold soon becomes dim, and the freshness of early days passes away. Yet it need not be so. If careful to maintain a good conscience before God; if watchful as to the first beginnings of departure from the place of communion; above all, if prayerful and dependent, the dew of youth need never be lost: or, if so, it will be but to give place to the more mature grace of a Spirit-filled old age. This is equally true of movements as of individuals; only the difficulty there is greater, because movements are composed of individuals, and only by each unit going on with God can the mass do so.

In Judah's case it had, as has been made solemnly patent, become far otherwise. "The precious sons of Zion, comparable to fine gold," were esteemed as earthen pottery. The glory had departed. There was no power to nourish the young. "The daughter of my people," complains Jeremiah, "is become cruel like the ostriches in the wilderness," who leave their offspring to shift for themselves. In vain the children cried for bread; no man gave to them; while the tongue of the babe cleaved to the roof of its mouth for thirst (vers. 3, 4). Unspeakably sad is the state of God's people when their assemblies are not like nurseries where new-born babes and young saints can find nourishing food such as is suitable for them. It is to be feared the needs of the lambs are often forgotten; and, alas, oftener still there is nought to feed them with because all is parched and dry. If older saints are living for the world, it is small wonder that the babes languish and succumb at last to the withering influences about them, so far as their joy and testimony are concerned.

Because of their own famished condition, the mothers of Judah could not nourish their children. "They that did feed delicately are desolate in the streets; they that were brought up in scarlet embrace dunghills" (ver. 5) ; so that their punishment seemed to be even greater than that of Sodom, which was overthrown in a moment, while with Judah the agony was long continued.

"Her Nazarites were purer than snow, they were whiter than milk, they were more ruddy in body than rubies, their polishing was of sapphire; their visage is blacker than a coal; they are not known in the streets: their skin cleaveth to their bones; it is withered, it is become like a stick" (vers. 7, 8). In order to understand what the prophet refers to in these verses, it is necessary that one be somewhat familiar with the law of the Nazarite as given in Numbers, chap. 6. To many of our readers this edifying portion of Scripture is familiar; but as it may not be so to some of them, it may be profitable to turn aside for a little to consider what is there set forth.

The Nazarite, as his name implies (from a root, meaning *to separate*), was one who was in a special sense separated to the Lord his God. All Israel were redeemed to be the people of God; but all were not Nazarites. *All* Christians, however, as Nazarites, are called unreservedly to devote themselves to the Lord. It is to every saved one that the apostle addresses himself when he writes, "I beseech you therefore, brethren, by the mercies of God, that ye present your bodies a living sacrifice, holy, acceptable unto God, which is your reasonable (or, intelligent) service. And be not conformed to this world: but be ye transformed by the renewing of your mind, that ye may prove what is that good, and acceptable, and perfect will of God" (Rom. 12:1, 2). It will be seen that actually this is far from being true of all believers, nor perhaps of any of them at all times. The Lord Jesus was the true Nazarite, separated to God from His lowly birth to His death of shame upon the tree. We are called undoubtedly to "follow His steps;" but it is sad indeed to realize how few maintain the Nazarite character.

There were three chief things in which the Nazarite of old was peculiar. (1) In Num. 6: 3, 4, it was written, "He shall separate himself from wine and strong drink." It is clearly specified that he was to partake of no product whatever of the vine tree, "from the kernels even to the husk."

(2) In ver. 5 we read, "All the days of the vow of his separation there shall come no razor upon his head." He was to let the locks of his hair grow long like those of a woman.

(3) Again, in ver. 6 we are told, "All the days that he separateth himself unto the Lord, he shall come at no dead body." It is particularly stated that he was not in this respect to make himself unclean even for his father, his mother, or any of his kin.

Each command has a distinct lesson in it. Wine, in Scripture, symbolizes joy (Judges 9:13; Ps. 104:15). The Nazarite must forego it. This world cannot minister to the joy of those who walk with God. Many Christians seem never to learn this. But such is the fact; and the sooner it is learned the better. The Nazarite is not without joy; but his are deeper, purer joys than this world's vines can offer. The wine of earth may stimulate and excite the fancy, thereby causing a thrill of pleasure for the moment; but it can never produce that deep-toned joy which characterizes the one who, like Enoch, walks with God. "The joy of the Lord is your strength" (Neh. 8:10), but it comes down from heaven. No plant of this sin-cursed scene produces it.

Secondly, the Nazarite allowed the hair of his

head to grow. According to 1 Cor. 11, long hair is the proper covering for the woman, telling of her place of subjection in the present order of things since the fall (Gen. 3:16; 1 Cor. 11:4-15). If the man has long hair, it is a shame unto him; but it is a glory to the woman, for "her hair is given her for a covering." The long hair speaks, then, of the place of dependence. In the Nazarite we see one who has voluntarily surrendered what man would call "his rights" and his independence in order to be wholly in subjection to God. The Lord Jesus is the great exemplar in this, as in all else, for He could say, "I came not to do Mine own will, but the will of Him that sent Me." This was the more remarkable in Him, as He was the only man who ever had title to do His own will: but He voluntarily surrendered that title; and humbling himself, became the dependent Man in the fullest sense. In the same way must the man of God lay aside his own thoughts and inclinations to make the will of the Lord supreme in his life.

Thirdly, the Nazarite was not to be defiled by the dead. So the believer who would devote himself to the Lord is called upon to walk apart from all the defiling influences of this scene. Hearing the word of Jesus, "Let the dead bury their dead, follow thou Me," it should be his to turn aside at once from everything that would grieve the Holy Spirit and dull his spiritual sensibilities, in order to be the Lord's alone. It is quite possible to be a Nazarite at times, and not at others. The balance of the chapter shows the solemn result of defilement. If brought into con-

tact with death, all the days of his separation
that went before would be lost, because his separation had become defiled (vers. 9-12). He could
only be restored to that place of special blessing
and privilege, as well as of responsibility, by
bringing the prescribed offerings, which set forth
the cross and the Holy One who hung there.

Not until the days of his separation were over,
was he to shave his head and be free to eat or
drink of the fruit of the vine. For the believer
this will only be when the wilderness journey is
over and the glory is entered. Then, with the
Lord who loved us, we shall drink the new wine
in the Father's kingdom, where pure joys, unsul-
lied by sin, shall be the portion of our hearts
forever.

Having before us the truth which the Spirit
of God would impart concerning the Nazarite,
we turn to the 7th and 8th verses of our chapter with a tender and sad interest. The past days
of devotion to God are contrasted with the awful
failure of their present condition. "Her Nazarites *were* purer than snow: . . . their visage *is*
blacker than a coal." How terrible the declension! Judah's godliest and goodliest sons, once
her proper pride, are now unknown in the streets,
so changed are they by famine and pestilence.
Their lot was even harder than that of those who
had been slain with the sword, for "these pine
away, stricken through for want of the fruits of
the field" (ver. 9). There is no hint of inten-
tional defilement on the part of the Nazarites;
but the dead were everywhere, and to escape becoming unclean thereby would have been impos-

sible: they share in the afflictions of the nation of which they form a part. In a still deeper sense is this true of those who, through the baptism of the Holy Spirit, are members of the Church, the Body of Christ. "If one member suffer, all the members suffer with it." The sin of Christendom is, in a way, our common sin; we are all in our measure accountable for its failure. It becomes us, therefore, not to spend our time pointing out for reprobation, or holding up to ridicule, the evils and follies into which our fellow-members may have fallen. Rather be it ours to confess our share in its sin and consequent ruin, and look to God for His mercy for revival and blessing.

In Jerusalem's distress, the fearful predictions made by Moses (Deut. 28: 56, 57; Lev. 26: 29) were again fulfilled, as they had been on several occasions in the past (2 Kings 6: 26-29). When "the hands of the pitiful women" could thus be stretched forth against their poor starved children, it is clear that the famine had done its worst (ver. 10). Therefore the next verse declares that "the Lord hath accomplished His fury; He hath poured out His fierce anger, and hath kindled a fire in Zion, and it hath devoured the foundations thereof. The kings of the earth, and all the inhabitants of the world, would not have believed that the adversary and the enemy could have entered into the gates of Jerusalem." But it was "because of the sins of her prophets, and the iniquities of her priests, who have shed the blood of the righteous in the midst of her" (vers. 11-13). In His righteous anger *God* had brought

Zion to the lowest depths, else, what could the nations have done against her?

It will be remembered that in Jer. 5:1 the Lord promised to pardon the city if even one person was found in it who executed judgment and sought the truth. One might wonder there were not to be found in Jerusalem a few righteous ones, as in a former day were found in Sodom; but, alas, they had all been slain or driven away by these ungodly priests and false prophets. A new translation, which we follow here, will make the following verses plainer: "It is for the sins of her prophets, and the iniquities of her priests, who have shed the blood of the righteous in the midst of her. They wandered about blind in the streets, they were polluted with blood, so that men could not touch their garments. They cried unto them, Depart, unclean! Depart, depart, touch not! When they fled away and wandered about, it was said among the nations, They shall no more sojourn there. The face of Jehovah hath divided them; He will no more regard them. They respected not the persons of the priests, they regarded not the aged" (vers. 13-16). The false prophets and false priests had put the just to death, or driven them into banishment. These faithful men "had trial of cruel mockings and scourgings, yea, moreover of bonds and imprisonment: they were stoned, they were sawn asunder, were tempted, were slain with the sword: they wandered about in sheepskins and goatskins; being destitute, afflicted, tormented; of whom the world was not worthy: they wandered in deserts, and in moun-

tains, and in dens and caves of the earth" (Heb.
11: 36-38). God's witnesses were despised and
hated by the very people to whom they sought
to minister. Isaiah, according to Jewish tradition, was sawn asunder. Elijah's life was sought
by Jezebel and Ahab; Obadiah had to hide the
prophets of the Lord in a cave; Amaziah endeav-
ored to intimidate Amos (Amos 7:12,13); Jeremiah was imprisoned on several occasions, and
would have been left to die in the pit but for
Ebed-melech; Baruch's life was declared forfeited. Thus, in a later day, Stephen could ask,
"Which of the prophets have not your fathers
persecuted? and they have slain them which
showed before the coming of the Just One, of
whom ye have been now the betrayers and mur-
derers" (Acts 7: 52). In rejecting those sent of
God they rejected the Sender: therefore the woes
that had come upon them.

Egypt is evidently referred to in ver. 17, as a
"nation that could not save us." To the last
Zedekiah and his ministers counted upon help
from Pharaoh, but in vain. God had said that
Egypt was a bruised reed, and so it proved to be.

The keen eye of the ever-present Babylonians
they could not escape. The steps of the men of
Judah were noted. They did not dare show themselves in the streets. Their persecutors were
"swifter than the eagles of the heaven:" on the
mountains and in the plains they pursued or laid
wait for them (vers. 18, 19). The king had been
captured, despite his effort to escape with a few
devoted retainers. "The breath of our nostrils,
the anointed of the Lord, was taken in their pits,

of whom we said, Under his shadow we shall live among the heathen (or, nations)" (ver. 20). Not till the true "Anointed of the Lord" comes, will there be a ruler under whose shadow His people can dwell in perfect security.

Edom had rejoiced in the day of Judah's calamity. The cup should soon pass to her. She must be made drunken and naked because of her exultation in the downfall of the city of God, and her manifold iniquities (ver. 21). The punishment of the daughter of Zion was accomplished. Restoration in place of captivity should soon be her portion, but Edom's judgment was just about to begin. "If the righteous scarcely be saved, where shall the ungodly and the sinner appear?"

CHAPTER XXXI

"THOU, O LORD, REMAINEST FOREVER!"

(Lam. 5.)

The detailed story of Judah's sufferings is spread out before the Lord in this last chapter, but the soul is stayed upon the fact that One remains, when all else is swept away. There is rest and confidence despite the wretched circumstances brought about by sin and waywardness. Everything has been gone over before God, and in Him the hearts of Jeremiah and of the few who are left of his people can find repose. He has not failed in all that He foretold as to the woes entailed by their wicked ways. He will not fail in carrying out His promises as to future deliverance and restoring mercy. The last few verses connect closely with the theme of chap. 3: 22-26.

The entire portion takes the form of a prayer, rather than a lamentation. "Remember, O Lord, what is come upon us: consider, and behold our reproach" (ver. 1). It is a great relief for the troubled heart to feel that there is One in heaven who observes every trial to which His children are subject, and that He has ordered all according to His infinite wisdom and love. There is rest in knowing that His eye is looking on, and that He is no unconcerned spectator.

Confidently, as knowing His deep interest in them still, though they have failed so grievously,

they enumerate the causes of their anguish and
reproach. "Our inheritance is turned to strangers, our houses to aliens" (ver. 2). The goodly
land, unappreciated, had passed under the dominion of the Gentiles. It was not that God delighted to have it so; but that His own might realize
the folly of departing from Him.

"We are orphans and fatherless, our mothers
are as widows" (ver. 3). This gave them special
title to the care of Him who is the Father of the
fatherless, and the Judge of the widow. In so
speaking of themselves they express their own
utter helplessness, and their confidence in Him
who had been the Guide of their youth. So earnest a plea would not be despised. None ever
called upon Him in vain when in felt need, and
truly repentant.

"We have drunken our water for money; our
wood is sold unto us" (ver. 4). All that this
world has for the soul away from the Lord comes
high. It may seem as though much is to be
gained by taking one's own way and casting the
fear of God behind the back. Satan will suggest,
too, that it costs too much to live for God, and
will allure with tempting baits the already unhappy heart that has begun to lust after other
things; but it will only be to prove in the end
that disobedience to God is a costly indulgence,
an unholy luxury, if we may use the term, that
none can really afford. They who here complain
that they have drunken their water for money,
had foolishly forsaken Him who is "the Fountain
of living waters" (of which all might drink freely), and had hewed out for themselves cisterns

that could hold no water (Jer. 2: 13). When they
sought it from the enemies of the Lord, a price
was put upon it that it burdened them to pay.
And then, of all that they purchased so dearly,
it could be said, "Whosoever drinketh of this
water shall thirst again;" while Jehovah's living
water satisfies the weary soul. Departure from
God is the most foolish and worst investment any
child of grace ever made.

"Our necks are under persecution: we labor,
and have no rest" (ver. 5). How could it be
otherwise? Was rest to be found in taking their
own way? It could not be. "Thou hast made
us for Thyself," said Augustine of Hippo, "and
our souls can never be at rest until they rest in
Thee." It is the most egregious folly to seek for
it anywhere else. That worldlings should make
such a mistake is no cause for surprise: they have
never known anything better than the alluring
enticements of Satan's realm: but for one who
has shared in the deep, true peace which the
Spirit gives to those that obey Him, to turn his
back upon the only source of rest and seek it in
the world from which he was once delivered, is
an anomaly beyond explanation, save on the
ground of hidden backsliding of heart long before. Such we know was the case of Judah.
Their heart went out after unholy things first;
then the feet soon followed. But they found, like
the dove sent forth out of the ark, no rest for
the sole of their feet. A raven, type of the evil
nature in every man, could rest upon a float-
ing carcass, while feeding on the carrion; but
the clean, pure dove, symbol of the Holy Spirit

and of the new nature which all God's children have received, could find neither rest nor food in such a scene, but must needs return to the ark, a type of Christ, for both.

"We have given the hand to the Egyptians, and to the Assyrians, to be satisfied with bread" (ver. 6). But Egypt soon failed them, and Assyria only oppressed them. All human props broken, the remnant were cast upon God alone, on whom they should have counted from the first.

Continuing in their confession, they own, "Our fathers have sinned, and are not; and we have borne their iniquities" (ver. 7). They were the children of wayward fathers, and had gone astray in the same unholy paths. Bitterly they complain that servants had borne rule over them, and there was no deliverer. At the peril of their lives they brought in their bread, "because of the sword of the wilderness" (vers. 8, 9). Famine-stricken, their skin became "black like an oven." The women of Zion and the maids of the cities of Judah were devoted to shame by the ravishers of the idolatrous armies. Princes were ignominiously hanged up by the hand; the elders were dishonored; while the young men and children were taken to be household servants (vers. 10-13).

The place of judgment and the place of merriment were alike vacant. The elders were no longer seen in the gate, and the song of the youths had ceased. The joy of their heart had ceased, and their dance was turned into funereal gloom. The voice of the mourner had usurped the place of the voice of the singer (vers. 14, 15).

Realizing keenly the immediate connection between their wrongdoing and their woes, they cry in contrition and penitence, "The crown is fallen from our head: woe unto us, that we have sinned!" (ver. 16). Thanks to a merciful God, blessing is not far away when the soul thus bends to the rod and confesses the justness of the punishment. "The Lord will not always chide, neither will He keep His anger forever." The surest way to find deliverance from God's governmental rod is humbly to bow in His presence, and frankly acknowledge how fully deserved the chastisement has been.

Judah had been brought very low; but He who cast them down can lift them up, when the needed lesson has been laid to heart and borne its fruit. Fainting in heart, with tear-dimmed eyes, "because of the mountain of Zion, which is desolate," and a habitation for foxes, they look up to Him from whom all their past blessings had come, and who found it necessary to pass them through all their sorrows: knowing He is their only resource, they exclaim, *"Thou, O Lord, remainest forever; Thy throne is from generation to generation"* (vers. 17-19). Everything else may have been swept away, but He remains forever.

What unspeakable consolation, dear fellow-saint, is in this precious fact for every tried and suffering child of God! Circumstances may be very hard; blow upon blow may strike; disaster follow disaster; until the stricken heart has not one earthly thing left to cling to. In such an hour Satan would fain lead the soul to believe that God too is gone: that it is no longer the object of His care, that He has left it to die alone. But no! It cannot be. Faith looks up and shouts, "Thou, O Lord, remainest!" for He abides the same "yesterday, and to-day, and forever."

There is an authentic incident related of a widowed Christian women who lived in Scotland years ago. Left with several dependent "bairns," she was at length reduced to great straits, and in order to feed and clothe her little household was obliged to practise the strictest economy. Yet withal, her heart was fixed upon the Lord, and both by precept and practice she taught the lesson of trust and confidence to her children.

But there came a day when the purse was flat and the cupboard bare. In the meal-barrel there was only left a handful of flour; and, like the widow of Zarephath, she went to get it to make a morsel of food to satisfy the craving of the hungry little ones, knowing not where the next would come from. As she bent over the barrel, scraping up the last of the flour, her heart for a moment gave way, and in a paroxysm of doubt the hot tears began to fall, and she felt as one utterly forsaken. Hearing her sobs, her little boy Robbie drew near to comfort. Plucking at her dress till he attracted her attention, he looked up into her face with wonder, and asked, in his quaint Scotch dialect, "Mither, what are ye greet-in' (weeping) aboot? **Doesna God hear** ye scrapin' o' the bottom o' the barrel, mither?"

In a moment her failing faith reasserted itself. Ah, yes, God did hear. All else might be gone, but He remained, and His Word declared her every need should be supplied. And so it was; for help was provided from a most unexpected source, when the last of what she had was gone.

It is the time of trial that tests faith; and never more so than when one is aware that the trial has been brought on by one's self. The spared of Judah feeling this, go on to ask, "Wherefore dost Thou forget us forever, and forsake us so long time?" (ver. 20.) But in confidence they add, "Turn Thou us unto Thee, O Lord, and we shall be turned; renew our days as of old" (ver. 21). If He shall turn them, all will be well. They are unable to trust themselves. They had ever been treacherous and false; but He can make them willing in the day of His power. Then they shall be as He would have them.

It would seem that neither in the Authorized nor in the Revised Versions is the last verse adequately rendered. As it stands in both, it would imply that they were hopeless of any recovery, and considered their rejection to be final and their prayer unavailing. "But Thou hast utterly rejected us; Thou art very wroth against us" is the way both read. But the margin of the R. V. is suggestive. It reads: "Unless Thou hast utterly rejected us and art very wroth." But we much prefer the interrogative of another translation. "For hast Thou utterly rejected us?" they ask; and the very question implies a confidence that it is otherwise, as Jeremiah well knew; though they justly add, "Thou hast been wroth against us—exceedingly." This was indeed true, but already His fierce anger was passing away. He was soon to arise, to be their Deliverer once more. This came to pass in part when, by permission of Cyrus, all who had heart enough for it returned to the cities from which their fathers and some of themselves had been carried captive.

But the day of Judah's lamentations will never be truly over until the Sun of Righteousness shall arise with healing in His wings, to dry their every tear, and to restore them to the land promised to Abraham for an inheritance forever. Then shall Zion put off her sackcloth; and, adorned with her beautiful garments, shall become the queen city of the world, when her King shall reign and prosper.

"In that day," in place of lamentation and wailing, "shall this song be sung in the land of Judah: We have a strong city; salvation will God appoint for walls and bulwarks. Open ye the gates, that the righteous nation which keepeth the truth may enter in. Thou wilt keep him in perfect peace, whose mind is stayed on Thee: because he trusteth in Thee. Trust ye in the Lord forever: for in the Lord Jehovah is everlasting strength" (Isa. 26:1-4). Then Jerusalem's mourning will be accomplished; her warfare will be ended!

APPENDIX I

An Attempt to Arrange the Writings of Jeremiah in Chronological Order.

(*a*) **Reign of Josiah** (B. C. 641 to 610).

B. C. 629   Chapter 1 - - - - - - Jeremiah's call.
           Chapters 2-6. Exhortations to Judah and Benjamin.

(*b*) **Reign of Jehoahaz** (Shallum) B. C. 610.

No specific portion in this brief reign of three months, but see Chapter 22: 10-12.

(*c*) **Reign of Jehoiakim** (B. C. 610 to 599).

B. C. 610   Chapter 26 - - - Arrest and Acquittal
    607(?) Chapter 35 - - - - - - The Rechabites.
    607   Chapter 36 - - - - - The Roll burned.
    607   Chapter 45 - - - The word for Baruch.
    607   Chapter 25 - - Seventy years' Servitude foretold.
    607   Chapter 46: 1-12 - Judgment on Pharaoh.
    605   Chapters 18, 19 - The Potter and the Clay.
    605   Chapter 20 - - Jeremiah's first Imprisonment.
    602   Chapter 13 - - - - The Linen Girdle.
    602   Chapter 14 - - - - - - - The Famine.
    601   Chapters 15-17 - - - Captivity foretold.
    600(?) Chapters 7-10 - - - Judgments predicted.
    600   Chapters 11, 12 - - - - Exhortations.
    600   Chapters 47-49 - - Against the Nations.

(*d*) **Reign of Jehoiakin, or Coniah** (Jeconiah)
B. C. 599.

B. C. 599   Chapters 22, 23 - Unfaithful Shepherds.

(*e*) **Reign of Zedekiah** (B. C. 599-588).

---

*Not written by Jeremiah. See comments.

APPENDIX II

For comparison we also give the moral order, as we have it in our Bibles. It will be readily seen by the spiritually minded that here we have no merely human compilation of scattered fragments, but a divine arrangement according to the subjects, in place of mere chronology.

The Divisions of Jeremiah's Writings According to Their Moral Order.

First Division.

The Call to Repentance and its Rejection.
Chapters 1-24.

Second Division.

The Judgments Coming through Nebuchadrezzar.
Chapters 25-29.

Third Division.

Future Restoration and Blessing.
Chapters 30, 31.

Fourth Division.

The Personal History of the Prophet and the Final Testing of Judah.
Chapters 32-38.

Fifth Division.

The Judgment Executed and the Spared Remnant.
Chapters 39-45.

Sixth Division.

The Prophecies as to the Nations.
Chapters 46-51.

Appendix.

The Historical Account of the Fall of Jerusalem.
Chapter 52.

Seventh Division.

The Sorrows of Judah and their Hope in Jehovah.

Lamentations.

57825